A guide to historical method

Edited by

ROBERT JONES SHAFER

DAVID BENNETT
NELSON M. BLAKE
C. VINCENT CONFER
ROBERT CRANE
SAMUEL EDDY
ROBERT G. GREGORY
ARTHUR LeGACY
JOSEPH LEVINE
RODERICK MACDONALD
PETER T. MARSH
FRED MORGNER
DIETRICH ORLOW
JAMES M. POWELL
JAMES R. SHARP
WILLIAM STINCHCOMBE
WALTER ULLMANN
JOSEPH VICTOR
WARREN B. WALSH
STEPHEN WEBB

All of the Department of History, Syracuse University

1974
Revised Edition

The Dorsey Press   *Homewood, Illinois 60430*
Irwin-Dorsey International   *London, England WC2H 9NJ*
Irwin-Dorsey Limited   *Georgetown, Ontario L7G 4B3*

Revised Edition
First Printing, January 1974

ISBN 0-256-01525-2
Library of Congress Catalog Card No. 73–87263
Printed in the United States of America

For Estelita

Preface

The gratifying reception of the first edition of this *Guide* demonstrated its need. We have, therefore, retained the basic organization, style, and point of view in this revised edition. A few changes in organization were made in response to comments by users. Additional information has been added dealing with the concepts and methodologies of the social and behavioral sciences, on epistemological studies, on the role of ideas in historical investigation, on the function of inference in historical reasoning, and on problems of exposition. Some of the figures, which were generously praised by users, have been revised in small ways to improve clarity. Additions have been made to the bibliographies.

The matter contained in this guide was developed over a period of two decades, primarily for beginning researchers in history. However, the experience of the authors in university teaching, cross-disciplinary research, government service, and private business strongly suggests the value of such training in research method for many other fields of activity as well. Our society demands huge numbers of professional researchers, data analysts, and report writers capable of reducing the record of assertion, belief, practice, and decision to understandable order.

Although this guide will be helpful to individuals trying to teach themselves research method, it will produce the best results when used in a tutorial situation in which the beginning researcher receives aid from an experienced scholar. The first problem of teaching method in the tutorial system is to move the beginning researcher quickly to the point where he can benefit substantially from tutorial sessions emphasizing analysis and interpretation. To provide such tutorial aid in the multiuniversity requires that we be prescriptive about some procedures, to force students quickly into research. Time is not available for drill in punctuation and grammar, carping about footnote styles, fatiguing repetition of simple bibliographic tips, and the like.* Much is gained and little is lost by prescription in these realms, so long as it is remembered that such prescription is designed to facilitate the development of orderly investigation and record keeping, in order to permit concentration on the essential business of encouraging anaylsis and the development of a critical attitude.

To get quickly into research, we find it desirable to *assign* research topics to students of method, by offering lists from which the students choose. Some instructors put exaggerated value on the process of topic selection for beginning researchers. Not all of the latter will become professional scholars. The process of topic selection consumes more time than it is worth at this level—both student and instructor time. We have, however, provided in Chapter VIII a discussion of the selection of research topics. Feasibility—in terms of library materials and student skills—is the criterion in compilation of research

---

* For useful additional information on such matters the student is referred to Kate L. Turabian, *A Manual for Writers of Term Papers, Theses, and Dissertations* (3d ed., rev.; Chicago, University of Chicago Press, 1967); E. B. White and William Strunk, *The Elements of Style* (New York, 1959). These are compact and sensible guides. Many other good ones are available.

topic lists for the beginning course in method. Most topics will be refined and redefined by the student, in consultation with the instructor, as work proceeds.

Where to begin is an agonizing problem for new researchers. Chapter I instructs the beginning researcher to use immediately some bibliographic aids (especially the library card catalog and major bibliographies), to locate a few good treatments of the research topic. Read quickly through one or more of these, taking sketch or orientation notes, and setting down questions, tentative hypotheses, and outlines, to help guide the research effort. Spend only a few days on this. You are trying merely to get some orientation, some notion of the character and dimensions of the topic. *Do not be afraid to read first the best studies of the subject;* professional scholars do. Your instructor will see to it that you also use contemporary materials or evidence.

The chapters of this guide may be assigned in a number of ways depending upon objectives, available staff, and time. Appendix A shows one possible arrangement of assignments. There is no magic in this suggested schedule, or in the specific additional guides to style and craftmanship suggested in the footnote above, or in the several other prescriptions offered in the text below. Substitutions on such matters can be made easily. Footnote method, rules of quotation, clarity in composition, a sound research note system, bibliographic techniques, and the like, are the necessary building blocks of good research method, but the heart of the enterprise is in critical analysis and interpretation.

December 1973   ROBERT JONES SHAFER

Contents

List of figures

I

The nature of history

Man views his past with boundless fascination, savoring its drama and victories, weeping at its failures and follies, probing it for clues to the meaning of human endeavor. We feel a tug of sympathy, a link of shared human experience, with Socrates drinking the hemlock for encouraging rebellious youth, or with Joan of Arc, repelling the invader, only to fall victim to man's endless willingness to proclaim the unimpeachable path of destiny. The pageantry and majesty of China's remote past take on new colors as we eye the wrenching changes of her recent history. The historical approach appeals to our feeling for the relationship of events in time, both for the continuity of human experience and its immense variety. It encompasses the recurrences of heroism and bigotry, the apathy and misery of vast peasantries, and the growth and vicissitudes of the ideas of justice and brotherhood. It celebrates the glittering careers of Napoleon and Caesar, Kublai Khan and Pericles; and the achievements of St. Francis of Assisi and Muhammad, of Mahatma Gandhi and Albert Einstein. In short, human interest in historical literature probably will never die.

1

The concern of this *Guide*, however, is chiefly with history as a discipline, a field of study and writing, with the ideas and techniques that are required for the accurate and forceful presentation of the past in the form of historical literature. The method and aims of historical inquiry have been much refined in the last two centuries, and the results codified and widely disseminated. Much of the method now is eminently teachable; as a result, historical inquiry has been professionalized, as the new techniques and concepts have become available to all. Much the same thing has happened in many fields in modern times. The result in historical studies is that the level of performance has improved, while abundant disagreement remains in those areas of judgment, morality, ethics, and religious and social belief that cannot be codified and "taught" in an agreed manner.

The catalog of achievements in the field in modern times is long. To name only a few: there has been a revolution in our understanding of ancient Egypt; vast improvements in our knowledge of technological and economic history; advances in our ability to grapple with the history of social groups; new vistas in the history of public health and medicine, and in the history of science; and strides forward in the development of historical demography. Who was aware, for example, a generation ago, that the introduction of European disease by the Spaniards to the great cultures of Indian America resulted in possibly the greatest demographic holocaust of human history?

This methodology now is used by many thousands of scholars throughout the world. They also build upon it, search for more sophisticated and precise techniques for the study of the human past. New concepts and techniques enable us to expand our understanding and our confidence in our findings. Michael Ventris is a recent example of the use of new techniques: in his case a combination of his knowledge of ancient Greek with the skills of a cryptographer, which he developed during World War II. This combination led him in the 1950s to the discovery that the language of the ancient Minoan Linear B script was not Minoan but Achaean Greek. This in turn enabled him to identify Linear B with Greek and read the script. This drove the history of written Greek back to about 1450 B.C., some seven centuries earlier than formerly believed, and indicated that Greek-speaking people had civilization many centuries before the great classical age.

A. History and other disciplines

The word "history" has several senses in English. First, it refers to the events of the past, to the actual happenings. Examples might be as recent as the removal of American troops from Vietnam or as remote as the Persian invasion of Greece in the fifth century B.C. Secondly, history means a record or account of events. Someone attempts to relate the events in Vietnam or to write a history of the Persian wars. Indeed, Herodotus, often called the father of history (that is, of history *writing*), set down his view on the causes and events of the war between the Persians and the Greeks. Finally, history means a discipline, a field of study that has developed a set of methods and concepts by which historians collect evidence of past events, evaluate that evidence, and present a meaningful discussion of the subject.

The methods used by historians in their research are not uniquely their own in most instances. They include methods developed over several centuries by humanistic scholars and others which have led to the great growth of the social and behavioral sciences during the last century. Insofar as historical study and literature are concerned with men, events, developments, and institutions for their own sakes as examples of human activity, they are humanistic; insofar as they seek regularities, generalizations, and even tentative predictability, they approach the social sciences. It is now less claimed than in the 19th century, that history is a science. Then the English historian Bury flatly declared history a science; the German von Ranke, who did so much to develop the attitudes and methodology of the new historiography in that age of scientific advance, hoped that historians could set down exactly what had happened in the past; the French historian Fustel de Coulanges asserted that "History is a science; it does not imagine, it only sees." The reaction against this view in the 20th century is seen in the statement of the English historian G. M. Trevelyan that "men are too spiritual, too various, for scientific analysis, and the life history of millions cannot be inferred from the history of single men. History . . . deals with intellectual and spiritual forces which cannot be subjected to any analysis that can properly be called "scientific." But Trevelyan made his methods—as do most modern historians—as scientific—that is, critical, objective, and systematic—as possible. Debate as to the "proper" tendency—humanistic or social scientific—for historical study and literature now seems antiquated and pointless.

History shares with the social and behavioral sciences the problem of grappling with highly intractable subject matter. Large-scale human activity involves huge numbers of interlocking variables. Observation of human activity, either directly, or indirectly by means of little glimpses in documents or artifacts, is imprecise. Experiments cannot be set up to control the environment or reduce the number of variables to manageable proportions. Historians cannot recreate the past to test hypotheses about behavior. The evidence available to the historian usually is not "fact" but *testimony* on the facts. The testimony inevitably is affected by the powers of observation, the mental state, and the veracity of the testifier. Courts and historians sigh when confronted with the testimony of children, the enraged, the mad, or the culpable weaving fancies to hide their guilt. Yet another difficulty is that often the witness is commenting on the mental state of others. And these difficulties are affected by the capacities and aims of the historian in a much more active and pervasive way than in the case of observations of evidence by the natural scientist. These considerations led two scholars to state that "historians are occupied solely with images,"[1] although nearly all of them are unconsciously so and under the impression that they are observing realities. Similar afflictions often are suffered by social scientists, who share with

---

[1] Charles Langlois and Charles Seignobos, *Introduction to the Study of History* (trans. by G. Berry, New York: Holt, 1912), p. 219.

historians the necessity of being wary of the supposition that
they know exactly what happened and why.

Both historians and social scientists are interested in regularities, tendencies, or repetitive elements in social behavior,
but the former also are concerned with the unique event and
person for their own sakes, and the latter are more uniformly
dedicated to identifying "laws" of human conduct. Proclaimed
general laws disconcertingly often are proved later to be rather
less general than originally claimed; and the infallibility of
"scientific" predictions is mostly a myth. Students of history will
discover that some excellent social scientists complain that the
massive effort to improve predictability in grappling with the life
of man in society is accompanied by an appalling multiplication
of jargon and by the construction of mountains of pretentious
and empty theory, with little improvement in predictability.
Economics is the most quantitative of the social sciences, often
described as the "hardest" (i.e., most nearly scientific), with the
greatest predictive capability, yet a Nobel winner in the field
could declare recently that "there is little warrant for the belief
that we know the laws of history well enough to make predictions of any great reliability."[2]

Despite this disclaimer by an eminent economist, much of
the most precise, systematic, and sophisticated work in recent
times on the motives, causes, regularities of human activity has
been done by social and behavioral scientists. They have developed methods of quantification (e.g., improved methods of
measurement and more sophisticated methods of statistical
analysis) and of the manipulation of evidence (e.g., in matrices
and by computers), and other methods and concepts that have
permitted promising new approaches to the study of man in
society. Historians necessarily have attended to the results of
social science and adapted its methods and concepts to historical
investigation.

New techniques of quantification currently are popular with
an increasing number of historians, following the lead of other

---

[2] Kenneth J. Arrow, in *New York Times,* 26 March 1973.

disciplines. Surely, this valuable tool should be exploited, although some historians view the effort with misgivings and acid objection. It is true that it is difficult to imagine useful direct quantification of some things: the motives of a president; the apathy of a peasantry; the alienation of an urban proletariat; racial prejudice; student unrest; deference in a rigid class society; the intensity of religious fervor. On the other hand, some of the apparent effects of these things can be quantified. And certainly we can hope for better figures bearing directly upon such matters as population, death rates, crop statistics, and correlations between the characteristics of legislators and their voting habits.

As another example, the concepts and experimental data of modern psychology are of great value to historians. The latter have been much influenced by interpretations of personality. An historian studying Sir Henry Clinton, British commander-in-chief during the Revolution, noticed a hesitancy in Clinton's execution of well-developed strategy. Unable to offer a satisfactory explanation, the historian asked a psychotherapist for help. The two specialists looked at the evidence together and settled on a mutually acceptable explanation that seemed to satisfy the criteria for interpretation in both fields. Historians also have been influenced by the work of social psychologists and sociologists in developing the concept of social norms and values as determinants of group action. Social norms include tangibles like clothing, housing, diet, ways of earning a living; and intangibles such as habits of thought, traditions, and ideas. Each social group has its own norms, and newcomers to the group must learn them. In addition, the newcomer learns the judgments which the group has made—that is, the social values which the group attaches to its norms. The majority in any group conform in general to that group's norms and values and it is this demonstrable fact which gives validity to limited generalizations about the group's behavior. Social norms and values in any living society are fluid, not static. Old norms and values are modified as a result of challenges; new norms and values appear in response to felt needs. One approach to history is to regard it as the study of the origins and development of social norms and values.

As still another example, recent social science work on polling methods is suggestive for the historian. Although an historian working on a 16th century problem cannot conduct a public opinion poll, an examination of questions used by modern pollsters to elicit certain types of information may suggest questions for which the historian might seek answers from old documents. A knowledge of modern sampling techniques may help in the weighting of data. At the very least, these types of knowledge of modern methods will force the historian to define more carefully the concept of public opinion.[3]

As a final bit of practical advice on this subject, let it be understood that a brief guide to historical method, intended primarily for beginning researchers, cannot usefully describe all the disciplines—e.g., geography, anthropology, economics—that may be of value to historical scholars. Two suggestions are offered, however: First, the beginning researcher is encouraged to search for materials on his subject produced by social and behavioral scientists, humanists, and even by natural scientists. Even without much knowledge of the concepts and methodologies of such disciplines, the beginning researcher will be able to use many of their findings, and exposure to their ideas and methods will be enriching. Second, the continuing and more experienced and more sophisticated researcher should acquaint himself with some of the concepts and methods of other disciplines. Of course, it is easy to say that there cannot be too much of this cross-disciplinary study, but as a practical matter such efforts usually must be tailored to the needs of individual students.

In any event, there is no need to suppose that either social scientists or historians have a monopoly of "knowledge based on the most careful examination of all available evidence."[4]

---

[3] See Chapter III c 2, below, on sampling.

[4] Morris R. Cohen, *The Meaning of Human History* (La Salle, Ill.: Open Court Publishing Co., 1947), p. 36.

Historians provide materials for social science activity, point out the shortcomings of some social science speculation that is based on improper selection of evidence or otherwise defective study of the past, and produce generalizations of their own. In sum, interrelations between the disciplines have tended to the enrichment of historical literature and pedagogy, rather than to their elimination.

Much of the antique part of historical literature (biographical and narrative) will long endure, regardless of the development of the social and behavioral sciences. History as a humanity and a literary genre exists almost independently of the social studies. But the fate of history as a discipline, capable of usefully answering questions about social conduct, either in investigations or in the classroom, is tied to a considerable extent to the development of the social and behavioral sciences. Historians need not use the concepts, methods, and findings of those disciplines quite as social scientists do, but historians will not be able, or wish, to ignore them. Much of the discussion in this *Guide* is influenced by the work of social and behavioral scientists.

B. Philosophy of history—metahistory

The term philosophy of history now embraces two very different things. One is recent work in the theory of knowledge (epistemology), mostly by philosophers, and less important activity in the realms of metaphysics (the nature of reality) and moral values. The other activity consists of a few, but often widely read and discussed, historical syntheses of all human experience, so unattached to empirical methods that they sometimes are called metahistory (metaphysical history). The metahistorians, also called monists or systematists, have little influence on historical craftsmen. The grand schemes of the metahistorians are too speculative for the methods and taste of the ordinary working historian. On the other hand, the work of modern epistemologists who specialize in the theory of historical knowledge, is taken seriously by working historians, but little used by them. The reason is that this epistemological work is too abstract for ready application to the inquiries of historians. It deals with the logic of language, the method of science, and the analysis of concepts. Thus the grand speculation of the older philosophy of history has been replaced by studies linked with the philosophy of science and the theory of knowledge, rather than with metaphysics.[5]

Historians do have personal, usually rather unpretentious, philosophies of history. No doubt these often would benefit from more rigorous elaboration. But historians do grapple with some of the thornier questions of causation and interpretation—and they frequently disagree. This is inevitable, since historians carry to such subjects differences of experience, often resulting in very different assumptions or prejudices; conflicting notions of the nature of man's social life; and different metaphysical views—for example, on the place of man in the universe. Such differences produce a variety of attitudes toward miracles, stock exchanges, race riots, and other matters of importance.

Determinism, or historical inevitability, and the question of free choice, is one of the large areas of disagreement. Most people—including most historians—largely ignore the question. Those for whom determinism is a matter of transcendent importance naturally believe that only the naive can ignore it in practice. Modern historians are at least interested to the extent that now most are aware that human choice is more limited—by heredity or by social and physical environments—than once was supposed.

A number of grand patterns or systems have been concocted since ancient times. They tend to locate the essence of causation in a single force, be it God, the spirit of the age, or the means of production. Often the system posits a scheme of stages through which human society passes in time (i.e., history). The system of stages may be either linear (i.e., ending in heaven, or the proletarian communist ideal society, or other ultimate per-

---

[5] Morton White, *Foundations of Historical Knowledge* (New York, 1965), 1–2.

fection), or cyclical or recurring (birth–growth to maturity–
decline to death, or spring–summer–fall–winter are popular).

Monistic, or single cause, explanation of the welter of human
history seems simplistic. The grand patterns are founded on
highly selective use of evidence. They also necessarily are founded
on most imperfect knowledge of the history of most civilizations,
since what individual really can know Rome, China, the Maya,
ancient Egypt, modern Europe, and antique Babylonia? But the
systematists are convinced they know how to select the essence
of each civilization, without bothering with detail. Also, the
most vaulting philosophies of history shine with imaginative
comparisons or even identifications of developments in different
civilizations, which most historians consider untrue if meant
literally, and often misleading if intended as analogies. The very
notion that civilizations are "born," or that they know "winters"
is poetry, not analysis. A civilization is a condition of culture
developed by successive generations of men. The men in the
civilization die, but the civilization continues. There apparently
is no logical reason (available to us) why the civilization could
not continue indefinitely. When a civilization weakens and dis-
appears, it is because the men within it cease to deal successfully
with their problems or are overcome by external forces too
strong to withstand.

The grand systems or philosophies of history do have some
value. They tend to stimulate interest in causation in its most
sweeping forms, in the broadest range of human history, and
offer some antidote to narrowly specialized historical scholarship. They also sharpen the critical faculties of conventional
historians who object to such systems. Insofar as the grand
philosophies of history tend to stimulate popular attention to
social development and the fate of man, they may be accounted
useful, even by those most dubious of their "accuracy." In any
event, such systems must be scanned for dogmatism and over-
simplification, however noble the motives of their creators.

Philosophies of history are created by individual human
beings in specific cultural contexts. Such systems therefore reflect the personal experience and central interests of those

individuals, and some aspects of the cultural biases and social problems of the societies in which they live. Thus Augustine (354–430 A.D.), a Christian bishop, in the *City of God* wrote out his personal search for a satisfying religion and a meaning for human life in a period when the ancient institutions of the Roman world visibly were crumbling under internal and external pressures. Augustine's concern was with the epic struggle between good and evil, seen in Hebrew-Christian terms. He saw man's earthly life as but a pilgrimage to God, with the end of human history the Last Judgment. Such a philosophy of history, if rigorously adhered to, makes many aspects of human activity seem too insignificant for serious attention. It permits little attention to causation except in terms of God's will. Augustine's view of human history ruled the Occident for more than a thousand years.

On the other hand, Karl Marx (1818–83) was very much a man of the 19th century, angered by the social ills of the industrial age, attracted to the socialist approach to their solution, and convinced that the scientific spirit of his day could be employed in the construction of a new world of plenty and justice. He asserted that man's history shows that his chief motive is materialist, and that the conflict of classes for control of the means of production is the key to human history. All else— ideas, beliefs, customs, laws—was "superstructure," essentially determined by the struggle for control of the means of production. This struggle, Marx asserted, ran through predestined stages. The capitalist stage of his own day would lead to increasing popular misery, economic crisis, and war. It would be succeeded by a dictatorship of the proletariat, followed by a withering away of the state and achievement of a classless, cooperative society.

This was an optimistic, monistic (one cause), essentially unprovable system. Its predictive value has been limited. There has been economic depression, but also a great improvement of levels of living in precisely the best developed countries which Marx believed first would become proletarian states. Communist regimes, ostensibly founded on Marxist doctrine, have

not formed classless societies. It is not clear that the terrible
wars of our time are primarily due to contradictions or tensions in the capitalist system. Personal frustration and the brute
urge to dominate cannot, in our present view, easily be dismissed
as superstructure determined by control of the means of economic production. So 20th-century interest in psychology modi-
fies economic interests inherited from an earlier day.

The development of "relativism" in the late nineteenth and
the twentieth centuries was especially influential in historical
theory. New knowledge from natural science, psychology, comparative religion, and other fields, resulted in a decline of interest
in metaphysics and to doubts about the capacity of the human
mind to deal with such problems. It led to the view that historians did not discover an historical reality that had an existence
apart from men, but that men themselves *created* (observed,
thought about, interpreted, composed) history. The English
philosopher R. G. Collingwood argued that the historian's criterion of truth was an innate *idea* of history, which "every man
possesses as part of the furniture of his mind." He contended,
further, that the historian uses this criterion in the light of his
own experience, to judge the value of authorities coming down
from the past, and in using his "constructive imagination" in
supplying gaps in the record.[6] Such contentions led the American historians Carl Becker and Charles Beard to declare re-
spectively that each man was "his own historian," and that history is "an act of faith."

To most historians, as a practical matter of teaching and of
research, such contentions boiled down to two commonly accepted propositions. One is that the historian's cultural experience or environment affects his interpretation of evidence on
human affairs, and that as a result interpretations of history
necessarily vary with the social environments of historians. The
other is that *inference* (i.e., supplying data not explicitly pro-

---

[6] R. G. Collingwood, *The Idea of History* (Oxford: The Clarendon Press,
1946).

vided by the contemporary writers or artifacts) must be indulged in with great care.

The researcher cannot, indeed, be too careful in bearing these propositions in mind. If the past must be interpreted in a variety of ways, the historian should be cautious about declaring the universal validity of his work, and thus cautious about the care with which he does his research and writing. As Collingwood pointed out, a modern historian's experience might lead him to reject ancient Greek accounts of killing infants by exposure, but the fact of such exposure, if it is a fact, existed independently of what any one may think. Assumptions regarding human standards—e.g., of cruelty or justice—must be used only tentatively. A beginning researcher today cannot, for example, be sure what infanticide might be acceptable in a future world made virtually unbearable by overpopulation. As for inference as imaginative connection between authorities or evidence, it also must rest on assumptions; hence, on the cultural environment of the historian.

Relativism, as we have stated, never seriously troubled most historians on the working level. On the theoretical level, relativism in the middle years of the twentieth century was rather modified by arguments by epistemologists and others that human activity shows some "probabalistic" regularities, permitting assumptions and explanations in which we may repose considerable confidence. There also has been a new emphasis on the knowability of certain things that are not metaphysical in nature; for example, election figures, or the capacities of oxcarts. To be sure, they can be linked with metaphysical questions, but that does not make them metaphysical in themselves.

Finally, we return to the proposition that although the Philosophy of History does not much engage the attention of working historians, the latter cannot write history without personal philosophies of some sort. To devote no attention to one's fundamental assumptions, it has been well said, is to remain prey to unformed ideas rather than to escape the influence of philosophical problems. In fact, to deny that any master plan for human activity exists is itself a judgment on the nature of reality; hence, a philosophical position. Most of the problems discussed in this *Guide* have philosophical implications; for example, what we can know of the past, to what extent the past exists in the present, what we mean by cause, whether there are events that can be said to result from pure chance. What the historian needs, therefore, is not less philosophy, but more, at least in the sense of rigorous analysis of his assumptions and methods.

C. The uses of history

1. History as experience

There is much to be said for the view that the greatest function of historical study is as an addition to experience, tending to an appreciation of the existence in the past of the race of many confrontations with problems similar to our own. We see how recurrent are such problems as the necessity but the danger of resistance to tyranny, argument over the values and perils of freedom of expression, greed in the development of property, abuse of labor, the rivalry of culture groups, the competition of individuals for eminence and power, the lurking danger of demagoguery in free societies. This broadening of experience promotes sophistication and judgment in the contemplation of public decisions, and tends both to the reduction of parochialism or insularity, and to steadiness in consideration of grand decisions by elimination of the supposition that all current problems are uniquely terrible in the history of man.

A New York City newspaper not long ago printed the following editorial:

A Wise Woman, Clio!

"Large populations, made susceptible by literacy to new ideas, but unable to discriminate among them, constitute perhaps the greatest single menace to modern culture," the leading review in a recent issue of *The* (London) *Times Literary Supplement* proposes. "Never, it may be suspected, has pretentious novelty had a better chance of being accepted at its face value," the review goes on to say.

If this needs to be said to Britons, how much more so to Americans, so many of whom date the beginning of time and human experience from 1900, or a decade or so later, it may be. A contemporary school of pedagogy tends to confirm their belief that history is wholly irrelevant to or merely an escape from the problems of the moment. Certainly it can be both or either for pedants or antiquarians; a brute accumulation of mere fact or a shameless lust for antiquity as such. But most history readers today are staring into the past, not wistfully, nor with pride of knowledge, but with a purposeful scrutiny. As a modern historian has recently said: "The prime . . . use of history is that it enables you to understand better than any other discipline the public events, affairs and trends of your own time."

History at least can save from severe disillusion those to whom every "new" idea or polity appears in the guise of a beautiful virgin. Clio, the muse of history, has known these meretricious hussies since the days of Herodotus. She has been around a lot and a long time. She knows that most of them are no better than they should be. In fact, she knew them when.[7]

It is precisely this sort of extension of experience through historical memory that dictatorial governments in our own and other times have recognized as a threat to their continuation. The protagonist of George Orwell's *1984,* that terrifying novel of technological tyranny, is a rectifier of history. He is a slave of the all-embracing, all-seeing government of Big Brother, spending his miserable days managing the record of the past. Especially he sees to it that the thin record contains nothing on mistakes of the past, or criticism of Big Brother's horror world, or even the memory of persons who disappointed him (they become "unpersons" as the record of their lives is erased), a fictional activity all too reminiscent of the removal of the names of unlucky Soviet officials from the official encyclopedia. Thus, the record always is favorable to the point of view of the omnipresent and omnipotent and omniscient state. There is no history out of which to condemn and convict the regime for usurpation, to compare it unfavorably with others (lost are the

---

[7] *New York Herald Tribune,* October 10, 1946.

virtues of Athens and Paris and Boston), to serve as a guide to
protest, to lift up the spirit with the thought of past revolt and
heroism (unpersons are Churchill, Ghandi, Washington, Sparta-
cus), to show the transience of regimes, to indicate the un-
changeability of change itself.

In brief, here is the horrible logic of the policy of uniformity,
starting with fear of heterodoxy, becoming regimentation of
opinion, hardening into a poisonous orthodoxy, and ending in
a pathological terror of contradiction not only by the recently
buried but by the most antique dead.

Many statesmen have testified that the study of history prepared them for what to expect, in a general way, from human
greed, cruelty, and folly, and from nobility and courage and
wisdom. It is clear that men who are ignorant of history are apt
to make superficial judgments—witness the views of the Germans Kaiser Wilhelm and Hitler regarding the martial qualities
of English and Americans. To be sure, history does not repeat
itself exactly; it does not give detailed guidance for action today. The past does not show us how to oppose Hitler tactically,
on a given day, but reveals the danger of bowing the neck to
tyrants and argues for opposition to tyranny even in the face of
great odds, often suggesting some means that might prove
valuable in gaining victory or pitfalls to be avoided.

Although there is little certainty in human affairs, and
sensible men do not expect it, current parallels with the past
may suggest common-sense courses of action. This is the case
with the assassinations of Presidents Abraham Lincoln and
John F. Kennedy. In both cases, some people emotionally,
even hysterically, insisted that deep conspiracy existed, and
hinted at hidden evidence and at serious danger to the republic and the social fabric. Material on the question of Lincoln's
assassination still occasionally is published. In the case of
Kennedy, a panel of excellent men carefully sifted the evidence,
and found the murder almost certainly the work of an individual. It is only reasonable to suppose that this is the probable
explanation. To assume either dishonesty or seriously slipshod
work on the part of the investigators flies in the face of their
character, the effort put into the investigation, and the manner

in which the work was done. But in the open society of Lincoln's and Kennedy's America we must expect unreasonable charges founded on ignorance, emotionalism, idiocy, vague fears, lust for attention, and hope of pecuniary and political profit.

Another danger is that, with our observation of the many value systems created by men, and the various actions taken with regard to governance, family, war, and other affairs, we may become "cultural relativists." Some regard this as no bad thing, a gain to sophistication and a prop to tolerance; others fear that the loss of faith in absolute values must lead into either cynicism or despair. This much-debated question scarcely can be resolved by pointing out that men have usually held to a core of ethical standards, or by arguing that our very humanity demands belief in such norms. If a man is capable of conceiving of ethical standards for humans, the study of history should reinforce his belief; if he is not, nothing will help him but religious revelation.

2. Other uses of history

History is much used in public life, nowhere more so than in the United States. Much of the belief, the action, and many of the leaders of our early history seem sufficiently contemporaneous to justify policy today. Our judicial system abounds in uses of history. Legislation is discussed and written in the light of precedent, recent and remote. Great political controversies swirl around passions roused by appeals to the sacred shades. When Daniel Webster and Robert Y. Hayne debated in the Senate the nature of the union in 1830, they appealed to the intent of the founding fathers. A century later, when Franklin Roosevelt was accused of trying to pack the Supreme Court, an almost unprecedented uproar arose over this asserted threat to the traditions of judicial independence and the separation of powers.

A powerful recent use of history was in a speech by Senator Flanders of Vermont in 1954,[8] scoring the activities of the demagogic Senator Joseph McCarthy as "contrary to Senatorial

---

[8] *New York Times,* July 19.

traditions," tending "to bring the Senate into disrepute," and calling for condemnation of his conduct. Flanders feared that the United States had entered into the "time of troubles" postulated by the historian Arnold Toynbee as indicative of a nation's decline. He compared McCarthy's exploitation of the communist issue with Hitler's and gave a picture of the senator as fuehrer. He pointed out that the Republican Party, of which Flanders and McCarthy were members, was a century old that year, and instead of the ideals of its first President (Lincoln) holding the spotlight, "We see the bright lights of television on the junior Senator from Wisconsin sitting at the table with his assistant whose lips are glued to his ear whispering, whispering, whispering." Flanders found his party now at a parting of the ways, to follow Lincoln or McCarthy. At least, Flanders concluded, the latter had done the great service of "giving us the opportunity to appraise our national political morality in this year of Our Lord 1954. For this opportunity we must ever be grateful." McCarthy was duly chastised for his irresponsible conduct, and the Senate and the country turned away from the witch hunt.

Historical studies long have served as weapons in controversy. The Protestant Reformation of the 16th century gave rise to a prolonged and often vitriolic literary dispute that extended almost to our own time. The character of Martin Luther was the object of intensive writing by Catholic historians, who often aimed at proving that he was an unworthy priest, guilty of vices that led to his break with the Church. Protestant writers seized on the weaknesses and immoralities of various Renaissance Popes to attack the leadership of the Catholic Church and to validate the Protestant rupture with the medieval Church. Another historical dispute developed with the rise of nationalism in the 19th century. Many scholars employed their talents to prove that their peoples had an historic right to political independence. Especially in eastern and southern Europe, nationalistic history often favored the position of one minority over those of others. The creation of a number of independent nations in that region following World War I did not settle the controversies between Czechs and Slovaks, Croats and Yugoslavs, or take historical argument out of political debate.

More recently, the controversy over United States entry into World War II gave rise to a polemic literature often more noted for its content of fury than for its attachment to historical evidence. There was much allusion to the experience of World War I as argument for or against involvement in World War II. Then, after World War II, an acute American awareness of the power of the Soviet Union, combined with a long-felt fear of communism, stimulated numerous theories of conspiracy concerning settlements among the great powers made at Yalta and Potsdam. Very often hindsight provided a perspective for evaluating defects in those agreements that in the minds of some were the result of sinister communist machinations, and the "historical" debate on the peace continues to enliven literature and politics.

As a final example, historical argument has been much used in the United States in recent years in connection with civil rights issues and the treatment of minorities. Historians, and their supporters in national and community affairs, often are divided into two schools of interpretation. On the one hand is a group asserting that in general American history shows a consensus on institutions and decisions, a pervading satisfaction and spirit of compromise. On the other hand, there is a group that declares that American history rather displays repression and violent protest as methods of action and reaction, and that violence is an indispensable and legitimate answer to bigotry and tyranny. Of course, it is not merely history showing one or the other of these pictures to be the more veracious, but the individual historians and others viewing that history.

Historians also provide data for public uses other than political polemics. They—together with social scientists, philosophers, and others—make various sorts of efforts to promote understanding of human society, and hopefully to suggest guidance for the future. Historical data are used to try to identify cultural conditions favorable to stated attitudes or institutions, in the hope that such knowledge can be used in decision-making in the future. Sometimes such data are prepared by historians directly for such projects, sometimes they are extracted from historical works by social scientists. In some cases, data can only be gathered and interpreted effectively by historians with the erudition to understand the time and place under consideration. In such instances, social scientists pluck raw data from the record of the past at their peril.

Historical studies provide background for many other subjects and disciplines—law, social and behavioral science, philosophy, and others. Also, history is one of the most powerful of studies for engendering empathy, an understanding of the motives, beliefs, frustrations, and hopes of other peoples. Yet another use of historical literature is in helping a person understand where he comes from and how, giving a sense of cultural self-knowledge.

Coins, stamps, monuments, newspapers, films, and television often employ historical themes and motifs. In many instances, the events are distorted or oversimplified. Sometimes, they are turned to the service of propaganda. But such uses only serve to illustrate the need for good historical writing. Many millions have found historical literature a pleasure to read. It provides something akin to the movement and variety of travel. It gives a sense of participation in the affairs of the race.

D. Varieties of historical literature

Man's fascination with his past is well illustrated in the many varieties of historical literature. From antiquity to the present, he has used whatever skills and materials were at hand, and often the approach reflected his purpose. It is not possible to categorize rigorously the rich variety of historical literature. Here we suggest some of the choices and combinations of choices that have been made and that lie open now to the historian.

Narrative history had its beginnings with Herodotus, and numerous other practitioners in the ancient Mediterranean world. This is a style that is literary and dramatic in character, though it is no longer thought proper to create dialogue in order to heighten the sense of crisis at key points in the narrative, as with the Melian dialogue of Thucydides, which so effectively illustrates the pride of the Athenians in dealing with the small states of their empire. Narrative historians, with their attention to story, to great events and human interest, and to individual heroism and depravity, have only biographers as near competitors for public interest. Gibbon's *Decline and Fall of the Roman Empire* was a best seller in the 18th century, as was Macaulay's *History of England* in the 19th.

Narrative history is important because it is a communication link between the scholar and the public. But there are fewer men capable of writing brilliant narrative history than of turning out competently done scholarly monographs. Thus it is that the public acclaims Bruce Catton's *A Stillness at Appomatox,* or the rolling periods, drama, and gusto of Winston Churchill's historical works. Nor are these authors devoid of scholarship, although their purpose is the creation for a wide public of a feeling for the great men and deeds of the past.

Biography has never been completely accepted as a branch of history, despite the obvious close relationship. The accepability of Plutarch's *Lives* or of Suetonius' biographies of the Caesars is considerably less than that of Tacitus' works, despite the bias in the last. Modern criticism of medieval hagiography, the lives of the saints, generally has been severe because of their uncritical acceptance of legend. Even modern biographers have all too often been overly sympathetic toward their subjects, and insufficiently critical. But biographers can, and often do, follow the canons of critical research, and respond to the latest concepts and methods of investigation and interpretation.

The scholarly monograph is the characteristic product of the modern professional historian.[9] Building on the development of critical scholarship in the 15th to 18th centuries, the monograph was refined by the "scientific" historians of the 19th century into approximately its present form. The emphasis

---

[9] Most historians were "amateurs" until the 19th century. There are critics who lament the change.

is on meticulous research into source materials. Often—though
not always—it presents an exhaustive treatment of a narrow
subject. It is, therefore, a child of science rather than of literature. Although influenced by the humanist tradition, it has, in
its essence, held to the dictum that accuracy is more important
than art. The training of the historian today aims at preparing
masters of the monograph. Historians who advocate a cultural
approach to history point to the failure of monographic history
to integrate its results into the broader framework of a period.
They and others also assert that the form, and the system of
training that emphasizes it, stand in the way of the production of
more stimulating narrative history. We find this a dubious thesis.
The apparently unslakable public appetite for good narrative
history probably tempts from the ranks of the monograph
writers most of the talent that exists. As a final word it must be
said that some monographic literature is well-written, even
lively, and that in any event the best of the narrative historians,
who find large audiences, must base their work on monographic
literature.

The growth of history as a discipline has witnessed an increasing tendency toward specialization in subject matter. The
professional historian may still write a general history of the
world or of a particular civilization, but this work is most often
prepared for use as a textbook. Increasingly, he tends to think
of himself not merely as a student of medieval history, modern
European history, or United States history, but also as a social,
economic, or intellectual historian. The broad avenues of political history that once held almost exclusive sway have had to
give way to the narrower specialties of the history of political
parties, of institutions, behavior, or the still important area
of international relations. Historians have also been much influenced by the deep stirrings in many parts of the world hitherto
little studied by European and American scholars. Africa, Asia,
and Latin America have attracted great interest in the period
since World War II. It is apparent that the historian is respon-
sive not only to influences from within the profession but that
his outlook is broadly shaped by fundamental changes in outlook and perspective within the society in which he lives.

At times the role of historian and philosopher become intertwined. The great speculators of the past attempted to see how history moved within a great design. While their basic premises were well within the province of philosophy, the conception was quasi-historical. From the *Scienza Nuova* of Giambattista Vico in the 17th century to Arnold Toynbee's massive *Study of History* in our own time, there have been numerous attempts to project a total view of human history, past, present, and future. The work of Karl Marx in *Das Kapital* has had a profound influence on modern historians, yet it fundamentally represents a philosophical effort to construct a historical system based on the view that conflict of materialistic forces is the primary determinant of social change and that the whole direction of future reality is determined by these same material forces.

But history is not philosophy nor is it the instrument for the working out of any predetermined system. History, by its nature, is an investigation whose results remain obscure and difficult to ascertain. Its validity as a discipline rests chiefly with the continuing effort of historians to improve their methodology and to lend greater precision to their techniques. In many ways, these strivings may be summed up in the life of the late Marc Bloch, the great French medieval historian killed by the Nazis in 1944 for his work in the French underground. Bloch early recognized the need for better historical methods. Together with Lucien Febvre, he founded the *Annales d'histoire économique et social* as a journal to open better communications between history and the social sciences. In *Feudal Society* and numerous articles he called for a comparative approach to historical study. All these efforts were part of his quest for a "broadened and deepened history which some of us—more every day—have begun to conceive."

E. Historical method

The elements of historical method as set down in our table of contents may be divided into those well-agreed-upon and those that are much more controversial. We present three well-agreed-upon elements of method. These are important, and must be learned if the investigator is to function effectively. They are not, as is sometimes naively supposed, just simple mechanics, requiring little brain. These relatively well-agreed-upon elements of method can be done much better with method than without it, and with great savings of effort. The efficiency with which these things are done clearly is in proportion to the careful intelligence carried to the tasks.

First is learning what the *categories of evidence* are, the critical elements that differentiate them, and what these mean to investigators. The very differences of view that the student may encounter with regard to the categorization of evidence should sharpen his capacity to judge the character and quality of evidence. It will be useful to observe what common features the categories of evidence possess, and the different problems they pose. Specialized concepts, points of view, or techniques may be required to deal with different categories of evidence.

Second is *collecting evidence*. Much, but not all, of this collection must occur early in the research effort. This involves bibliographic search, description, control, and analysis or annotation. Huge accumulations of aids and techniques makes this field much more manageable than in the past. This element of method also involves means of recording evidence, of deciding what to record, and how and how much to process the material at this point. On both the collection and the recording of evidence there are many useful suggestions that can be made without much fear of contradiction. One of these is that bibliographic method is not child's play, or mindless paper shuffling, and that even professionals vary widely in their domination of such skills. Another suggestion is that good research notes do not simply drip from the unthinking and inexperienced pen. Taking good research notes is something few doctoral candidates manage until near the end of their dissertations. Both bibliographic method and note-taking can be taught, using well-understood concepts and techniques; neither is likely to be handled well by the uninstructed without a long and wasteful period of trial and error, which is quite unnecessary today. Finally, since so much of a researcher's time inevitably is consumed by bibliographic work and note-taking, rationalization of even the smallest processes may pay handsome dividends.

Thirdly, the *communication of evidence* also is a subject that can in important measure be taught according to well-accepted standards, at least in its essence, which is lucidity. Most human beings can improve their lucidity—that is, unambiguous expression—with thought, study, and practice. Without these operations, only miraculous intercession will contrive the same result. The opportunities for ambiguous expression in historical studies are appalingly numerous, much more so than in such fields as physics and chemistry. The need for training and method is correspondingly acute. As for the graces of exposition —that is, style, we will here only note that they are scarcely a feature of many historical writings. Lucidity is an essential and learnable part of historical method, style is "merely" desirable, and possibly a gift of genetic roulette.

The less agreed-upon, more controversial elements of historical method are more difficult to perform, and to talk about or teach. We have chosen to put all these elements under the title of "using evidence," and under that three major sub-categories: external criticism, internal criticism, and synthetic operations. Within these categories we discuss the problems that all guides must deal with, although they disagree considerably as to how they should be labeled, arranged, and treated.

External criticism determines the authenticity of evidence. It gets evidence ready for use in the examination of human affairs—that is, prepares it for the processes of internal criticism and synthesis. In the case of documents, external criticism essentially authenticates the evidence and establishes the text in the most nearly accurate form possible. It may deal with problems of forgery or the garbling of texts in copying. The concept of authentication is not difficult, but the process can be complex, and it may call for great erudition and special skills, for example, in languages or in calligraphy.

Although the difference between the aims of external and internal criticism can be simply stated—authenticity of the evidence as against its credibility in the explanation of human fairs, the processes share some interests and many mental operations. External criticism especially means determination of authorship and date of evidence, and these things are important also in judging the credibility of evidence. Such mental operations as analysis, assumption, inference, and synthesis, which are difficult and often hazardous, are common to both external and internal criticism. Although the beginning researcher probably will not engage in external criticism, he must know what it is, develop the habit of thinking in terms of the critical approach used in authenticating materials, and know some of the problems of external criticism as an aid to avoiding some of the pitfalls of internal criticism and synthesis.

The other two categories of what we have labeled "using evidence," are internal criticism, or the determination of meaning and value, or credibility, of evidence; and synthesis, here meaning the blending of evidence into an account that accurately describes historical events or solves historical problems. These operations call not only for erudition and technique, but for intelligence, powers of discrimination, imagination, and sophistication. They necessarily are riddled with subjectivism, with value judgments, some of them acknowledged by the historical scholar, and some of them unacknowledged but nonetheless operative. These operations are the subject of much debate, within the individual historian, and between historians. It is in these areas that some historians most bitterly contend that some one and only that one conception of operations is proper. It is of these areas of what may be called types of interpretation that sometimes it is said that most working historians have relatively little interest in methodological theory.

Such comments are misleading. It is more accurate to say that many historians are lukewarm toward metaphysical and epistemological problems, and especially to efforts to schematicize research and interpretation as a whole. On the other hand, many historians who are tepid toward the more ambituous efforts to explain or integrate method, have a lively interest in discussions of portions of methodology—for example, bias, selection and relevance, organization schemes (chronologic, topical, geographic) in their influence upon interpretation and assignment of possible causation, probability, contingency, the uses of working hypotheses. It is for this reason that in this *Guide* we put much of our material on methodological theory in sections dealing with *aspects* of method.[10]

We contend that even some parts of the more difficult areas of historical method can be discussed by most historians without debilitating differences of opinion; for example, bias, probability, the importance of knowing the time of composition of documents, the difference between literal and real meaning, and the usefulness of at least some corroboration, whatever the difficulties of determining what is true corroboration, or what constitutes enough. Some of these aspects of method have, after all, in modern times been much refined. To give only a few examples: the conceptualization of groups in human activity; the partial penetration of the complexities of individual motivation—conscious and unconscious; the nature of prejudice; the interaction of factors in human society; the naiveté of meta-history; appreciation that economic or religious phenomena need not result simply from economic or religious "causes," but are a part of a total culture and its experience; a nearly revolutionary increase in our understanding of statistical methodology, hence of the role of quantitative factors in historical explanations.

We contend that for those parts of the method that may always be subject to bitter and comprehensive debate, the student can be carried little further than an understanding of the fact of disagreement, the characteristics of some of the positions taken, and the necessity of sometime arriving at his own views both on the substantive questions and on the importance of the questions to his own activity as a working historian. There simply are some things that guides to method cannot do.

---

[10] See David Hackett Fischer, *Historians' Fallacies. Toward a Logic of Historical Thought* (New York, 1970), for a sophisticated but sometimes rather "theoretical" effort to deal with aspects of historical methodology; Cohen, *Meaning of Human History,* for an especially lucid treatment of broader theoretical considerations, by a philosopher.

F. First steps in the research process

The stages of an historical investigation, as was pointed out
in the Preface, can not be delimited precisely into chronological
blocks. Thus, while much of the collection of data is concentrated in the early stages of an investigation, some is likely to
continue well into the stage of final composition. Also, collection merges into analysis when the first research note is
taken that consists of more than simple copying. Because of
these overlaps, this chapter ends with comments on first steps
in the research process, dealing briefly with matters that will
be discussed more fully later.

Assuming the subject of research to have been chosen,[11]
quickly locate a few good treatments of the research topic. This
may be done by using the library card catalog and major bibliographies. Bibliographies may offer comments on the items
listed, which will help in choosing what to read first. Or a few
articles in major scholarly journals of history and the social
sciences may be selected for this early reading. The fact of
publication in such journals is at least a minimum guarantee of
quality. Or, when a book title is located that looks promising, an
effort can be made to find reviews of it in scholarly journals in
the year or two following the book's publication. Finally, the
researcher may simply look at a book with a promising title, and
quickly estimate its quality, and its probable suitability for this
early reading. This process of quick estimation, or screening,
will be discussed further.

A few such items having been selected, commence reading.
This may be thought of as *orientation reading.* The object is
to get some notion of the character and dimensions of the subject, of some of the attitudes toward it adopted by investigators,
and of problems of evidence and interpretation. Notes should
be taken, but at this stage they will not be the type of research
note discussed later in this chapter. Think of these early notes
as orientation materials, understanding that they will not form

---

[11] For advice on the selection of topics, see Preface, and Chapter VIII (A).

a part of the body of evidence used in composition of the final paper. If careful research notes are wanted on the materials read quickly for this early orientation, it will be necessary at a later time to return to the materials.

If the orientation process is thought of as involving the quick scanning of several hundred pages in about a week, it is clear that note taking must be sketchy. Try to get some idea of the *major subdivisions* of the project—chronologic, geographic, topical. If the subject is "United States Intervention in Latin America since 1898," it quickly will become apparent that different types of intervention have occurred. So a note might suggest a preliminary classification into economic, military, cultural, and diplomatic intervention. Also, it will be seen that certain chronologic divisions are evident: (*a*) much direct intervention to about 1933, (*b*) cessation of such intervention from 1933 to 1954, (*c*) direct intervention since 1954.

Such simple patterns, set down in writing, should in effect be *questioned by the researcher*. Why did this periodization occur? Was it because of developments in the United States, in Latin America, or elsewhere, or a combination of these? Was it because of economic, military, political, cultural, or diplomatic developments? Were the causes different in one period than in another? This preliminary questioning process might result in construction of a simple outline indicating the causes of intervention in specific cases discussed by the authors read.

At the same time the researcher should be considering two other matters: (*a*) does there seem to be difference of opinion on the character and results of United States intervention in Latin America, and (*b*) is it apparent that there are some problems of evidence in connection with study of the subject? The researcher should be able to jot down a number of problems in connection with these questions if he has read even a hundred pages in a standard college textbook of United States–Latin American relations. For example:

a) Has U.S. intervention in Latin America ever been successful?

b) How can scholars define "success" in intervention? Will this be different from the definitions of journalists, Secretaries of State, corporation executives?

c) Are there "schools of thought" among scholars on U.S. intervention in Latin America in general? In Haiti in 1915? In Guatemala in 1954?

d) How much, and in what ways, have Latin Americans expressed resentment of U.S. intervention? How is this related to the problem of "success?"

e) Do views on intervention vary in accordance with an individual's political party, occupation, income level, religious faith?

f) What is the evidence for the view that private business induced Theodore Roosevelt to declare and act on his "corollary" to the Monroe Doctrine?

g) Are there special problems of evidence in connection with the local communism that ostensibly was all-important in recent U.S. interventions in Guatemala, Cuba, and the Dominican Republic? How great was local communist influence in each case? How much of a threat did it pose to the U.S. in each case?

Such questions come, then, from what the researcher reads —by historians, social scientists, journalists, and others; and from his own thought processes. They are developed to give shape and direction to research. They will be applied to the evidence as it is collected, helping to determine what to look for, and what to take down as being relevant. Some of the questions may be adopted as tentative hypotheses quite early in the research process. In any event, from the beginning of his work the researcher should try to make sense of it by inquiring what it means, how it came about. If this is not done, there will be no basis on which to select from among the mass of data available. The researcher should not be disturbed by the thought that some of the early questions will be abandoned or changed and new ones developed later. This is unavoidable.

Either during this initial brief period of orientation reading and questioning, or early in the following process of collecting materials, it often is helpful to construct a tentative outline of the subject. This not only will help in the development of more questions to ask of the evidence, but it may very early in the research effort suggest that the subject ought to be drastically modified, probably reduced in size. This should be the case with the subject discussed above on intervention in Latin America. Clearly it is too large for a research paper of moderate length.

Developing questions to put to the evidence, and to the publications of scholars who have used some part of it, is a challenge to the researcher's sense of the fitness of things, of priorities in human affairs, of the ways in which men judge their own actions and those of others. Do not be afraid to ask the most important questions. Was the United States justified in invading the Dominican Republic because of a communist menace there? Has business been too influential in the making of intervention policy? Such questions give meaning, life, and interest to research. Of course, they shape research by setting up standards of relevance. That is much better than having no standards, and pretending to follow the impossible policy of collecting "everything," an error that has afflicted not only individual historians but huge government research and intelligence agencies.

After this orientation reading, with its attendant development of questions and of tentative outlines of at least portions of the subject, *systematic bibliographic work* must be started. A small amount only will have been done in searching for materials for the orientation reading. A thorough search for materials requires a knowledge of bibliographic method and bibliographic aids, which are discussed later in this *Guide*. Here it is necessary to point out that the bibliographic effort necessarily must proceed hand-in-hand with some research note-taking from materials located. Research notes are discussed in a later chapter.

One reason that research notes must be taken before the bibliographic work is completed is that improvement of knowledge of the substantive aspects of the subject is necessary to guide the search for materials. A deepening knowledge of the research subject may well change the emphasis of research or alter the interpretation of evidence, with effects upon the search

for materials. The difficult problem for the beginning researcher
—and often a considerable problem for the experienced investigator—is to decide when to suspend the search for materials in
order to take research notes and analyze some of the data found.
It probably will work reasonably well if the beginning researcher locates—and makes working bibliography cards for—
the materials on his subject that appear to be of major importance in the library card catalog and the major bibliographic
aids appropriate to his subject.

Very likely the number of items located during this effort
will be fairly large. It must, of course, vary with the subject,
with the bibliographic aids available to the student, and with
the latter's diligence and skill. But it is not uncommon for a
student to spend a week on orientation reading, then another
week on bibliographic work resulting in from one hundred to
two hundred working bibliography cards. During this bibliographic effort it is necessary to develop some ability to screen
or rapidly scan and estimate the worth of material. Such procedures present dangers; but so does an effort to explore thor-
oughly all materials encountered. Some screening can be done
from bibliographic data in the card catalog or in other bibliographic aids: titles may show what a book covers, or its intent
(e.g., levity or popularization); the publisher may indicate quality (a university press probably will avoid the frivolous, a communist press probably will view reality in terms of the expected clichés); the length may be indicative (110 pages is
short for a useful economic history of Europe); the date of
publication may indicate authorship too early for the chief
area of interest of the researcher; editing by a well-known
scholar suggests quality.

Many items must, of course, be examined. This sometimes
can be done quickly. Coverage often can be judged by a scanning of table of contents and index. Quality can be judged
tentatively by sampling pages and observing the method of
dealing with evidence. Prefaces, introductions, bibliographies,
and footnotes may give quick indications of the desirability of
taking research notes from an item. After such a preliminary

examination of an item, a judgment of its quality should be entered on the working bibliography card. If no further use need be made of an item—whether a study or contemporary evidence—that should be so stated, to avoid a second examination due to failure of memory.

From this first set of working bibliography cards should be culled (without discarding the others) the most promising items in the light of knowledge to this point, and in consideration of the emphases developed in the initial week of orientation reading. Research notetaking should be begun in these items. Usually it will be best to begin with the studies by other scholars which appear most promising, leaving the contemporary evidence to a bit later.

The beginning researcher must identify as many items of probable value for his subject as he can, *whether or not they are in the holdings of the libraries he will be able to use.* There are three major reasons for this bibliographic effort: (*a*) to identify a large part of the materials, so as to permit a selection from the apparently best materials, either those immediately available, or possibly available through travel or by interlibrary loan or in microcopy; (*b*) training in bibliographic method, which is to some extent independent of "use" of the materials identified; and (*c*) it probably will enlarge and improve understanding of the dimensions of the research project itself.

II

Facts and ideas, proof and probability

No facts speak for themselves to lighten the historian's task, not even facts as objects—a chariot wheel or a baby's crib—to say nothing of facts as events or ideas. So, facts must be made to speak, in the light of historians' varying purposes, erudition, abilities to deal with problems of proof and probability, and sense of the fitness of things. This chapter deals with some of the problems involved in thinking about historical inquiry.

A. Facts as values, ideas, objects, events

Just give us the facts, some people (even some historians) say. The difficulty in doing so begins with the character of historical fact itself. There can be no all-embracing and all-acceptable definition of historical fact. There are no measurable and unvarying units as in communication theory or chemistry. Each fact, on examination, turns out to be made up of a variety of facts. The Battle of Waterloo was a fact as event, but made up of many smaller facts as events (drum rolls, charges and retreats, heads mashed by cannon balls, orders shouted by officers); and it also was made up of facts as objects (field guns, boots, food depots, bandages, hills, streams, cadavers); finally, it consisted of ideas and values, which shaped the actions of men on the field—even the officers' shouted orders. And each of these facts as object, event, or idea can be further subdivided. So the Battle of Waterloo is only a single "fact" in certain contexts decided upon by the historian; e.g., the Battle of Waterloo demonstrated the genius of Wellington.

One of the great problems of historical inquiry is that ideas in the life of man are facts as surely as are atomic bombs and chocolate soufflés. Ideas (and values and motives, as types of ideas) may be subjective facts, but they are real in their effects upon history. Remember, however, that even in the case of objects we often have only the mental images of them recorded by witnesses. In the case of ideas, we have impressions of states of mind. In the case of motives, we often make do with sheer guesses based on actions, incidental and tangential statements, or suppositions regarding character and intent. That is, we move from demonstrable proof to inference. And all this we put into language, itself a system of symbols.

The activity of individuals, and the institutions, quarrels, decisions of man in society are determined not only by the physical conditions of existence—the weather, mineral resources, soil types, virus disease, sun flares—but by the ideas men hold of their relations with each other, of their hopes of life, of the nature of property, of the sources of the territorial jurisdiction of political units, of the nature of governance. How much of the triumph and disaster of human history has been molded by the ideas of the divine right of kings, equality, freedom, nationalism.

In a sense, it can be asserted that the life of man—especially, but not exclusively, civilized man—is almost entirely a history of ideas, that these are the engines that chiefly determine the direction of human movement. This means political ideas, regarding representative government, woman suffrage, nepotism; social ideas, as slavery, class distinction, incest; or spiritual or metaphysical conceptions, as damnation, or nirvana.

It certainly is the case that much of the activity of man in society, actions involving organized groups and institutions, is dependent upon agreement on ideas. Without this agreement, effective action is difficult. An electoral process will not work well if there is no firm agreement to accept the results. There is no physical safety without agreement on rules of conduct. There can be no discussion if opponents can howl down debate.

In sum, although there are discoverable facts as events (battles, births, deaths, famines, voyages, inaugurations) that often can be agreed on regardless of the views of the historian, they can be interperted only in the light of theories about society and man therein. Historians carry different theories to the raw material of event. Thus, interpretation in the later 20th century is not the same in the Soviet Union, China, and the United States. And the views of the historians of a given nation change over time, so that history constantly is being reinterpreted, the same events judged, weighed, ordered, generalized upon in different fashions.

This is another way of saying that the interpretation of history is selective, that within the vast mass of raw material emphasis is placed on those items that seem meaningful to the historian in terms of his conception of human society, in terms of his own ideas. So it follows that historians often disagree. But this is no reason for not reading history. We do not abandon politics because statesmen fall out, or resort to witch doctors because medical doctors dispute, or repudiate science as its new findings cancel some of the old.

Also, we may say that (as if all the above did not offer difficulty enough) ideas are slippery things to grasp, often too slippery for the imprecision of language. In addition, ideas are difficult to identify, detect, weigh in individuals, because they involve often unexpressed, or poorly verbalized, beliefs, hopes, attitudes. Further, social changes over time bring new meanings both to words and to ideas. We must remember that words and ideas have histories.

We must distinguish between "single" (or bare) facts and linkages of objects and events with ideas. Fortunately for the

historian, it is possible to feel confident about the bare facts
of the place and date of the death of Napoleon, and about much
of the physical scene at the Battle of Warteloo; it is much more
difficult to discuss the role of morale in the great battle or the
later problem of frustration as a cause of the death of the ex-
emperor.

The historian's own sense of values, we must emphasize
again, affects his search for evidence and his understanding of
that evidence. This makes difficult obedience to Ranke's famous
injunction to the historian to put down the "facts," and sternly
resist the temptation to judge or to moralize. Values and facts
cannot always be conveniently compartmentalized. Senator
Barry Goldwater voted against the Civil Rights Act of 1964, a
fact easily verified by checking the *Congressional Record*. But
its significance as a fact hinges upon the value placed on his act
by various groups of citizens. To millions of Negroes it was a
hostile act demonstrating Goldwater's lack of sympathy with
their situation; to millions of Southern whites it was a cour-
ageous act demonstrating his dedication to states' rights and
constitutionalism. The influence upon the presidential election
of 1964 of Goldwater's vote against the Civil Rights Act hinges
not upon the fact itself but upon the value judgments associated
with it. These value judgments are, in this sense, themselves
facts and must be considered by the historian.

But how does the historian's own sense of values enter the
situation? As a person, he may either approve or disapprove
Goldwater's civil rights stand; as a historian, he would do well
to heed Ranke and avoid moralizing upon it. But he cannot
avoid including it and evaluating its influence—not if he wants
to explain an election so bizarre that a Republican candidate
carried four states in the deep south and only one in the rest of
the country. Twentieth-century American historians cannot help
but believe that elections are important, that the factors by
which they are determined ought to be understood, and that
legislation affecting the status of millions of people is of significance. This is what we really mean by saying that a system

of values, usually implicit rather than explicit, always dictates the historian's selection of materials.

To be sure, as we have said before, certain facts can be treated almost without reference to values; e.g., the date of John Adam's death, or the weight of a nuclear weapon, or the time required for a given journey to the Moon. Such matters can, however, by linkage with other events, objects, and ideas enter into considerations involving value judgment; they may even be turned into aspects of a metaphysical question.

B. Probability, plausibility, certainty

Imagine that you are a third party listening to a conversation betwen Bill and his girl friend Mary. The mental comments that you might be making are indicated in brackets.

Mary: Hello, Bill, how are you this morning? [Does this salutation mean that Mary is really deeply interested in Bill's health, or is it merely casual politeness?]

Bill: Oh, I'm OK. How are you? [Is Bill really feeling well, or is he concealing a hangover? Why?]

Mary: I'm not feeling very well. I have a headache. [Does she really, or does she want sympathy? Why?]

Bill: Sure is raining hard, isn't it? [It's probably really raining. Why would Bill tell an untruth that would be immediately apparent? But maybe the issue is how *hard* it's raining. Is Bill trying to talk Mary out of doing something he doesn't want to do? How much rain is the weather bureau registering?]

Mary: Oh, I think it'll clear up. [Does she really think so, or is she trying to persuade herself and Bill that they can carry through their plans?]

Bill: That's a pretty hat you have on. [Mary probably does have a hat on. Bill wouldn't be mistaken on this. Or might he be, hairdos being what they are? But does Bill really think that it is pretty, or does he want to please Mary?]

Mary: Thanks. I borrowed it from my roommate. [Probably she did. What difference does it make?]

Bill: I'm sorry that I forgot your birthday. [He probably did

neglect the poor girl's birthday. Otherwise why make himself look
bad? But did he *forget* it or did he just *not bother* to get her a present?]

    Mary: Oh, that's all right. [Is this Mary's true feeling? Probably
not. She's more likely to be hurt or angry.]

    Bill: Yesterday at the lecture you cut Professor Smith announced
an hour examination for April 15th. [Is this accurate? Was Bill there?
Did he hear correctly?]

    Mary: Guess what! Last night I saw a flying saucer land on the
campus and five little men with pointed heads got out. [I just don't
believe it!]

Obviously, even the most casual conversations are made up
of all kinds of statements, some probably true, some probably
false, some probably accurate, some probably inaccurate, some
plausible, some implausible. In dealing with people—even those
we like and trust—we are constantly evaluating their statements.
We have to make continuous judgments, sometimes consciously, sometimes unconsciously.

Yet unthinking people tend to accept statements that they
see in print or in writing. They are much quicker to give
credence to what they read in books and newspapers or in
letters and diaries than to what they hear in conversation. To
a degree, this preference for the written over the spoken word
may be justified. Conscientious people may make a special
effort to be truthful and accurate when they are committing
themselves to writing, especially if the document is to be published. But the basic problem remains the same. Writers have
the same personal biases, the same private interests, the same
frailties of observation that conversationalists have. Indeed
there may often be a stronger temptation to conceal the truth
in a formal written document than in a candid conversation
among friends.

The commonsense evaluation we make in everyday situations therefore has its direct counterpart in the internal criticism
of documents. It will clarify the discussion if we realize that a
single statement ought never to be accepted as true beyond the
shadow of a doubt. Even the most truthful of men may conceal

or distort the truth under certain circumstances; even the most accurate of observers will sometimes be mistaken. The researcher must make the best judgment he can on every statement that is important to his investigation. In each case the judgment is one of varying degrees of *probability*—probably true, probably accurate, probably untrue, probably inaccurate. In actual practice many statements will fall in the intermediate range: they are perhaps true and accurate, perhaps untrue or inaccurate; they are statements to be handled carefully and compared with other evidence.

Some statements are inherently plausible; that is, we find them easy rather than difficult to believe. This is particularly true of statements that are consistent with other information that we have about the situation, the known ideas and behavior of the parties, what has happened earlier and later in a series of events. Yet the test of *plausibility* does not substitute for that of *probability*. The plausible statement is by no means to be accepted as necessarily true. Indeed the clever liar tries to make his untruths seem as plausible as possible. At most then, the fact that a statement is plausible merely adds to the probability of its truth.

The opposite case is that of the implausible statement, the statement that we find difficult to believe. Statements are implausible if they do not fit with the rest of the evidence. Such statements are probably false or mistaken, yet they cannot be dismissed out of hand. Readers of detective stories will remember the numerous occasions on which the incongruous piece of evidence proves to be not only true but the key to the mystery. In historical investigation this dramatic turn of events occurs less frequently, but it occasionally happens. The careful historian will remember that a piece of evidence may seem implausible only because of a mistaken interpretation of previously known evidence. Even more implausible are statements that run counter to our best scientific knowledge—statements about witchcraft, extrasensory perception, flying saucers, and the like. Certainly the trained investigator will deal with all such stories with a very high degree of skepticism. They are probably false or mistaken. Yet he should temper his skepticism with a bit of humility. The history of science is a history of changing ideas about what is possible and what is impossible, and the evidence of an extremely improbable event just might be confirmed by further investigation.

Although at best, single statements may be evaluated as no more than *probably* true and accurate, documents are capable of a different kind of analysis in which we may accept a measure of *certainty*. Even a completely untruthful document reveals the ideas and concepts available to its author. If he writes about flying saucers and little men, he is familiar with the concepts of flying, saucers, and men, and has an idea of size. For contemporary documents such analysis is not very helpful, but for documents about ancient or little known societies it may provide a useful tool of investigation.

Certainty is not to be found on the larger historical problems. The best historians have been able to judge when they have accumulated about all that could be expected with reasonable effort for the construction of an explanation that was highly probable. They realized that their own values and assumptions affected their choices and interpretations at every stage of their activity, but thought it more productive to press forward with the inquiry rather than constantly wrestle with epistemological questions. Specialists with a bent toward the latter activity may deplore this, but they do not write much history. There is another sort of laborer in the historical field who does not write history: the scholar who collects for a lifetime, finding refuge in an impossible search for all the evidence, and the attainment of an unattainable certainty.[1]

C. Some historical ideas and explanations

We are interested in ideas because (a) they influenced past events; (b) they influence the historian's interpretation of past events; and (c) difficult problems of proof arise in connection

---

[1] See VI E, below, on corroboration, and judgments regarding sufficiency of evidence.

with the effort to show the influence of ideas in human affairs. We have selected for discussion a few ideas that are important in themselves and to historians, but also are illustrative of the problems of historical interpretation and proof, which are, after all, at the heart of the craft. Commenting on such problems is a way of getting into some of the intricacies of methodology.

Continuity and change

History often seems to deal only with change. We hear it said that history is being made at a rapid rate today. What is meant, of course, is that the map of Africa and Asia is burgeoning with new nations, astronauts are being orbited in space, Negro demonstrators are on the march, college students are restless.

All this is true, yet change is only a small part of the human picture. Suppose, that instead of the familiar greeting, "What's new?" we ask, "What's old?" Obviously much of human behavior is immensely old. People marry and divorce, laugh and weep, work and play, worship and sin in 20th-century America, and they carried on these same activities in first-century Rome. Also old are our basic social and political groupings (family, village, city, nation, empire), our instruments of written communication (letters, books, magazines, newspapers), our educational institutions (schools, colleges, and universities).

The complaint of the disenchanted youth that he is born into a world he never made has an obvious basis. Yet it is fortunate that this is true. If each generation had really to make its world anew, creating from nothing all its patterns of behavior, all its means of livelihood, all its political and social institutions, mankind could do little more than struggle to keep alive. One of the great advantages of being human is that we inherit all these aspects of our culture. Each generation leaves only a thin accretion on the huge reef of humanity's experience.

Respect for what is old gives us perspective on what is new. We soon perceive that the completely new in human affairs is rare. The 1961 achievement of the Russians in first orbiting a man through space around the earth was a notable triumph, but both Russia and America had experimented earlier with unmanned space vehicles. Nor were the so-called artificial satellites themselves wholly novel. Their launching would have been impossible without earlier experimentation with long-range ballistic missiles and military rockets. The not-too-distant ancestors of today's mighty Saturns were the high-arching rockets that delighted our grandfathers on the Fourth of July. Equally necessary for modern space triumphs was the patient accumulation of scientific knowledge during earlier generations, knowledge about the laws of motion, the composition of the atmosphere and space, the uses of mathematics, and the transmission of electronic commands. So viewed, the question of who *invented* space travel becomes pointless. Man's curiosity and inventiveness over many generations played a much larger part than any single man's genius.

Impressed by this fact of the *continuity of history,* the historian sees every problem in long perspective. He finds the roots of today's racial tensions in lines of development that go back not merely to the Civil War but long before. In trying to understand Russian domestic and foreign policy, he studies not only Marxist ideology but the conditioning experience of hundreds of years of Czarist history. But the idea of continuity is a modern idea; it will not be found—except for hints and isolated anticipations—in ancient and medieval historians.

It is a 19th century idea, this concept of continuing incremental change in human society, of history as a developing process, of linkage rather than periodization, of the existence of the past in the present. It should be noted that even when historians speak of "discontinuities" or "real" or "profound" discontinuities in human affairs (e.g., the revolutions in Russia in 1917, Mexico 1910–17, or China in recent years), they do not mean that all the past was eradicated, but that the rate of change was abruptly increased. Much that was old remains. Scholars need to examine the continuities (often heavily camouflaged) as well as the discontinuities or changes in such post-revolutionary societies. In short, an historical approach is a vital component in the study of current affairs, giving adequate attention to both continuity and change.

The individual and society

Once upon a time it was thought that the good prince made good times and the bad king corrupted society. The element of truth in this notion is now much modified by the view that while devils and saints frequently twist human affairs, they do not all by themselves form or shatter the foundations of society. Ancient Hellenic and romantic Victorian historians who subscribed to the "Great Man Theory" of history tended to give insufficient weight to the role of society (institutions) and culture (values) in forming the ideas of leaders, in structuring the problems they faced, and in molding the solutions they might attempt and achieve.

All men are, of course, born into society, into what anthropologists call a culture. Each culture has many institutions and values—that is, customs, associations, relationships, complexes of values or norms that are enforced in various ways. A man acts, consciously and unconsciously, in the light of the institutions and values of his culture—affected, to be sure, by his own qualities. Great innovators, leaders, villains, can move other men only within limits imposed by the culture—religious, economic, scientific, technological, and political. Julius Caesar could not start automobile manufacture. Muhammed could not have foisted Zen Buddhism on the Arabs. Adolf Hitler born into Samoan society in 1600 might have been simply an indifferent fisherman.

What are sometimes called "social forces" are the outcome of persons acting for change in the context of existing customs and forcing others to do the same. It is obvious that human institutions have varied tremendously in place and time; there are no unvarying social forces, except in the sense that institutions of some sort will deal with certain broad classes of human needs for example, food, sexual gratification, and procreation. There have been many societies with numerous important institutions that involved groups of people dedicated in at least some of their activities to maintaining and extending the rights and obligations of the group. It may be a church, a military institution, a chamber of commerce. Such organized groups have been much studied in recent times. We are better equipped than formerly to examine their organization and structure, membership, doctrine, leadership, and linkages with other institutions.

There are three overriding requirements in the study of individuals and institutions: (1) That they be conceived of as interacting, but with the power of the individual much inhibited by the organized and established strength of the ideas and interests of men grouped in institutions; (2) That it be clear that the historian cannot understand an historical figure except in the context of that figure's own culture. Slavery and permissive homosexuality were facts of ancient Hellenic society, to be understood in that context, not in that of Victorian England; (3) That it be clear that historians are products of their own times— that is, of the institutions of their specific cultures, even if their culture encourages them to study others. Even in a culture that encourages individualism, men are not entirely free, either physically or spiritually.

Generalizations and laws

"History repeats itself" is a saying more popular with nonhistorians than with historians. Franklin D. Roosevelt won the presidential elections of 1932, 1936, 1940, and 1944, an example, presumably, of history repeating itself. Yet if we compare these elections, the dissimilarities may impress us more than the similarities. In each election the Republican candidate was different, the issues were different, the campaigning was different, the popular and electoral votes were different. The same may be said of the numerous instances in human history of warfare, political assassination, religious persecutions, and many other phenomena. So the historian often will regard them more as illustrations of the uniqueness of human events than as proof of the uniformities of history.

Certainly history differs strikingly from the physical sciences. Space travel is possible because the course of a projectile and of a body moving through space repeats itself in a far more dependable way than the course of historical events. By the application of mathematics and "laws," certain results can be reliably predicted from certain antecedent causes. But history deals with so many independent variables, impossible of measurement or control, that it lacks this element of predictability.

Actually, the search for laws of history usually reveals some navieté. The metahistorians are most ambitious in this quest. Even in the field of science the idea of "law" is misleading; the more sophisticated scientists of the 20th century prefer to think in terms of statistical probability. Most, although by no means all, historians regard the search for "laws" of history as a futile endeavor.

Yet there is ample room for a less pretentious kind of historical generalization. Able scholars have written comparative studies of revolutions, demonstrating strikingly similar patterns of events. More limited historical generalizations can be cited. Farmers usually favor inflation; bankers usually oppose it. Lawless men are attracted to the frontier; vigilante justice is often administered there. Wartime periods encourage hasty marriages; postwar periods are likely to experience a rise in the divorce rate.

Such generalizations often involve some fairly simple relationships of cause and effect that the historian can have considerable confidence in. Or they are statements of statistical regularity, non-causal explanations. In any event, they are generalizations in terms of probability, not unvarying "laws." They should be carefully formulated so as not to outrun the evidence. This fault—outrunning the evidence—may be due either to poor conceptualization or to sloppy and unthinking exposition; e.g., extreme terms such as "never," "every," "all," "forever" must not be used unless they are irrefutably justified. This will seldom be possible with three of those terms; in the case of "forever," it will never be possible.

Causation

What caused an historical event? Every student will recognize this as a favorite examination question, and it is an equally favorite question for historians to ask themselves and each other. *What* happened is supposedly an easy or elementary question; *why* it happened is much more difficult and challenging. What were the causes of the fall of the Roman Empire? Of the American Civil War? Of American entry into World War I? Each of these has become a sharply controverted question resulting in a flood of books and articles.

Nor are historians the only persons concerned with the causes of past events. Practical statesmen make implicit judgments about the past whenever they adopt a policy. Undoubtedly the belief that a major cause of war is weakness and division in the face of threatened aggression has been a reason for the abandonment of American isolation, for the organziation of NATO and other defensive alignments, and for American involvement in Korea and Vietnam.

Simple people give simple answers to these questions of causation. Asked why World War II broke out in September, 1939, the unthinking student will be satisfied to answer that the war resulted from Hitler's order sending German troops across the Polish frontier. This is not an adequate answer. During earlier months, Hitler had ordered German troops into Austria and Czechoslovakia, yet no war resulted. What was different on the later occasion? The difference was Polish resistance to German attack and the decision of France and Britain to go to Poland's assistance. But instead of putting an end to our curiosity, such answers only raise new questions: Why was Hitler so determined to move against Poland? Why had British and French leaders decided that German expansion must be halted?

In short, the historian is led beyond the "precipitating" or "immediate" cause of the war—the invasion of Poland, to look at the "underlying" causes that made England and France accept that invasion as a reason for action. He will find himself exploring the Polish question back through the Versailles treaty, and on back to the partitions of Poland in the 18th and 19th centuries, and even back to the migrations of Germans and Slavs during the Middle Ages. Similarly, he may trace German militarism back through Bismarck to Frederick the Great and beyond, and Adolf Hitler's twisted mentality back through the horrors of trench warfare in World War I, frustrations in youth, to the unnourishing social environment into which he was born. To understand the mood of Britain and France in September, 1939, the scholar would have to understand the impact of the Munich crisis and its aftermath, the earlier hope for appeasement, the French alliance system, and a whole antecedent chain of events over many generations. Not only will the search for the causes of World War II ramify backward into time, it also will spread out in space as the historian ponders the influence of such factors as Russia's relations with Germany and with England and France, Franklin Roosevelt's struggles with Congress over American neutrality policy, world economic conditions, and the state of military preparation in various countries of the world.

All of these may seem likely causes, but often it is difficult to prove an agency connecting events. It will not do simply to *correlate* them. This is a vulgar error. Many ridiculous correlations have been observed, such as between the incidence of bathing and great changes in national attitudes or institutions (e.g., in Rome and the United States), or between rainfall and baseball scores. Some correlations, however, have been so striking as to lead to a presumption of causal relationship, and to a search for the link, as in the cases of cigarette smoking and various disorders of the human body.

The historian, therefore, believes in *multiple causation*. He mistrusts the glib amateurs who are always ready to write a book proving that Pearl Harbor resulted from the machinations of Franklin D. Roosevelt, or that Secretary of War Stanton was responsible for the assassination of Abraham Lincoln. Similarly, he is hesitant to believe that the influence of the frontier is the sole cause of American democracy and individualism, or that the pocketbook interest of the founding fathers is the sole cause of the American constitution. He finds instead a plurality of causes behind historical events. Moreover, he always finds a chain of causes; that is, each cause has antecedent causes, and the latter are preceded by still earlier. Theologians or philosophers may postulate a final cause, but such speculation today is considered outside the province of the historian.

If historical events have so many causes, how can the historian discuss cause intelligibly? The answer is that the historian cannot hope to ferret out all of the causes of complex events. Nor can he always demonstrate that his explanations of the relationships between data is causal—it often will merely seem probable, or, even more weakly, plausible. It sometimes helps to accept a logician's definition of the cause of an event as "the sum of the necessary and sufficient conditions for the event's occurrence." If the circumstance is not necessary for the event —that is, the event could have taken place without it—it cannot be the cause; if the circumstance is not sufficient to bring about the event—that is, if the circumstance could have occurred without the event following—it cannot be the cause.

This definition often is difficult to use in historical inquiry. It will yield little as applied to the problem of Hitler's invasion of Poland as a cause of World War II. It may be used with somewhat more confidence in connection with another alleged cause of the war. In the early weeks of the war the German government published a collection of documents intended to prove that the Poles had been guilty of atrocities against the German minority living in Poland. According to the Germans, these atrocities cried out for German intervention, thus were the real cause of the war. There are two problems here. Did such atrocities actually occur, or was the evidence of the German documents fabricated? This is a problem of historical fact, dealt with elsewhere in this book. But the other problem is one of causation. Even if such incidents actually occurred, were these the necessary and sufficient condition for the German action? On this, the evidence from captured German documents seems clear. Hitler was determined to seize Polish territory in any case, and the alleged atrocities served as a pretext rather than a true cause for his action.

The issue of the alleged Polish atrocities involves also the fallacy which logicians call *post hoc, ergo propter hoc* (after this, therefore because of this). Even if it could be proved that the German attack came *after* Polish atrocities, it would not necessarily follow that the attack occurred *because* of the atrocities. A series of causes is not a mere succession of events in time. Some kind of logical dependence of one upon another must be demonstrated.

Medical experimenters, testing the efficacy of the new Salk polio vaccine, conducted controlled experiments and subjected the results to statistical analysis before asserting that the vaccine gave immunity from polio. The historian finds it almost impossible to duplicate this procedure. Dealing with past events that never exactly repeat themselves, he cannot conduct controlled experiments. Yet under certain circumstances he can apply statistical tools. Suppose, for example, his problem is whether the Negro vote was the principal cause of Johnson's victory over Goldwater in the state of Virginia in the 1964 presidential election. The researcher could probably design a study based upon comparison of voting districts with high Negro registration with districts of low Negro registration, working in a comparison between this election and earlier ones, as well. The result of his investigation might well be a convincing set of correlations between the percentage of Negro registrants in a district and the amount of Johnson's majority in that district. Statistical analysis would then tend to support the hypothesis of the decisiveness of the Negro vote. But several cautions must at once be offered. Even in the hands of experts, statistical analysis has many pitfalls, and for the amateur the perils are multiplied. Consider, for example, a possible rival hypothesis that low-income voters played the decisive role in the election. Then the fact that districts with a large Negro registration might also be low-income districts would be a confusing factor in the analysis. More careful study might resolve this difficulty, but other problems probably would be encountered. The purpose of these remarks is not to discourage the student from using statistical tools, but to warn him against superficial or shoddy thinking. Mere correlation does not establish causation; a logical connection between the two series of events must be established.

Not only does the historian have to distinguish between true and spurious causes; he must also attempt to make meaningful generalization about the particular causes that he has identified. In this way, he may group together the attack upon Poland and earlier episodes and find convincing evidence of the aggressive character of the entire Nazi movement. Or generalizing still further about German, Italian, Japanese, and Russian behavior, he may find a larger cause of war in the rise of totalitarianism. In a similar way he may make some generalizing statement about the kinds of action taken by Britain, France, and the United States in response to this totalitarian threat. The failure of the democratic powers to take a strong united stand in earlier years may seem to him another major cause of World War II.

The problem of causation, the most vexatious facing the historian, is beyond complete "solution"—that is, to the permanent satisfaction of all manners of men. It bristles with philosophical and practical difficulties. Are human events "determined," or can individuals choose paths to follow? Apparently the best we can do is assert that we seem to come nearer to free choice on some questions than on others. Could events have developed differently than in fact they did? Yes, if the antecedent causes had been different—which gets us no place. Is there any *absolute* way of determining decisive causes? Probably not; it depends on value systems. Should we therefore abandon efforts to find causes? Some historians do, preferring to deal in non-causal explanations. But to abandon the search for causes would be other than human (that is, it is not likely to happen), and it would leave us with formless and meaningless historical literature. Why should we not regard the search for cause, with appropriate vigor and modesty, as the greatest of the conceptual and technical challenges posed to the craft? At least historians now know more about the causes of many complex historical events (eg., the Protestant Revolution, World War I, the disruption of the ancient Roman world) than did the participants themselves.

Motivation

Since history so often deals with an individual's actions, sometimes it is relevant to probe his motives. For example, on January 1, 1863, President Abraham Lincoln issued the Emancipation Proclamation. Did he do this because of abhorrence of slavery and a determination to end it? If so, why did he wait almost two years after his inauguration to take the step? Or, even more pertinent, why did he limit the proclamation to regions within the control of the Confederacy, excluding exactly those districts where his authority was respected? The historian, analyzing Lincoln's motives as best he can, probably will decide that Lincoln's dislike for slavery is not an adequate explanation, since that dislike was held in check by a sense of duty to act within the Constitution, and by a sense of political realism that deterred him from antagonizing the border states. He may find more convincing motivation in Lincoln's desire to recruit Negro troops, weaken the Confederacy, and strengthen the moral standing of the North in English eyes.

But most of the evidence for all this is indirect; we are working by inference; it is better than nothing, but the historian will be troubled. Even when the person under study leaves testimony as to his motives, we cannot be sure that he is trying to tell the complete truth; in any event, some of his motivation may have been obscure to himself, if only because men often are driven by irrational considerations, or because his motives were too mixed for him to disentangle accurately.

Attribution of motives is seen to be a hazardous business. Our confidence in the result is weak. Of course, the historian is not alone with this difficulty. People often find it difficult to understand their own mixed and confused motives; or they may be unwilling to face them, and leave "false" testimony to confuse the historian. Nor do students of the human mind give us unambiguous guidance. A psychiatrist, after long observation, may find his patient's motives obscure. Psychology has not agreed on a single theory of human personality. It gives us insights, but not answers. Historians thus will be cautious about blanket assignment of human motivation to self-interest, the will to dominate, or altruism.

Motivation may be seen as a special case of causation. But often the researcher must ask himself: Do the motives of this individual much matter in the interpretation of the events under consideration? In many cases it will be decided that it does not much matter, unless simple biography is the objective. For example, if the objective is examination of the reception and practical consequences of the Emancipation Proclamation, Lincoln's motives in issuing the document are of little importance. Nor does it matter much—from most points of view—how much, if any, political motivation was involved in President Franklin Roosevelt's advocacy of Social Security.[2]

Contingency

Although most events in history appear to have their logical explanation in the continuous chain of cause and effect, an occasional event may seem to have a chance or accidental character. Consider the assassination of John F. Kennedy. As soon as the tragic event occurred, men began to speculate on its cause. Since the President's political and social program had antagonized many Southern whites and since Dallas, Texas, was a center of such opposition, it seemed to some men logical to suspect that right-wing extremists had conspired to kill him. Quite different, but inviting to other men, was the conjecture that communists had plotted the President's death because he

---

[2] The beginning researcher should be aware that some professional and many amateur historians would dispute, or at least grumble at, this attitude toward the motives of notable personages.

had been opposing communist ambitions in Germany, Cuba, and Asia.

Yet the facts, as far as the Warren Commission could determine them, would fit no neat pattern of logic. The President's presumed assassin was, to be sure, a professed believer in Marxism, who had at one time renounced his U.S. citizenship. Yet he was as much a misfit in the Soviet Union as in America. The crime was apparently the senseless deed of a mentally twisted man, no more to be explained in terms of a communist plot than in those of a right-wing conspiracy. Not only did the murder seem to have no rational cause, but the circumstances seemed singularly fortuitous. By what unlucky chance had the President chosen to visit this particular city and to travel past the very building where this dangerously abnormal man had recently found employment? By the merest accident the paths of John F. Kennnedy and Lee Oswald seem to have crossed on November 22, 1963. And insofar as the sudden and unexpected death of the President changed the pattern of subsequent events, we may argue that an accidental factor had changed the course of history.

Yet a few comments on this episode, and on contingency in general, are in order. In the first place, the events of the assassination separately considered are not so causeless as we might at first assume. If we ask why the President was in that city and on that street on that day, we will discover an adequate chain of causes. And if we ask why Lee Oswald was lurking in a warehouse prepared to shock the world with a dramatic act of violence, this phenomenon too has its undoubted sequence of causes in his heredity and experience. It is only the convergence of these two lines of causation that gives the assassination its seemingly accidental character. The life of man is full of the crossings of such independent chains of cause and effect. This is what we mean by contingency.

A second point would have to do with the general behavior of presidents and psychopaths. In order to provide effective leadership, all presidents seem compelled to dramatize their role by appearing before applauding crowds. The presidential motorcade has become a fixed pattern of American political behavior. Just as presidents seem to think it necessary to play the role of president in a certain way, a certain percentage of psychopaths with homicidal tendencies and delusions of grandeur always will be present in the population. The underlying cause of the Kennedy assassination lies not in acts of this president and this assassin, but in general behavior patterns, which make such tragic episodes from time to time almost inevitable, however vigilant the Secret Service.

In the third place, we should note that contingency in history usually is of limited long-range significance. Even the sudden and unexpected removal of a popular young president probably did not interrupt major historical sequences. In Germany, in China, in Alabama, events continued to follow events in a way that was probably little different from what might have been expected if Kennedy had never visited Dallas.

Notions of fate, or demons, or other supernatural agencies interfering with human affairs have little currency today, at least among historians. It is, of course, recognized that historical persons have believed in such interventions, and that such belief has had important consequences. In colonial Massachusetts the belief in witches possessed by the devil led to the trials and executions at Salem. At the very least, it must be agreed that human history is strewn with unexpected and unpredictable "accidents."

Progress

During the 19th century a widely postulated "law" of history assumed mankind's majestic progress toward a perfect society —a society where poverty and crime would be unknown, where wars would cease, where government would be based upon the free consent of all, where social justice would be achieved, and human intelligence would find a solution for every problem.

This idea of progress was unknown to earlier ages. Greek and Roman thinkers were more likely to imagine a golden age in the past than in the future, or else they inclined toward cyclical theories of history in which periods of happiness were followed by periods of trouble. During the Middle Ages churchmen-scholars found history's meanings in the purpose and judgments of God. Perfection would be achieved, not in this world, but in a world to come.

Thus, it was not until the Renaissance that writers began to find in history a record of man's progress from barbarism and ignorance toward civilization and knowledge. Confidence in man's potentialities grew stronger during the 18th-century Enlightenment. It reached its apex during the 19th century, when scientific and technological innovations were transforming life, humanitarians were achieving the abolition of slavery and other reforms, governments were granting constitutions and widening the franchise. Progress appeared to be not only a fact but a law of life, a corollary to Darwin's theory of evolution.

Intellectuals of the 20th century have become skeptical of the notion of progress. Again the reasons are clear. Are Nazi gas ovens and Soviet purges evidence of increasing humanitarianism? Are guided missiles and nuclear warheads evidence of the beneficence of science? Pessimists, fearing that mankind is tobogganing toward disaster, often have appeared to make more sense that optimists looking forward to a golden age. Still, while the idea has been under attack, it retains strong partisans in the United States; it is at the bottom of boosterism and propaganda for optimism, and condemnations of pessimism as "un-American" and debilitating.

What are the proofs for this very large idea, this veritable philosophy of history? The evidence of improved knowledge, production, medicine, and at least some social institutions, we have mentioned. Did they not "prove" progress in the 19th century? Most historians would agree. The error was in letting the generalization outrun the evidence, by focusing on too narrow a time-range, by not being sufficiently historical. The indications of such progress before the 19th century were at the best ambiguous, and there was no proof that the conditions of the 19th would continue indefinitely.

Actually, a long view of history supports neither the optimists nor the pessimists. Destructiveness and irrationality seem to be recurring constants in human affairs. Periods of progress have been interrupted by periods of retrogression; empires have flourished and declined; learning has flourished and withered. The sensible conclusion would seem to be that progress is neither automatic nor inevitable, but that it is always possible provided men use their intelligence. Actually, progress ought to become more rather than less possible because of the continuity of history; that is, each generation has at its disposal a larger cultural inheritance and a longer body of experience.

National character

The much discussed subject of national character is useful for consideration because it involves difficult, possibly insoluble, problems of argument and proof. Some scholars consider that national character is an idea without objective reality; others assert that national character is verifiable by the presence of certain characteristics in individual human beings which explain their actions. Much ink has been spilled—and, not too indirectly, considerable blood—in argument over the American, French, English, Russian, Chinese national characters. Many men have believed that such a thing exists, and that Germans should be hated en masse as natural slaves in internal politics and booted brutes in foreign affairs; or Latins dismissed as volatile, Russians as sad, and the English as stolid.

Many problems face the researcher trying to assess national character. There is disagreement as to the definition of nation. Also, there are problems regarding the heterogeneity of national populations, and variations in heterogeneity over time, with it being obviously the case that many cultural groups within the political bounds of nations were so included as the result of military or diplomatic action and not because of the similarity of their cultures to that of the older nucleus of the nation-state. For another thing, there is the problem of defining the critical individual personality traits for description of national character. Then there is the problem of obtaining evidence on the presence of those traits. The effort to apply psycho-analytical techniques, for example, to time past labors under the difficulty that no living subjects are available for the process. For these and other reasons, the subject of national character bristles with difficulties in the collection and interpretation of evidence. Finally, much apparent testimonial or observational evidence from the past probably is suspect because the witnesses or commentators were either unwilling or unable to observe and interpret accurately.

There is general agreement that if national character exists it is an assemblage of characteristics attaching to individuals. Until a few years ago the following assertions (with parenthetic cautions) also were common: If a large proportion of the individuals in a national group (not always so easy to define) possess enough (whatever that amount may be) of these characteristics (not so easy to select) in sufficient strength (however that may be measured), we may say that these are characteristics of that nation, hence of its national character. These postulates did not dispose of the question of whether the mix of characteristics was very different between nations. Nor did it tell us how individuals would act in specified situations. It was more a statistical average (it was hoped) of characteristics found in a given population (undoubtedly assumed by extrapolation from a sample—hopefully representative of the whole).

The parenthetical difficulties indicated in the preceding paragraph were serious enough. New ones have been pointed out in recent years. One very striking one includes the proposition that most persons in the larger nations possess similar personality patterns, and that the characteristically different patterns occur only in small minorities of the totals. This suggestion from psychological research thus concentrates national character in the "modally extant," that is the most frequent (but found in only a small minority of the population) personality pattern. This psychoanalitical technique poses weighty methodological problems, both in measuring individual patterns, and in providing meaningful samples when the techniques are so difficult and time-consuming, and some of the national populations

are so large and diverse. And it has been pointed out that for all
we know the most prevalent pattern in one nation might turn
out to be the same as the most prevalent in another nation. Or
suppose, if this were the case, that the frequencies in the two
nations were considerably different, even though both were
quite low? How would we interpret that?

There has been much variation, over the years, in the selection of characteristics thought to be important in a national context. The older, and the continuing vulgar, interest is in such
things as laziness, deceitfulness, volatility. These are difficult to
define and identify. No one today takes seriously the frequent
19th century English suggestion that American public spitting
was indicative of weakness in the national soul. A recent view
of a political scientist is that the chief attributes of national
political character in modern times are particularism, atomism,
orderliness, otherworldliness, restraint, a sense of mission, herr-
envolkism, mysticism and humility, anthropocentrism, material-
ism, egalitarianism, traditionalism, logicism, empiricism, ex-
perimetalism, and resoluteness.[3] Such heterogeneity may be
balanced by reference below to efforts to boil American national character to one or a few fundamentally distinctive
elements.

It is heartening to observe that at least now it is the pre-
dominant scholarly view that national characteristics are determined largely by social conditions operating upon our common pool of psychic resources and limitations. The older view
(not dead today) is that such characteristics were conferred by
God on nations, or resulted from peculiar climates or soils, or
somehow were "inherent" in Romans or Gauls or Italians, something like a national soul present in the infant at birth, equally
present in all individuals in the nation, and unchanging over
time.

Inability or unwillingness to observe and interpret accu-

---

[3] James C. Charlesworth, "National Character in the Perspective of Political Science," pp. 23–29 in *National Character in the Perspective of the
Social Sciences,* March, 1967, issue of *The Annals* of the American Academy
of Political and Social Science.

rately is common in writers on national character. Superpatriotism, self-esteem, jealousy, frustration, obscure thousands of pages of dogmatism on the subject. In addition, the subject simply is too difficult for many persons who attempt to grapple with it. It is precisely the sort of matter Adolf Hitler quite incorrectly supposed himself to understand.

What characteristics, in what combination, demonstrate a national character different from that of other national groups? How to prove the existence of these characteristics in individuals? From their utterances? From their actions? Are these superficial or fundamental indications of the characteristics in question? Are a few statements or actions by an individual sufficient to demonstrate that the characteristic is present in force? In how much force? What is it likely to lead the individual to do? How many individuals must be "proven" to possess the presumed proper mix of characteristics in order to permit a confident assertion that the majority of the population possesses this mix of characteristics? Are there significant ethnic or social variations?

Not only is it difficult to get sufficient proof of the presence of given characteristics, in a large enough sample of a national population, and with a determinable strength or force, but we find that the mix apparently changes in time. The English of the 17th century had a reputation for instability. Did they not execute and exile kings? But in the 19th century the accepted view of the English national character was of a stable, reliable, even stolid people. The Mexicans of the 19th century often were thought indolent; today they seem more energetic than many Latin Americans. So national character changes as social conditions change, unless we wish to return to the old foolishness about God's favoritism or changing climates or mysterious emanations.

It should be observed, also, that testimony on characteristics varies widely with the witnesses. In the 19th century Charles Dickens criticized American characteristics that Domingo Sarmiento of Argentina, observing at the same time, praised. This almost certainly was because Dickens considered English cul-

ture superior to American, whereas Sarmiento admired the
United States as a model for his more backward homeland.

Controversy on American (i.e., United States) national character is illustrative of the difficulties of the subject. Some scholars believe that Americans ask "Who are we?" more fervently
than some Europeans because American history is short, its
traditions thin, the backgrounds of its population varied due to
rapid, heavy immigration; that all this leaves Americans self-
conscious and self-critical. These scholars assert that in trying so
hard to find out who they are, Americans sometimes find themselves prescribing who they ought to be. The fact of a House
Committee on Un-American Activities, according to this analysis, reveals more than fuzzy thinking; it denotes insecurity,
which may itself be an American characteristic. Are there
French, English, or Italian committees on "unnational" activity?

Other scholars find the foregoing suggestions superficial and
undemonstrable. They assert that American harping on national
character may originally (i.e., in the decades after the Declara-
tion of Independence) have been partly due to a consciousness
of lack of tradition, and sensitivity to European sneers (not
quite the same thing); but that quite early it also was founded
on pride in what was conceived as American superiority, and
that this element long has been apparent. Further, other new
nations, less successful than the United States, as Argentina and
Mexico (who, incidentally, resent the United States appropria-
tion of the term "American"), now seem more interested in the
issue of national character than the United States. Finally, it is
not clear that the surfacing of xenophobia, anti-Communism,
conservatism, and other phenomena in a swirl of activity about
the Un-American Activities Committee proves by itself that
these phenomena are absent in France, Spain, and Germany.
To put it mildly, these phenomena are strongly present in the
nations named, and in many others.

The notion that the American was a new man acting upon
new principles, new ideas, new opinions, was long ago expressed
by the French visitor Crèvecoeur and, somewhat later, by the

historian Frederick J. Turner. According to Turner, free land drew Europeans west in America, and there the frontier transformed his habits, language, and customs. The process was repeated for three centuries, so long as free land existed in the west, and the American who emerged was rugged, impatient, successful, materialistic, and, most of all, individualistic. But Turner's critics declared that he neglected the influence of community life, which Americans did not merely suffer, as Turner implied, but created for mutual benefit. They contended that community-mindedness long has been evident in habits of co-operation and control imposed by group life and its pressures. Whereas Turner emphasized freedom, for some of his critics the central American concept was equality, and this was secured through the physical and social pressures of group life.

In recent decades there have been a number of suggestions that competitiveness has been the truly formative element in American life, as compared with other societies. This competitiveness is asserted to have come not only from relative lack of tradition, prescription, social rigidity, but also from relative material abundance, which increases the putative rewards of competitive action. It is claimed that the emphasis on competition, and the rapid economic and social transformation of America, created especially severe contradictions between the older and the newer values, thus accounting for various social phenomena, from violence and crime to passion for psychoanalysis. Such suggestions seem at least as persuasive as Turner's appeal to the freedom of the frontier, or Schlesinger's emphasis on community-mindedness.

A current interest of some critics is whether the American character is being departed from, diluted, or violated if and when Negroes are offered less freedom, equality, or opportunity to compete. If this is the case, and if it always has been the case, then the American character must be defined to include the prescription that participation must be limited on racial grounds. If, on the other hand, Negro Americans have been moving toward greater participation in such characteristics, they must be acknowledged to have been affected to some extent by the environment and to partake to some extent of the national character.[4]

---

[4] See David M. Potter, *People of Plenty: Economic Abundance and the American Character* (Chicago: University of Chicago Press, 1954), for a discussion by an historian that makes considerable use of the work of social and behavioral scientists. But Potter has recently been strongly and persuasively criticized, for example, for depending too much on inference, on "argument from logic," rather than on "data-reinforced" statements. See David E. Stannard, "American Historians and the Idea of National Character: Some Problems and Prospects," *American Quarterly*, XXIII (May 1971), 202–20, and for remarks on the modal personality concept. Another useful introduction to the large literature is "National Character in the Perspective of the Social Sciences," *The Annals* of the American Academy of Political and Social Science, March 1967: 165 pages of discussion, from the points of view of various disciplines, and with articles on the national characters of 13 countries.

III

Historical evidence

This chapter not only categorizes the evidence used by historians, but in so doing introduces the beginning researcher to the processes of analysis. Categorization requires examination of the character and quality of evidence. Nothing is more important in research. We are here concerned both with the different *forms* of evidence, and with the social and individual psychological factors that determine the *quality* and *credibility* of evidence.

A. The categorization of evidence

1. There are a number of schemes for the classification of historical evidence. Many of them have value, but three seem most useful to us.

a) Our broadest classification in this chapter is into "documents" and "other," in turn divided into sub-classes. We use this classification on the grounds that our students (and, indeed, our History faculty) use little but documentary evidence in their research. This has been so nearly true of most historians that in the 19th century Langlois and Seignobos in their well-known *Introduction to the Study of History* scarcely considered that the training of historians required attention to other forms of evidence, because "documents [are] the sole source of historical knowledge."

b) More important to analysis is distinguishing between the witness or participant in events, and testimony by others. "Others" in this sense means both men living at the time the events under consideration occurred, but who did not witness or participate in them; and historians who may live centuries after the event. To be sure, nonwitnesses contemporaneous with the events often leave us a record of their conversations with witnesses, or relevant evidence on encircling events or environment. Thus "contemporary evidence" is a useful category to bear in mind, encompassing witnesses, nonwitnesses, and a third class of nonpersonal documents (e.g., constitutions) and artifacts (e.g., bludgeons, coins, feather capes) produced at the time. It is suggested, therefore, that the most useful categorization with this purpose in view is into "contemporary materials" ("materials" is more neutral than "sources") and "studies." We suggest this, for example, for the bibliography. The value of this division is little frayed by the fact that occasionally a "study" is done by an historian who was a witness of or participant in the events he describes and analyzes. Finally, it must be remembered that various mixtures of evidential categories exist (for example, an account of events left in writing by a witness may include both his statements based on observation and also his recording of hearsay).

c) There is some value in thinking of types of evidence as falling into the two classes of the consciously or deliberately and the unconsciously transmitted. The supposition is that bias is more common in consciously than in unconsciously transmitted evidence. Both this supposition, and the assignment of many sorts of evidence, or specific examples in the subdivisions, bristle with difficulties. Consideration of such division is, however, a critical exercise of some worth. Figure 1 shows the division into these two types of evidence.[1]

Figure 1. Consciously and unconsciously transmitted historical evidence

---

   I.   Consciously Transmitted
      A. Written: annals, chronicles, some inscriptions, diaries, memoirs, genealogies.
      B. Oral
         1. Traditional: ballads, tales, sagas
         2. Contemporary interviews
      C. Art Works: historical paintings and mosaics, portraits, scenic sculpture, coins, medals, some films

  II. Unconsciously Transmitted
      A. Human Remains
      B. Written: "mere" records (e.g., business, military, government)
      C. Oral: e.g., wiretapped conversation
      D. Language
      E. Customs and Institutions
      F. Artifacts
         1. Artistic works
         2. Tools, etc.

Based on John Vincent, *Historical Research*, 1934 ed., pp. 21–23.

2. Figure 1 deliberately leaves out of account many of the tags traditionally used in categorizing historical evidence. The student must be prepared to encounter and to be initially confused by such labels as source, contemporary source, secondary source or work, original source, primary source.

3. As will be seen below, documents should be considered to consist of materials in writing,[2] and especially there should be no question that the term includes materials set up in type.

---

[1] Another classification of some value is that which distinguishes between evidence involving words (written or oral) and evidence lacking them (tools, pottery without inscriptions, etc.).

[2] And even for some purposes to include much "unwritten but verbal" material (e.g., tape recordings).

To use document as a synonym for manuscript was a practice—
fortunately moribund—arising out of a desirable emphasis on
better use of archival material, but also out of both snobbery
and sloppy analysis.

4. Historians must be prepared to use "tainted" materials,
and lies. Forgeries may be interesting in themselves as evidence
of interest in a subject, and they may include veracious details.
And who would not like to have tape recordings or shorthand
notes of the lies told to historian questioners by Nero, Napoleon, and Cleopatra? The admissibility of historical evidence is
not restricted in the fashion of legal evidence, where the rules on
direct, circumstantial, hearsay, and original evidence are designed not only to elicit the "truth" but to protect contestants
and to secure for society decisions of approximate justice within
tolerable periods of time. It is clear that historians are entitled—
indeed, required—to indulge in conjecture (properly identified
as to degree of probability) in a way that courts could not tol-
erate.

5. The evidence—documentary or other—available on the
past often touches but fitfully the activities of man. We cannot
know, of course, what or how much occurred of which we have
no trace. In any event, no sane historian would want evidence
on all of human actions, mental and physical, even if such a
possibility were imaginable. But what we do have is unevenly
distributed, and often in a merely accidental way. Much evidence that once existed has been destroyed, accidentally or purposefully. In many areas of human activity poor records or no
records are kept, either because of the state of the culture (e.g.,
religious taboos against certain types of record), or because it
was thought expedient to minimize records (e.g., in the world
of espionage). The conversational activity of man leaves but
intermittent traces (even in our age of "bugging"), and these
often set down tardily and inaccurately. It is an old bad joke
that it is easier to write the history of the ancient Mediterranean
world because the record is relatively scanty. On the other hand,
the historian of recent times often has the opposite problem in
that the mass of evidence confronting him demands a selection

process at once imaginative, soundly related to the purpose and the records, and operable within a lifetime.

B. Documents

This *Guide,* as noted above, deals largely with that class of evidence called documents. Most methodological problems and processes can be illustrated from documents. It will be clear that the following discussion is tied primarily to fairly recent documents, although much of what is said can be applied, with modification, to earlier times. We have observed that one definition of document is any written language. The student is reminded, however, that the term sometimes is taken to refer to writing on paper-like materials, and the term inscriptions is used to denote the class of documents inscribed on hard materials.[3]

Men developed writing independently in several places; apparently first in Sumeria in the Middle East in about the mid-fourth millenium B.C.; somewhat later in Egypt; later yet in the Indus Valley, possibly in the mid-third millenium; in China in the late third millenium; in the Maya area of Central America, possibly about the time of the birth of Christ.[4] The Mycenaean Greeks had writing possibly in the early second millenium B.C., the Minoans of Crete somewhat later. Alphabetic writing, in which symbols (letters) represent single sounds (rather than ideas or syllables), greatly increasing the effectiveness of communication by script, apparently was invented by Semites in the Palestine-Syria area about 1100 B.C.[5] From this old Semitic alphabet descended Greek, Etruscan, modern European, Arabic, and other alphabets.

It is obvious that the beginning of true writing in a culture provides an important dividing line between the types of evidence available to the historian. With the production of docu-

---

[3] See Chapter V (B) for discussion of inscriptions.

[4] Some of these dates are conjectural, as are the possible influences of one script on another.

[5] Cf. David Deringer, *Writing* (New York: Praeger, 1962), for discussion of scripts having phonetic elements without being truly alphabetic.

ments, the nature of the record is changed; it becomes much
more detailed, and it becomes more additive or accumulative
—the generations can learn more effectively from each other.
The culture develops a greatly expanded memory. Civilization
is difficult without writing, without the transmission of masses
of data and ideas. The languages and the scripts used in this
writing all have separate histories (though sometimes affecting
each other), that is, they changed in time.[6]

Both design and accident have had roles in the preservation
of documents. The amount of material extant for a culture
today does not bear any *necessary* direct relationship to the
quantity originally produced, although sometimes, in fact, quantity has been a factor of consequence in the preservation of
documents. The other factors involved in determining preservation are: (*a*) the physical materials used for writing, (*b*) the
nature of the storage system, and (*c*) social conditions. The
first of these requires little comment. It is plain that baked clay
documents in dry climates may last a long time, and that writing
on linen in a damp climate will soon be destroyed by decay.
Also, huge stone stelae are difficult to move, and may for that
reason be preserved. This last consideration is, however, much
affected by social conditions: e.g., by the presence of a population desirous of mining ancient stone structures for materials for
erection of new buildings. As for storage, we may say that the
ancients seldom were concerned with providing an historical
record except as this was involved in magical or religious or
familial considerations, or some limited governmental purposes,
and some business transactions. Storage often was secretion.
Hoards of secreted documents keep turning up in modern times.
Conditions of preservation may be especially favorable if the
documents were hidden in a dry location. Documents of metal
sealed in jars in the Palestine area have proven rather resistant
to the rots of time. Skin and paper-like materials also came
down the ages well if secreted in dry airtight containers.

Social conditions affect the preservation of documents in

---

[6] See Chapter V (B) on paleography, linguistics, diplomatics.

many ways. Religious partisans (e.g., those of the Inquisition) or political groups (Nazi or Communist parties) may burn or otherwise destroy documents, or prevent their creation. Preservation may be aided by a fad for collection, as in the Renaissance. In the United States today, the illuminated pages of medieval hymnals may be bought separately in cellophane wrappers at Macy's department store.

The amount of documentation does play some role in preservation. This relates to the number of literates, the requirements they have for documents (individually and as operators in institutions), the technology of documentary production, and prices. Requirements for documents may be affected, among other things, by the general nature of the economic and social system, or by such specific social phenomena as censorship or representative government. Requirements may also bear some relationship to storage and retrieval methods. There would seem to be no point in producing more documentation than can be handled effectively.

It is precisely this situation that threatens us today. Data handling techniques barely have kept up with the increase in the production of documents. Recently, the population, information, educational, bureaucratic, and scientific explosions have vastly increased the pace of document production, the copies required or desired in each case (or of each edition), and the transmission of documents from place to place. This includes material in letterpress, offset printing, mimeograph and other machine duplication processes, typescript, etc. It includes materials that are published and sold, that are scattered almost broadcast to the general public by pressure groups and advertisers and political parties, that are directed to large but specialized "publics," that are circulated only within business or government offices, and materials that are given security classifications by government officials and that scarcely circulate at all. The storage files of governments (national and local) and international organizations (United Nations, Organization of American States, NATO), of General Motors and Fiat, of Chambers of Commerce, of fraternal organizations and social clubs, are crammed with the wordage of the bureaucratized culture.

Great expenditures of money and of technical talent are being made in efforts to bring this Niagara of verbiage under control. Mechanical, magnetic, photographic, and electronic methods of storage and retrieval have been devised to permit the rapid and accurate manipulation of documentation. Unfortunately, the indexing and cataloging of the kinds of documents and forms of evidence used by most historians have not kept pace with the new hardware of storage and retrieval. Historians of the future may do much of their collecting of evidence by electronic means. A greal deal of drudgery may thus be eliminated. On the other hand, the historical craft may be required to contribute to the process of putting the material into proper form for electronic manipulation—or at least to help plan ways of doing this for given types of material.[7]

In our present period of transition, however, the historian—especially of recent times—must hone a sharp edge to his skills in the use of the prodigious volume of documentation available to him. Classification of documents assists somewhat in locating, selecting, and judging the general quality of documents. There is no magic in the "categories" of documents suggested here; they are merely a convenience for getting into the subject. They are in fact, primarily of use as an entry into the processes of verification and verbal analysis discussed in later chapters.

The student must know the difference between published and unpublished documents. The latter have been enormously multiplied in recent times. This is a distinction founded upon whether or not there was public issuance; it has nothing to do with whether or not the documents are in manuscript or are printed or typed. Huge numbers of documents are produced by the great bureaucracies, public and private, of the modern

---

[7] Actually, all major data-producing agencies may be required to put their material in common machine language; some day, hopefully, the data may be at least partially indexed by electronic means.

world, sometimes using printing presses, but reserved for private circulation (that is, never published for public use).

There is the distinction between printed and manuscript material. Were words marked down in type by a machine, or inscribed by hand with a pen or pencil or crayon? Manuscript materials, as we noted earlier, once were thought by some scholars to be the really important documents for historical research. This view no longer obtains.[8] There may be little difference between a memorandum handwritten by Secretary of State John Quincy Adams and a memorandum dictated by Cordell Hull to a stenographer and transcribed by a typist. There is, however, a certain charm about the use of handwritten documents, especially those composed by famous persons. There is also a certain difficulty in their use in repositories around the world, as several of the authors of this manual have discovered. There are aggravations involved in deciphering badly spelled, poorly written and much abbreviated 18th-century Spanish from paper warped by subtropic heat and humidity, ink faded and smudged by time and handling, and pages riddled by worms.

Documents sometimes are categorized in terms of (*a*) time of composition in relation to observation of the matter observed, or (*b*) the audience for which the document is intended, or (*c*) the intent of the composer. Such classifications are only marginally helpful. The time of composition in relation to observation is important in the use of documentary evidence, but it does not aid much in the classification of documents. The same is true of the confidentiality of documents. A bit more can be done with classification by intent.

The intent of the composer of a document is an important part of the process of judging its credibility or plausibility. Many documents are composed not just with the intent of telling as much of the truth as possible, but of editing or distorting the facts, either to improve communications (which may often be laudable and proper), or to make a point or create an im-

---

[8] Manuscript materials may still be of especial interest if they indicate: (*a*) relative privacy of testimony; or (*b*) documents not yet edited and printed for general use.

pression (this may range from minor fudging to towering lies).
There are, however, some documents that are composed either
in a spirit of neutrality with regard to the facts, or with a sincere
effort to hew to the line of truth. These include simple records,
commands or instructions, and more or less neutral "business"
reports. The terms are imprecise, but efforts to tighten the categorization lead to subclassifications that create more confusion
than order.

"Simple" record in this context means only or merely a record; that is, a record that may be erroneous, but not because of
intent on the part of the recorder. Tape records obviously have
no intent; they reproduce sounds. There is a presumption that
the machine got what was said in its range. Of course, their sensitivity is not infinite (whispers will be missed, noise may cause
confusion), they are subject to malfunction, and the tapes can
be doctored or edited to in fact tell lies. There is a presumption
that a shorthand record is taken and transcribed with no intent
to deceive. Not many stenographers are spies, jealous of the
boss, or insane. Cameras and film have no intent, but their users
may introduce such an element.

There is a presumption that commands are issued to accom-
plish action, so that the issuer does not lie to his subordinate.
Of course, some commanders do lie, and many of them issue
ambiguous orders; and some orders are given for symbolic,
hortatory, propaganda, or ceremonial reasons. Still, the general
rule remains. Most corporation executives try to frame their
orders in relation to fact in order to assist in obtaining what they
want. So important is this objective that cadets in military colleges are rigorously schooled in the composition of succinct and
unambiguous orders. They also are told of many instances in
the history of military activity when poorly framed orders either
caused confusion because they could not be interpreted correctly, or had no effect because their ambiguity invited dis-
obedience. It may be remarked that this is only one of many
fields in which the systematization of methodology and instruction in modern times has improved the performance of professionals, even when they are men of no more than average
talent.

What does "more or less neutral business report" mean? Merely that a common type of document results from the activity of men in institutions (government agencies, business firms, military establishments, churches, etc.), in situations in which the impulse to torture the record occurs relatively seldom. Examples are: the counting of barrels of flour by an employee of a large milling company, the report of a professional accountting firm on the financial condition of a corporation that hired it to make such a report, a report by an ambassador to his home government on the preparations he has made for a visit by his president to a foreign country. Most business receipts also are meant to be neutral and unambiguous.

We have moved from neutrality (but not certain absence of error) in the cases of simple records, to some (conceivably much) possibility of intent to deceive in instructions or commands, to a greater likelihood of cases of intent to deceive in what we call more or less neutral business reports. In the last case we have no doubt passed the line of usefulness in the categorization of documents in terms of neutrality or probable absence of motive for deceit. Probability, as we frequently stress, usually is the most we can hope for in historical research.

Government documents constitute a class that deserves comment. They may pertain to national, provincial, municipal units of government, or to special districts (water, sanitation, education), or to international organizations. The student is reminded that government documents are composed by men, not by disembodied entities. Government documents can and often do contain distortion and error due to selection and bias and mistaken facts and mechanical errors. They can contain lies, God knows. The *Congressional Record* reports as having been spoken on the floor of Congress words merely supplied the printer in typescript by an absent congressman's administrative assistant. The student must not assume that the published report of congressional committee hearings contains all the record of its activities. In short, we must put away the assumption that government documents are especially entitled to uncritical acceptance, just as we must abandon the notion that the appearance of anything in print somehow sanctifies it.

The press produces a special class of document (newspapers and magazines). It contains various sorts of data. There is more or less straight reporting—reprints in full in the *New York Times* of speeches or legislation, or rather full and objective accounts by reporters of events they witnessed or men they talked to. There are cartoons, with or without captions. There are signed columns of interpretation, ranging from the profound to scurrilous superficiality. There are editorials, which are unsigned (usually) columns by the ownership or editorship of the newspaper or magazine. There is fiction, fashion, song, poetry, photographs.

The press sometimes is examined by beginning researchers with the hope of deriving from it intimations of public opinion. This is too much to expect. Samples of editorial opinion on given subjects give leads to what newspapers and magazines of well-known orientation consider it desirable to print on those subjects. The inference may be made that usually they will not depart too widely from the views of the majority of their readers lest they lose their allegiance. But any specific case may be one in which the editors have departed widely—purposefully or involuntarily—from the views of a large part of the publication's usual audience. In the best of cases, this sort of sampling merely gives insights into the views of publishers and editors of known political affiliation or orientation, or with a specific religious interest, or an economic or occupational bias. Precisely how much they reflect or influence public opinion cannot be known.

Private business documents are important sources of data in many countries. Access to this kind of record is, on the whole, difficult to arrange. Often, a corporation's files are almost as closely guarded as the strategic plans and logistic and personnel minutiae of military general staffs.

Enough has been said about documents as a type of evidence to suggest the many difficulties involved in their use. And it is *use* that is required for the development of skill and judgment in research. No manual of method can do more than assist the student in developing his skills through practice.

C. Other evidence

1. Physical remains

What is meant here is physical remains that offer no language:[9] man's own bones, his artifacts, the remnants of cultured plants, natural objects man has collected or moved, or traces of astral, geologic, or climatic conditions or events that may have influenced human existence. This sometimes is called *mute* evidence. Use of the term "physical remains" in this sense is merely a convenience, since in its plain meaning the phrase might be taken to include documents, inscriptions, and tape recordings. Items of evidence in the category of physical remains sometimes are called nonlinguistic sources, relics, or artifacts. The first of these (nonlinguistic) will cover all that we include in the first sentence of this paragraph; the other two will not.

Physical remains in our sense generally are collected and judged by specialists—e.g., anthropologists, archeologists, "prehistorians," epigraphers, paleographers, paleontologists—making use of techniques not available to students using this *Guide*. A few of our students do archeological research; a few do work on art or architectural history where they use the mute evidence of physical remains. Obviously, the specialists who use physical remains often also use evidence containing words. A numismatist will uncover coins with and without inscriptions; his study of either type probably will require the use of documents.

Physical remains must be judged in part in terms of whether they were intended to convey meaning to future eyes. Most physical remains are unpremeditated or unintentional sources— i.e., they were not created with the thought of leaving a record. This clearly is the case with all physical remains other than artifacts, and even with most of the latter. Among artifacts there are, of course, exceptions (e.g., public edifices are erected at least in part for the edification of posterity). Still, we may as-

---

[9] Except that language itself may be said to be a physical remain that gives mute testimony (i.e., some leads to human activity in time may be found in the elements of languages and in change in them over time).

sume that most artifacts are "unbiased" in the sense of deliberate effort to mislead. They are, on the other hand, highly biased in the sense of reflecting the culture patterns of the society in which they were constructed; they are "culture bound."

Our modern exploitation of physical remains has no meaningful parallel in the past. Research is more systematic now; it is on a larger scale; better records are kept; many new scientific techniques are used. Photography and improved printing techniques have revolutionized this type of research. Improved organization of research includes the better circulation of results, with the effect of permitting greatly improved comparison of data; it also greatly facilitates the corroboration of physical and documentary evidence and vice versa.

The use of physical remains other than artifacts was virtually unknown until recently. Historians do little of this work; they use the results. Anthropologists sift anthropoid bones, dating man's forebears by the carbon decay of ashes, by geologic strata, and by the known chronology of biologic species. Botanists trace the origins of maize from wild grasses, offering illumination of the growth of American Indian culture. Data are found in the traces of volcanic eruptions, tree growth rings, and sunken coral reefs.

It is from artifacts, however, that the historian derives most of the evidence from physical remains. Things made by men (artisans) include weapons, buildings, vehicles, clothing, religious objects, toiletries, medical equipment, jewelry, coins, fishing gear, and toys. Some artifacts are especially impressive, either by their great size, large numbers, or unusual quality. The great pyramids of Egypt and of the Maya and other pre-Columbian Indians of Middle America cry out beyond question the high level of social organization of their builders. From many types of remains we derive data on a culture's level of technological skills (by the quality of an iron sword, a wheeled cart, a woven cape, an arched stone bridge), its esthetic standards (are artifacts formed and decorated in an effort to please, and, if so, with what purpose—artistic, religious, political?), its social ideals, religious attitudes, economic organization.

Mute artifacts may either require corroboration or explanation from documentary or other materials, or they may provide corroboration for documentary evidence. Swords of Saracen craftsmanship found in the ruins of a Frankish castle may be with some confidence thought to argue relations between Franks and Muslims. It may be more difficult to learn whether they were friends or foes, or both at different times. Were the swords gifts, acquired through trade, or booty of war; or all of those things at different times? All sorts of supporting evidence, including documents, might be needed to solve the problem. On the other hand, mountains of fragments of pottery types made by one society, but found in the trash of another, may well be thought more persuasive evidence of trade between states than an inscription on a monument stating that distant commerce flourished under King Thom the Great. And we have many examples in investigations of ancient and medieval European history of data derived from examination of the mute remains of ships, carts, and roads, that provide impressive corroboration of the often incidental comments on economic life by chroniclers and official historiographers, whose orientation was political, civic, or religious.

2. Orally transmitted fact, error, myth

Orally transmitted data are used primarily for the study of preliterate cultures (ancient and contemporary), and for examination of our contemporary mass, literate society. Historians and anthropologists are prominent in the former type of work; they are joined in the latter by political scientists, sociologists, psychologists, and commercial pollsters.

For preliterate societies orally transmitted evidence is our only verbal material. It gives us more than a mere record of some past events. In the form of myth, epic, ballad, fairy tale it is also a form of entertainment, and a vehicle for cross-generational value transmission. In fact, the value of such oral record as an account of past events, is often very limited, and tends to be less in proportion to the distance in time between the account and the event—if, indeed, such an event ever occurred. Each generation of story-tellers or troubadours embellishes the inherited account and the original core of "truth," which is increasingly hidden by the overlay. On the other hand, all such oral traditions cannot be dismissed as inventions. Heinrich Schliemann did excavate the ruins of Troy by using the orally transmitted Homeric epics as guide for the archeologist's shovel.

More significant, however, is the use which historians make of the orally transmitted data of preliterate societies in establishing changing value systems. Although such data often are "bad" history, they are excellent material for the historian (or the historically oriented anthropologist) to use in determining the positive and negative societal values of preliterate societies, following the changes that occur from generation to generation. Thus, the endless variations of the *Nibelungen* sagas are indications of changing values among the numerous Germanic tribes that claimed the epic as part of their heritage.

Considerably more controversial are the more recent attempts by anthropologists to use orally transmitted data of preliterate societies to establish a typology or model of the functioning of the human mind itself, or to use such data as mirrors of the human subconscious mind. Jung attempted to establish a collective folk soul on the basis of German fairy tales. Joseph Campbell's *The Masks of God* is an even more ambitious effort to construct the cross-cultural subconscious value base of all religious sentiments.[10] Perhaps intellectually even more exciting is the project of the French anthropologist Claude Lévi-Strauss to use South American folk myths to establish the binary, computer-like logical workings of the human mind. Professional historians generally have left such ambitious integrative projects to their colleagues in other social science disciplines, but a recent work by Traian Stoijadonovich, *A Study in Balkan Civilization,* uses Balkan myths as part of his source material in sketching a cross-generational portrait of Balkan civilizations.[11]

---

[10] Three volumes (New York: Viking, 1959–64).
[11] New York: Knopf, 1967.

In analyzing developments in our contemporary, literate mass society, orally transmitted evidence offers several advantages. First, there is the obvious usefulness of interviewing the leading participants in great affairs. This means not only the five-star generals and presidents, but the numerous staff officers and advisers who participate in the complex decision-making process of our times. Second, it permits a new approach to understanding the popular mind, as a step toward estimating its effect on affairs. This is a matter of obvious importance in countries where there is overt broad participation in public affairs; it is, in fact, also more important than might be supposed in modern "command" societies, as the U.S.S.R., which has a varied and highly educated population. Third, the appalling quantity of material produced by typewriter, mimeograph machine, tape recorder, printing press, drives us to all devices that may permit reduction of the traditional practice of reading "everything" on the subject in hand. Fourth, and rather curiously, certain types of valuable written materials have been reduced by the use of the telephone and air travel. Fifth, there has been some recent increase of the "historicity" purposefully injected into documents by public figures concerned with their place in history.

Oral evidence, especially when preserved on tape, often allows an historically prominent individual to record his observations informally with a minimum of effort shortly after an event has occurred. Such recordings are memoirs, offering the advantage to the historian of often shortening the time span that elapses between event and memoir publication, and of supplying, through the timbre of the recorded voice and facial expression (if the oral evidence is video taped or filmed), emotional nuances that are not always evident in written memoirs.

Often more useful to the individual historian is the personal interview conducted by the researcher with an eye witness to the events he is studying. Such interviews are not without pitfalls, and must be carefully prepared. The interviewer must establish a balance between the dangers of possibly antagonizing the witness with aggressive questions and allowing the latter to deliver a monologue in an attempt to instruct an ignorant visitor. For this reason it is usually helpful to test the respondent's memory and truthfulness by beginning the interview with questions about matters which are uncontroversial and for which the interviewer already has verified answers from other sources. This establishes that the historian is familiar with the events under discussion and, in addition, induces the subject to transfer himself mentally into the events that are the main concern of the interview. After this sort of rapport has been established, the interviewer proceeds to question the subject about more controversial matters which require more emotional, nonverifiable responses. This type of interview is usually most effective when conducted by an individual historian pursuing a single subject; at times, however, a more institutionalized format can be useful. The Institute for Contemporary History in Munich has systematically collected a large number of "witness reports" by individuals who either participated in or were eyewitness to the major events of the Nazi era in German history. Scholars may consult these reports but the persons interviewed seldom are available for direct contact. A number of American universities have established oral history projects in recent years, recording answers of prominent men to questions posed by historians.

The interview technique also has been used to study the opinions and values not only of existing tribal cultures, but of poor urban groups in modernized communities. The anthropologist Oscar Lewis used it extensively, using tape recorders, to penetrate and describe the "subculture" of the poor in Mexico and the United States. The chief aim of this type of interview is to discover the values of a group in society that is not a part of the mainstream of events. Among other things, it suggests the types of reactions, or lack of reaction, to be expected from such groups given certain political or economic developments.

For the individual historian the interview technique is limited by his physical inability to question many persons in depth. To ascertain the opinions of large segments of the public, social scientists must use mass interviews and sampling techniques. The most common sample devices are the quota type and the random sample; both often are conducted by research institutes using professional interviewers. The quota type requires more elaborate preparations before the interviewing begins. First, the structure of the group to be studied is analyzed to establish the percentage of men and women, age groups, etc. From this a microcosmic model is constructed which is meant to correspond on a reduced scale to the larger group, hopefully in all significant respects. If the entire group had a population of some 25 million, the model might consist of 1,500–2,000. It is hoped that the small group is representative of the total group. Only the members of the model are interviewed, and because they are asserted to represent a microcosm of the larger group, the tabulated results are said to be valid for determining the views of the entire 25 million. So-called random sampling, on the other hand, relies almost entirely on statistical probability for the validity of its findings. In this method—far cheaper than the quota method—researchers select a numerical percentage of the entire group, supposedly without reference to the characteristics of individuals (e.g., by picking every 100th name in the census reports), and this sample is then interviewed.

Both quota and sampling techniques can be valuable to the historian. But they require careful use and interpretation. The usefulness of samples taken before 1945 is very limited, since the emergence of relatively reliable sampling techniques is largely a post-World War II development. Then, too, while the questions posed in large-scale polls are always of great current interest to the interviewer or institute, later historians may decide that the issues were really of peripheral concern in the larger perspective of history. Also, most sampling interview efforts are constructed to make the answers easily quantifiable—i.e., the respondent is allowed only a limited number of choices. This usually distorts nuances of feeling that may be important, particularly in gauging developing shifts of opinion over a larger span of time, which is, after all, a primary concern of the historian. Again, there is great difficulty detecting certain types of distortion in testimony, even if many detailed answers are allowed. For another thing, determining which qualities (age, sex, occupation, race, place of residence, religion, education, etc.) of a population are critically important in establishment of quotas is difficult, as witness the poor models—and erroneous "answers"—of some interview projects. Another point is that so-called random samples sometimes are highly structured and selective. Plucking names from a United States telephone book means that a significant fraction of the population (non-phone owners) is excluded. Use a Mexican telephone book and nearly all the population is excluded. Finally, it is often pointed out that shallow interviews and questionnaires frequently do not measure "intensity" of opinion. The respondents have no stake in their answers and they can, and often do, answer irresponsibly; thus, their answers are a poor guide to their probable actions. One answer to this problem is the interview "in depth." But subjects for this procedure are more difficult to find, and the time-consuming nature of the process reduces the size of the sample.

IV

Collecting historical evidence

The Preface and chapter I have pointed out that the stages of an historical inquiry overlap.[1] In the case of the collection of evidence, much of the activity is concentrated in the early part of an investigation, but some will occur later. Furthermore, collection merges into analysis when the first research note is taken that consists of more than simple copying. Collecting evidence is not, then, a simple process that may be delegated with a few instructions to secretaries or research assistants. When teams of collectors are available—for example, in large United States military history projects—their work must be planned and supervised with great care. Many decisions made during the collection of evidence will, at least ideally, require a sound methodology and sophisticated reasoning, and will have profound effects upon the results of the investigation.

A. Recording bibliographic information

Here, we are talking about *working bibliography cards*. Their purposes are (1) description, (2) control, (3) analysis or anno-

---

[1] The student at this point should review I F, "First Steps in the Research Process."

tation. Each of these purposes is important, and all are looked
for by the instructor in inspecting the student's working bibliography cards. These cards are not only critical to the control of
the bibliographic effort, and important tools for the assessment
of the character of evidence, they also will be used to make up
the bibliographic essay and the formal, annotated bibliography.
The following injunctions do not cover all the techniques of
recording bibliographic data; they do constitute a teachable
core that will put the student on the road to effective activity.
As with most of our techniques, we do not expect that each
working bibliography card display all the devices available;
only that some of them be so complex. Remember, when first
encountering a new and apparently promising item (in card catalog, a bibliography, a footnote, etc.), make out a bibliography
card. It takes a bit of time, but it pays.

1. Description

Each item will have its own card, and it is recommended that
the form of the card catalog be followed, with such deletions
and other modifications as may be appropriate. A 3- x 5-inch
card usually is adequate. It will work best to file cards by author
(the author, last name first, will be at the top of the card). At
the minimum, the card must carry author (or editor or compiler), title, place and date of publication, publisher, volumes
(if more than one), edition (if other than first; and occasionally
the first must be mentioned), series of which a part (if appropriate). If the item is taken from the card catalog it usually will pay
to enter the call number in the upper left (this seems a burden
to professional researchers, too, but it does pay in the long run).
Sometimes the number of pages should be recorded: e.g., if an
indication of length will be useful as an estimate of coverage;
or, to distinguish between editions of a work. Some scholars prefer always to enter the number of pages. The following procedures will be valuable:

a) Conserve space in entering bibliographic data, to leave
maximum room for later entry of descriptive and analytic data.

b) Abbreviate. It is necessary only that you be able to read the cards. You can interpret them for the instructor. An occasional loss through over-abbreviation must be risked in a large research job.

c) Do use both sides of the card, but put "over" at the bottom of the obverse. This is better than two cards tied with a clip although sometimes this cannot be avoided.

d) Neatness may be valuable; it is not essential. If cards done in script, with blots and coffee stains, are legible, there is no point doing them over in typescript.

e) Do include a separate card for each of the most important bibliographic aids used. This will be necessary for control purposes. It also will have the pedagogical function of helping the instructor to discuss such aids with you.

f) All signed articles in scholarly journals will have individual author cards. On the other hand, only one card is required for a newspaper; and often only one card is required for a popular magazine when a survey has been made of its contents and points of view and the individual authors or articles are not important.

g) Sometimes it will be thought possibly useful to enter an indication of where an item was located: e.g., if an item seems possibly incorrect, or possibly little known, a note can be made that it was found in such-and-such a bibliography.

h) Working bibliography cards should be filed alphabetically by author in a box where they are easily accessible. It is desirable to divide the file into at least "bibliographic aids" and "other." The latter may also be subdivided topically, chronologically, geographically, by types of materials, etc. Among the types of materials that it is most often convenient to keep in distinct alphabetic files are public opinion materials (newspapers, popular magazines), government documents, and manuscript materials. There seldom is any reason to separate scholarly journal articles from "books," as some scholars do.

2. Control

The control of bibliography, in a large research task, requires meticulous attention to detail. It shows what has been

done, and permits quick reference thereto. In a large research
task it is all too easy to forget whether an item has been used,
and to what extent. This record is useful on single-volume
works; it is indispensable for widely used newspapers and popular magazines, multivolume histories or sets of documents,
many types of manuscript collections. It is impossible to remember what has been done in such complex materials without a
written record. Also, a card should be kept for each bibliographic aid (bibliography, government document guide, card
catalog), showing when used, what categories looked under,
and at least in general what principle was followed in taking
cards from the bibliographic aid (e.g., "took all items on economic aspect," "prob got all will ever need on all aspects,"
"only took on 1789; see again later").

3. Analysis or annotation

Some working bibliography cards require annotation, if the
items have been looked at. The annotation may amount to no
more than "no use"; or it may point to need for further exploitation (e.g., "see ch. iv for excellent material on weegies"); it may
indicate a bias of the author; it may indicate hiatuses in the
coverage; it may judge the quality of the work; or it may describe the arrangement of large sets of materials; and there are
other types of annotation. Of course, some of the "control" material discussed in the preceding section also is annotation.

A critical attitude toward materials is indispensable to research. Certain types of analysis of the item itself (as apart from
analysis of parts of the item) belong on the bibliography card.
It is very important to include views regarding the general character of the item that are generated in the course of research
note-taking. Such general views should be transferred to the
working bibliography card. Thus, it is best if the bibliography
file is at hand while research is going on. Of course, this is not
always possible, so a separate note to put the judgment on the
bibliography card should be made. Does all this mean that judgments regarding the item will not be put on research notes?

Certainly not. Only certain general judgments will go on the working bibliography card. Some of these later will appear in the bibliographic essay and in the formal, annotated bibliography appended to the final research paper. This process of bibliographic analysis and annotation requires labor, thought, and method. Your instructor will be looking for these things on your working bibliography cards (remember, only on some of them—those you have used, and that were worth elaborate annotation).

B. Bibliographic aids[2]

Our modern bibliographic aids are a boon to the investigator. The immense labors of modern indexers, catalogers, compilers, editors, from which we benefit, constitute a great difference between historical research today and in earlier times. New techniques—such as pushbutton catalog searching, possibly of scores of associated libraries—promise further advances. The Bird Library at Syracuse University (opened 1972) has consoles available to students by which they query the computerized catalog and circulation systems to locate items in the collections.

It is important for the researcher to think in terms of *categories* of bibliographic aids. This necessarily involves consideration of the types of evidence likely to be useful for the given research task. These are by no means the same for all studies: newspapers, government documents, business records illuminate some subjects, but not others. Once the researcher grasps the principle of category in this context, he can apply it to any research task, looking for *items* within the identified *categories* of aids (e.g., Poore's *Descriptive Catalogue of the Public Documents of the United States* within the category of indexes or guides to public documents).

---

[2] For additional bibliographic aids see Appendix B; American Historical Association, *Guide to Historical Literature;* and appropriate headings in library card catalogs (e.g., "United States" as subject, "History" as subcategory under it, and "Bibliography" as further subdivision under "History."

Figure 2. Sample of author entry in card catalog
  This is *not* the same as a "working bibliography card" in a researcher's own files, although they have some elements in common.

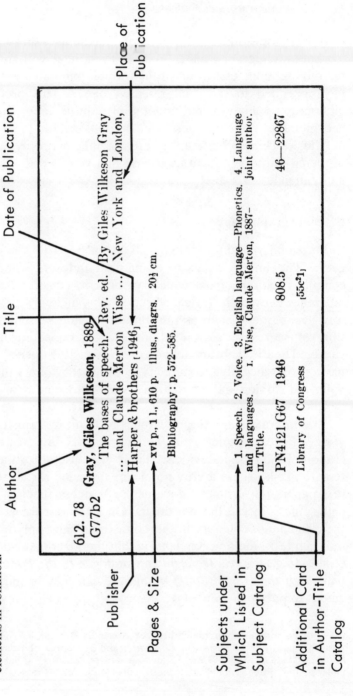

Author   Title   Date of Publication

Place of Publication

612.78
G77b2   **Gray, Giles Wilkeson,** 1889–
      The bases of speech. Rev. ed. By Giles Wilkeson Gray
      ... and Claude Merton Wise ... New York and London,
      Harper & brothers [1946]
      xvi p., 1 l., 610 p. illus., diagrs. 20½ cm.
      Bibliography : p. 572–585.

      1. Speech. 2. Voice. 3. English language—Phonetics. 4. Language
      and languages.   I. Wise, Claude Merton, 1887–   joint author.
      II. Title.

      PN4121.G67 1946   808.5   46—22867
                            [55c²1]
      Library of Congress

Publisher

Pages & Size

Subjects under
Which Listed in
Subject Catalog

Additional Card
in Author–Title
Catalog

Figure 3. Sample working bibliography cards

Following are 12 examples of working bibliography cards. Some data are standard on all such cards: e.g., author, title, publisher, date and place of publication, number of pages. The annotations vary with the nature of the item and the character of the research task; possible variations thus are so numerous that the few examples given here can be no more than suggestive. No diacritical marks are put on these example cards, on the grounds that scholars familiar with the languages will supply the marks when required in a manuscript. Students not firm in their knowledge of the rules for such marks should include the marks on the cards as they go along. The 5th, 9th, and 11th examples are bibliographic aids, which pose special record-keeping problems.

```
          Hennery, George
          A history of Spain.  NY: Macmillan, 1944.
                  626pp

Seems good. May want see for treatment of the May
riot, pp 66-90. No notes yet.
```

A few injunctions will be useful to the beginning bibliographer. (1) Diligence, system, intelligence, even imagination are needed in bibliographic work; without them, the aids will not be well used. (2) Be sure to use the prefaces and keys and other explanatory data in bibliographic aids; learn how the aid is organized, in how many volumes, what is covered and what excluded, and how the indexes work. (3) Do not try to determine library holdings by puttering about in the stacks; all the books on your subject will not be grouped in a few places, and

Figure 3—*Continued*

```
924.1         Gonzalez, Carlos T. & Jeremy K. Smith eds.
SU has 2d     Coleccion de documentos ineditos para la
ed, with v.29 hist. de las constituciones de Mexico
missing       35 vols Mexico, 1942-49

XXXV: iii-vi, essay on sources; viii-cvi, Bibliog (div
into: works on Mex consts., fed and state; texts of fed.
consts; text state consts). A very few annotated.
I, iv-lvi: Intro: discn purpose, and genl discn hist Mex
state & fed consts. Primary aim bring tog texts. Discn
hist emphasizes 'legalistic' aspects; remarks on fed
consts. standard, unexcptl; remarks on state consts. exclt,
full of new insights.
I-VI: texts fed. consts., incl. not only those adoptd, but
those suggestd (ie by major gps or convetns); and constl
amends suggestd but not adoptd. Texts in ea case taken fr
best available source, with fn discussn of source, its
status, accuracy, etc.
```

```
VII-XXXIV: texts state consts.; again fr best possib source,
with discn source; here had much diffic locatg reliable
texts of many early state consts; and of total 116 state
consts since 1822, lack any text of 12.
   A very few fns to texts of consts; so few that wonder
why incl any. Those few seem to be concentrated in the secs.
dealg with indiv liberties, and show some effort 'prove'
fine Mex record in this regard....And intro does same, by
stressg constl provns without adeqtly referrg to failures
to implement.
   3 state consts in 1940s incl; all others before 1940.
IX: Michoacan and Jalisco.

 Jan. 65: took full notes everything on indiv liberties in
19th cent. in Michoacan.
 Mar.65: full notes on indiv libs. Jalisco in 19th cent.
Also detd that nothing else of value for those states except
XX, iii-vi, LX lxi-lxiii, some of I ((took full notes all
these cld use))
```

some that the library owns will be missing during your visit. The library card catalog is the bibliographic aid designed to give you the library's holdings. (4) Keep records of what bibliographic aids you use, and how you use them (e.g., what subjects you scanned in the index, or what years you covered), or you will lose track of what you have done. It usually is most convenient to keep this record on a 3 x 5 card for each biblio-

Figure 3—*Continued*

(reverse of preceding working bibliography card)

```
            Smith, Clark P., "Whaling in Argentina in the
         Nineteenth Century," Hisp. Am. Histcl Rev.,
         Summer 1955, pp 350-398.

 Definitive on number Arg vessels, amt catch, values, taxes,
 etc.  Took full separate notes. Basd on Arg govt records.
```

```
         Martinez, Lazaro
            Los cristeros.    Mexico: Editorial Graza,
              1943.    193 pp

   No value on substance of the movement and actions; but
   excellent example of a sympathizer's attitude.  Took a
   few notes on this; no more needed.
```

graphic aid, filed with the working bibliography (see the 5th, 9th, and 11th examples in Figure 3). (5) Librarians are a help, but seldom have the time or specialized knowledge to do much of your bibliographic work for you.

Some of the many types of bibliographic aids are clumped

Figure 3—*Continued*

```
              Guide to documents in the archives of
              the Stark County Historical Society.
              Canton, Ohio:   Blucher Typographical, 1956.
                             201 pp

Apparently done at least in part by employees or officials
of the Society.
    Excellent organization, by topics within chronological
divisions.   Index of names only.
Jan. 66: used secs.  1 & 2 thoroly (took notes & cards)
for econ history subjects on all townships exc Plain and
Goward (tho material there).
Mar 66: used secs 3-4 as in Jan. 66 above.
Feb 67: used secs 1-4 for Plain & Goward twnships on
econ subjects.
Nothing anyplace on separate Amish activities.
```

```
              Feldman, Percy
              Exports thru London in the 19th century.
                  London: Beverley, 1922.   567 pp

 Basd on wide variety contemporary materials, esp govt
records. Judicious. But value of sections varies consid.
due to unevenness of evidence available.
 Esp good on hardware (pp44-69), textiles (101-165), &
processed foods (204-245); and have full notes on all
these....Much less valuable on other commodities, and took
no notes on them. Prob neednt look at again.
```

below into categories: (1) library catalogs; (2) bibliographies; (3) government publication guides and indexes; (4) press and journal indexes; (5) indexes to books published; (6) manuscript and archival guides; (7) indexes to doctoral dissertations; (8) scholarly journals; (9) guides to reference books; (10) booksellers' lists; and (11) item locators. The first seven

Figure 3—*Continued*

```
            Johnson, Paul
               Military clubs in Tibet.  St. Paul, Minn.;
                  Pine Tree Printery, 1934.   133 pp

   no use
```

```
            Smith, Max
               Lumber booms of the northwest.
                  NY: Putnams, 1924.   234 pp

    Baker, Hist Oregon, says not worth consultg; but S.
   Dobbs, The Bibber Company, says useful for IWW.
         ((prob shldnt bother to find?))

   Oct 66: Got copy. Baker right. Sec on labor of marginal
   use. Took few notes--all that worth.
```

of these are probably the most commonly used types of aids; the rest are of rather less frequent application.[3]

---

[3] There are many other categories of bibliographic aids. Some of these have an obvious, specialized importance: e.g., guides to law and legal literature (Edward Schuster, *Guide to Law and Legal Literature of Central American Republics,* New York, 1937). There are guides to the appraisal of books (as the *Book Review Digest,* 1905–   ). Many other categories are either rather esoteric (*Numismatic Literature,* published by the American Numismatic Society, 1947–   ), or are of minor significance for bibliographic work (encyclopedias, biographic dictionaries). Library journals often contain list-

Figure 3—*Continued*

```
              Readers Guide Per Lit

Jan. 65: took cards on all stuff in index under NICARAGUA
in 1917-29.
Sept 65: took cards on Literary Digest stuff only as in
index under NICARAGUA in 1930-33.
Dec 65: under LATIN AMERICA and INTER-AMERICAN AFFAIRS
 in index took everything for 1917-33 that might touch
 on Nicaragua-US affairs.
```

```
      Confederacion de Camaras de Comercio de los
              Estados Unidos Mexicanos
                 Boletin de la....

1a. epoca, no. 1919-20, t.I, No. 1 (1 enero 1919) -
 t. II, No. 9 (Sept 1920). Took full notes my interests.
2a. epoca, quincenal, No. 1-12 (Jan.-June 1923). Used
 all.
3a. epoca, quincenal, No.1-52 (jun 1923-oct 1925). Much
 bigger format and more pp than 1st 2 series. Took
 full notes.

      Heraldo Comercial.  Successor to Boletin.
 Quincenal; every 2 wks fr 10 jan 1926 to 25 may
 1932, when ceased publcn.
      Took full notes all relevant subjects.
```

The items listed under these categories are merely illustrative. We cannot cover here even the more important bibliographic aids. (A few more are listed in Appendix B.) It is quite simple, however, to learn the *categories* of aids, and to search for items within those categories.

---

ings or discussions of rare materials, but this is not a category of aid that ordinarily would be used in a simple investigation or in the first stages of a complex study.

Figure 3—*Concluded*

```
              Jones, Paul V.
                 Index of historical materials in
              Argentine periodicals.   3 vols. Buenos
              Aires, 1963.

  Covers all that cld find in 12 libs in BAires and 3 in
  Cordoba that "likely" to have such material.  Does not cover
  "some low-grade" periodicals.  No nwpers (not even wklies).
  Only minor efforts cover govt periodicals.  Does incl univer-
  sity periodicals.  Almost 0 bef 1850, but he believes bec
  little pubd. 90% material in post-1900.
      Index quite genl, and mostly basd on titles of articles
  rather than analysis content articles.
  Jan.65: took cards on all under MONEY, BANKING, TAXES,
   JOSE CARRANZA. Appar no other useful index categories for
   1886 money scandal ((tried several)).
  Fb 66: lookd under VICTOR MARIATEGUI and made several
        cards.
```

```
              Lockwright, George P
              A history of Arg-US relns.
              NY 1953.

  Scholarly; well doctd; good bibliog; well org; marred on
  close exam by bias vs US 'appeasement' of Arg in 1943.
      Author in Arg with Emby 1946-48...Suspect doesnt like
  Args....Really assumes Peron wld have knuckled under to
  stronger US line, but without giving reasoning.
      But exclt for resume and discusan (most things) Arg-
  US since XVIII.
  65-69: good analysis Arg natsm[took sep notes]
  75-79: on Arg milit; a miserable polemic; he hates Arg
  milit, and can hardly describe their role because so busy
  deplorg it[took no notes - not nec].
```

1. Library catalogs

Library catalogs are bibliographic aids in two senses: (*a*) they assist *identification* of materials, and (*b*) they show the *location* of items. The distinction for beginning researchers is important in that many assume that the holdings of a library necessarily represent a large part of the extant items useful for a subject; in fact, of course, most libraries are too small and heterogeneous in their holdings for this to be possible.

Most library catalogs today are *dictionary* catalogs—i.e., items are arranged on cards or on pages under one dictionary arrangement from A to Z, with many subordinate A–Z arrangements. An older and usually less efficient type is the handwritten book or ledger catalog. This last, in its worst form, is a list of items set down as acquired; clearly, it may be necessary to scan the entire catalog to learn the library's holdings.

The *card,* and the *printed* catalog are the most common types in the United States today, and nearly all are dictionary catalogs as well. Some printed catalogs are merely reproductions of cards. The printed catalog is valuable in permitting a scanning of the holdings of libraries not directly accessible to the researcher. Some are catalogs of a library's entire collection; some are catalogs of special collections. An example of the latter is: University of California Library, *Spain and Spanish America in the Libraries of the University of California, a Catalogue of Books* (2 vols., Berkeley, 1928–30).

The printed catalogs of national libraries often are of especial value, both because these tend to be among the best libraries in a country, and because they usually have large holdings touching on national subjects, holdings often not found elsewhere in the world. Sometimes publishers are required to deposit copies of all their issues in the national library. The Library of Congress is the "national" library of the United States. Its enormous collections may be scanned through its printed catalogs, the hundreds of volumes of which are widely held by libraries. The volumes have been issued in several series, beginning with *A Catalog of Books Represented by Library of Congress Printed Cards Issued* [from 1898] to July 31, 1942 (167 vols.); a supplement to this for acquisitions from August 1, 1942 through 1947 (42 vols.); continued as *The Library of Congress Author Catalog* for 1948–52 (24 vols.); *Library of Congress Catalog . . . Books: Authors,* 1953–55; and *The National Union Catalog: A Cumulative Author List, 1956–* . These printed author cards were supplemented, beginning in

1950, with the *Library of Congress Catalog: Books: Subjects* (73 vols. for 1950–66).

Following are some of the things to learn about the use of a card catalog:

a) Beginning researchers tend to use the catalog poorly; they underestimate its complexity, do not understand how it is organized, and fail to realize that its proper use requires patience, care, imagination, and some (as much as possible) knowledge of the subject being investigated. Beginning researchers commonly miss many items in the card catalog through improper procedure.

b) Your library will have guides (often posted near the catalog) to the organization and use of the catalogs.

c) You will be well-advised to take down all or most of the data on the catalog card, and approximately in the order and positions found there. Usually, less work is involved in discarding data than in revisiting the catalog. Do omit data useless to your purpose (e.g., size of book, and usually the subject headings under which the card also is filed elsewhere in the catalog). Abbreviate as much as possible.

d) The catalog will contain several cards for each item: an author card, title card (beginning with the first word of the title that is not an article), and cards cross-filed under subject headings, and possibly cards under co-authors, editors, compilers, or a series title.

e) In searching the catalog under either author or subject it is important to note subdivisions. *United States* as author will have various agencies (e.g., Department of State) as subdivisions within the overall category, and each subdivision in turn will be arranged A–Z, and may have subdivisions itself. *United States* as subject will have many subdivisions, with these in turn subdivided. Not all subdivisions are marked by raised index tabs; they may merely be indicated by headings on the cards themselves, and must be searched for diligently. The complexity of the arrangement under such headings as United States or Great Britain makes evident the prudence of keeping records of how the catalog was used (especially what categories and subcategories were searched, and whether cards were made on all relevant items found).

f) Most libraries post the rules for entries in the catalogs: e.g., articles (the, la, el, die, etc.) as the first word of a title are not counted (e.g., *La Historia de España* is filed under H); if a word is a person, place, and thing, cards are filed in that order.

2. Bibliographies

Bibliographies may be published separately (as books or articles), or they may be included in other works; here we deal with the former, although researchers are, of course, also interested in the latter. Five categories of bibliographies are discussed below.

Bibliographies of bibliographies. These are lists of lists. Where such aids exist, they are an excellent place to commence bibliographic research. Examples are: Edith M. Coulter and Melanie Gerstenfeld, *Historical Bibliographies, A Systematic and Annotated Guide* (Berkeley: University of California, 1935; ii, 206 pp.); Cecil Knight Jones, *A Bibliography of Latin American Bibliographies* (2d ed., Washington: Government Printing Office, 1942; 311 pp.); Robert L. Collison, *Bibliographies, Subject and National. A Guide to Their Contents, Arrangement and Use* (New York: Hafner, 1962; 168 pp.).

Bibliographies of countries or areas. There are many bibliographies that cover a country or culture-area, or some subdivision (e.g., chronological or geographic) thereof. The arrangement of such aids varies: some are summaries of all work done to date, some are lists of new work published in a given period, some are combined bibliographies and discussions of trends and events of history. Examples are:

Handbook of Latin American Studies. Harvard University Press, 1936–47; University of Florida Press, 1948– . An annual, covering publications in each year, beginning with 1935. Later volumes include materials for more than one year. Covers many disciplines, including history. Selection and annotation by many scholars. Only the more important items included. Books, articles, some printed documents listed. Includes material published in many countries and languages.

Handlin, Oscar, *et al. Harvard Guide to American History.* Cambridge, Mass.: Harvard University, 1966. A combination of guide and bibliographies.

Richardson, E. C., Grace C. Griffin, *et al. Writings on American History.* Publications for 1902–03, 1906–40, 1948– ; various publishers since 1904. Irregular in later years. A major bibliographic annual. There is an *Index to the Writings on American History, 1902–40* (Washington, 1956).

Bibliographies of chronological periods. Examples are Louis J. Paetow, *A Guide to the Study of Medieval History* (rev. ed.; New York, 1931), a combination guide and bibliography, confined geographically or culturally largely to the Occident, although it contains some Islamic material; Lowell J. Ragatz, *A Bibliography for the Study of European History, 1815–1939* (2nd ed.; Washington, 1946).

Bibliographies of local history. There is a large bibliographic literature on subdivisions of nation-states. Examples are: James H. Easterby, *Guide to the Study and Reading of South Carolina History: A General Classified Bibliography* (2 pts.; Columbia: Historical Commission of South Carolina, 1949–50 [i.e., 1953]); Charles Gross, *A Bibliography of British Municipal History* (New York, 1897); Joaquín Díaz Mercado, *Bibliografía general del estado de Veracruz. t. I, 1794–1910* (Mexico, 1937), a bibliography of one state of the Mexican federal republic.

Bibliographies of other subjects (than the above). There are many types of specialized bibliographies in addition to those categorized above. Examples include Karl W. Deutsch, *Interdisciplinary Bibliography on Nationalism* (Cambridge, Mass.: Technology Press of M.I.T., 1956); Monroe N. Work, *A Bibliography of the Negro in Africa and America* (New York, 1928); the American Historical Association's *Guide to*

Historical Literature (New York, 1961; 854 pp., double-columned), was done by many scholars, is highly selective and annotated, and it covers all culture areas and all times of recorded history, with sections on pre-history, auxiliary disciplines, and other subjects.

3. Government publication guides and indexes

These come in many forms. Some nations are better served than others. The student should carefully read the prefatory material in such aids to try to learn what is included. Often much material has not been covered, and not infrequently the aid does not make this clear. There may be separate indexes or listings (even separate volumes) for legislative, executive, or judicial publications; or the publications may be divided in other ways. Some governments have state printing offices that print all government publications; others permit various agencies to handle their publications separately (even using private printers). There may have been several indexes in the history of a country. For the United States the indexes are: Benjamin Perley Poore, *A Descriptive Catalogue of the Government Publications of the United States, September 5, 1774–March 4, 1881* (Washington: GPO, 1885); John G. Ames, *Comprehensive Index to the Publications of the United States, 1881–93* (2 vols.; Washington: GPO, 1905); United States Congress, *Catalog of the Public Documents* (Washington: GPO, 1896–).

Guides (as opposed to indexes) to United States government publications follow: Anne Morris Boyd, *United States Government Publications* (3rd ed., rev. by E. Rips; New York, 1949); Everett S. Brown, *Manual of Government Publications, United States and Foreign* (New York, 1950). The Brown item obviously treats a number of governments, as does Jean Meyriat (ed.), *A Study of Current Bibliographies of National Official Publications* (comp. by the International Committee for Social Sciences Documentation, and published by UNESCO, 1958).

4. Press and journal indexes

This category includes indexes to newspapers, popular magazines, and specialized (including scholarly historical) journals.

Newspaper indexes, not numerous, include: *New York Daily Tribune Index* (30 vols.; New York: Tribune Associates [1876–1907]; the *New York Times Index* (New York: New York Times Co., 1913–), published monthly, then cumulated (years before 1913 indexed later and now available on microfilm); Lester J. Cappon and Stella F. Duff, *Virginia Gazette Index, 1736–1780* (2 vols.; Williamsburg, Va.: Institute of Early American History and Culture, 1950); Herbert O. Brayer, "Preliminary Guide to Indexed Newspapers in the United States, 1850–1900," *The Mississippi Valley Historical Review,* XXXIII (Sept., 1946), pp. 237–58. The Brayer guide was being brought up to date by W. R. Griffin and J. L. Rasmussen.

Indexes of magazines and journals are of many types. Care must be taken to understand the coverage of each index. Examples include: *Poole's Index to Periodical Literature, 1802–1881* (rev. ed., 2 vols., Boston, 1891; later supplements cover 1882–1906) covers United States and English periodicals; *Reader's Guide to Periodical Literature* (New York, 1907– ; monthly, with annual cumulations), chiefly indexing popular magazines of general circulation, and probably of value mainly for public opinion estimates; Columbus Memorial Library of the Pan American Union and the New York Public Library, *Indice general de publicaciones periódicas latinomericanas* (1961–), a quarterly cooperative index of Latin American periodicals; Franklin D. Scott and Elaine Teigler, *Guide to the American Historical Review, 1895–1945: A Subject-Classified Explanatory Bibliography of the Articles, Notes and Suggestions, and Documents* (Washington: GPO, 1945); *Social Sciences and Humanities Index* (New York: H. W. Wilson, 1916–), originally (covering years 1907–1919) *Reader's Guide to Periodical Literature Supplement,* then *International*

Index to Periodicals (covering 1920–65), and continuing under the present title to cover more scholarly journals than the *Reader's Guide; Public Affairs Index* (Bulletin of the Public Affairs Information Service; New York, 1915–), issued as weekly bulletins, with cumulations five times a year, the fifth forming the annual volume.[4]

5. Indexes to books published

This category might also be titled "National Bibliographies"; it encompasses aids that help one to learn what has been published in a given country. "Helping" is used advisedly, since no national bibliographical system covers all items published. The aids available vary widely from country to country, and over time in a single nation. In many cases, this is one of the more difficult bibliographic tasks. Only professional bibliographers are likely to have a firm grasp of the intricacies of national bibliography in many countries. Both public and private agencies may be involved in the preparation of lists that contribute to a national bibliography. The national bibliography usually will exclude some categories of publications (e.g., comic books are commonly excluded), and may exclude others (they often exclude government publications). On national bibliographies in many lands, see Helen F. Conover, *Current National Bibliographies* (Washington, 1955); LeRoy H. Liner, *The Rise of Current Complete National Bibliography* (New York, 1959).

National bibliography is apt to be a complex and frustrating matter for nations that have had printing since the 15th century (see Appendix B for national bibliography in several countries) and difficult because of poor organization of society in general and of printing and library and scholarly work in particular in modern underdeveloped countries. For the United States national bibliography may be followed with a considerable degree of coverage and accuracy in: Charles Evans, *Ameri-*

---

[4] *Ulrich's Periodicals Dictionary* (8th ed., New York, 1956) not only lists periodicals by subject, but states whether abstracted or indexed, and in most cases gives collective indexes that exist.

can Bibliography: A Chronological Dictionary of All Books, Pamphlets and Periodical Publications Printed in the United States of America from the Genesis of Printing in 1639 down to and Including the Year 1800: with Bibliographical and Biographical Notes (14 vols.; Worcester, Mass.: American Antiquarian Society, 1903–59), arranged chronologically; Joseph Sabin, *A Dictionary of Books Relating to America, from Its Discovery to the Present Time* (29 vols.; New York: Bibliographical Society of America, 1868–1936), covering to the mid-18th century, overlapping Evans, but with additional items, and arranged by authors; Ralph R. Shaw and Richard H. Shoemaker, *American Bibliography: A Preliminary Check List for 1801–[1819]* (New York: Scarecrow Press, 1958–); Orville A. Roorbach, *Bibliotheca Americana; Catalogue of American Publications Including Reprints and Original Works from 1820 to 1860 Inclusive, Together with a List of Periodicals Published in the United States* (4 vols.; New York; Roorbach, 1852–61), organized by author; James Kelly, *The American Catalogue of Books, Original and Reprints, Published in the United States from January 1861 to January 1871* (2 vols.; New York: Wiley, 1866–67); this last was continued by annual issues of the *American Catalogue of Books* (9 vols. in 13; New York, 1877–1911), listing volumes in print in 1876–1910; *The United States Catalog* (New York, 1900–28); *The Cumulative Book Index* (New York, 1898–), listing United States publications, and since 1928 including books published in English in other parts of the world; *The Publishers Weekly: The American Book Trade Journal* (New York, 1872–).

6. Manuscript and archival guides

This class of aid is represented by many thousands of items, some of them modest, some large and complex. Professional scholars depend heavily on manuscript and archival guides. Three examples follow: *Guide to Records in the National Archives* (Washington: GPO, 1948), with later supplements; Grace G. Griffin, *A Guide to Manuscripts Relating to Ameri-*

can History in British Repositories Reproduced for the Division of Manuscripts of the Library of Congress (Washington: Library of Congress, 1946); Lino Gómez Canedo, *Los archivos de la historia de América. Período colonial español, I* (México: Instituto Panamericano de Geografía e Historia, Publicación Num. 225, 1961).

7. Indexes to doctoral dissertations

Many doctoral dissertations never are published; some are not published until long after the degree is granted.[5] It is often important to search for dissertations in more than one discipline (e.g., history, economics, political science). Dissertations in history in the United States and Canada in recent years may be found in: *List of Doctoral Dissertations in History Now in Progress at Universities in the United States* (Washington: Carnegie Corporation, 1902–38, annual volumes; American Historical Association, 1941– , usually triennial volumes); *Doctoral Dissertations Accepted by American Universities, 1933–55* (New York: H. W. Wilson, 1934–56), an annual; *Dissertation Abstracts: A Guide to Dissertations and Monographs Available in Microfilm* (Ann Arbor, Mich.: University Microfilms, 1952–), an annual, continuing the preceding item, and representing an expansion of a microfilm abstract guide for 1938–51.

8. Scholarly journals

Searching scholarly journals ordinarily is not an efficient way of compiling bibliography. The exceptions are with materials of very recent publication that have not yet appeared in bibliographic compilations, or those underdeveloped countries that lack such compilations. Scholarly journals (e.g., *The Hispanic American Historical Review, The English Historical Review*) do have other bibliographic uses: e.g., reviews of books,

---

[5] Unpublished dissertations may be borrowed or microfilm copies bought.

descriptions of manuscript collections, discussions of fields of historiography.

9. Guides to reference books

Guides to reference books sometimes are of considerable help to the historical researcher. They generally assist him in finding specialized materials dealing with aspects of his subject. Listings of reference books are in American Historical Association, *Guide to Historical Literature;* and Constance M. Winchell, *Guide to Reference Books* (7th ed.; Chicago, 1951; and supplements in later years). And see Louis Shores, *Basic Reference Sources* (Chicago, 1954); A. J. Walford, *et al., Guide to Reference Materials . . . with Emphasis on Current Publications and on Material Published in Britain* (New York, 1959); Helen J. Poulton and Marguerite S. Howland, *The Historian's Handbook. A Descriptive Guide to Reference Works* (University of Oklahoma Press, 1972).

10. Booksellers' lists

Sometimes booksellers' sales catalogs list items that pass quickly from one little-known (or even entirely private) collection to another: e.g., Maggs Brothers, *Spanish America and the Guianas* (London, 1935; listing 800 items in 118 pp.). And see Archer Taylor, *Book Catalogues: Their Varieties and Uses* (Chicago, 1957).

11. Item locators

These aids show the researcher where to find examples of materials that he has identified previously. Ordinarily, they are not usefully consulted to identify items.

a) Union lists: These set down materials found in an area: e.g., *Union List of Serials in Libraries of the United States and Canada* (2nd ed., 1943, with supplements in later years), a much used locator; Louis F. Steig, *A Union List of Printed Col-*

*lections of Source Materials on European History in New
York State Libraries* (New York, 1944).

b) *Microprint guides:* These may or may not also be union
lists. An example: United States Library of Congress,
Newspapers on Microfilm (2nd ed.; Washington, 1953), listing holdings in United States libraries of foreign and domestic
newspapers.

C. Research notes

The making of research notes involves both relatively simple forms and quite complex analysis. It thus is both a set of
procedures and an art.

1. The mechanics

Memory alone will not serve in historical research; the evidence is too abundant, too diverse, and too ambiguous. The
mechanical side of note taking must be accepted in the sense
that practice is accepted by musicians and the sanitary and
materials-handling aspects of chemical research are accepted
by its practitioners.

Three types of notes may appear in the files: (*a*) research
notes proper, containing substantive data; (*b*) notes referring
to other parts of the research note files; and (*c*) notes directing
the attention to the possibility of further research on a stated
subject in a given source.

There is no size or material for research notes that is best
suited to all tasks. Whatever suffices is appropriate, with the
following provisos: (*a*) that all the sheets or cards be of the
same size, for ease of filing and indexing; (*b*) the size be suitable to the materials of research (e.g., certain types of statistical research can employ quite small note cards); (*c*) that
index cards and file drawers can be found for the note material
selected; (*d*) that the weight and expense are bearable; (*e*)
that the material will take a proper impression and will stand
the expectable amount of wear.

We require students to use sheets the size of one-half a page of typewriter paper on the grounds that it is cheap, readily available in many forms and colors (typewriter paper, foolscap pads, etc.), light in weight, large enough for nearly all purposes (some researchers consider it *too* large), desirable from the standpoint of uniformity. Although most researchers today prefer loose-leaf note materials, some perform quite acceptably with bound notebooks. Loose-leaf materials have the advantage of permitting physical shuffling of materials.

The following injunctions will be helpful:

a) Adopt a standard method of recording things, including a set place on the note sheet for the elements involved (source, pages, heading, etc.). We prescribe a system here, for pedagogical reasons, but many other procedures are equally acceptable.

b) In the upper left corner put the source, abbreviated (full data will be on the working bibliography card).

c) Put a short heading or descriptive phrase in the upper right corner. This describes the content of the note, aids in filing and organization (not the same things), and obviates the need to read long notes over every time you contemplate using them.

d) Put pages and volumes of source. If this is put only in the source citation in upper left, it will apply to the entire note. If more than one page and/or volume of citation is involved, it should be put to the left of the part of the note to which it applies.

e) Abbreviate as much as possible, and be telegraphic (e.g., by elimination of articles).

f) Do not use reverse for materials that require a different heading (indexer) from that in the upper right corner. But do use the reverse so long as the continuation material is on the same subject.

g) Material that you interpolate into quotations should be in brackets.

h) Quotations that contain quotations should be so indicated by single quotation marks within double.

i) Legibility (to the researcher) is necessary, beauty is not. Do not type over notes that have been taken in longhand simply to improve their appearance.

As nearly as possible use a note sheet for only one subject.

This generally accepted principle is easier to state than to demonstrate. What is a subject? Think about it. The fact is that it is impossible to follow this injunction with all notes. Sometimes it simply would be too much labor. Sometimes the definition of subject changes in the course of research. But it is a tremendous help to follow this principle as nearly as possible. It permits the physical grouping for analysis and composition of a major part of the evidence on a part of the subject. It also greatly simplifies the problem of cross-indexing, a heavy chore in any sizable research project.

Notes must be filed by categories, divided by indexers, if they are to be easily usable. Some classifications will be suggested by the descriptive titles of research notes and by the divisions of working outlines. The first file categories set up almost certainly will be modified later to some extent, and some notes shifted. Another problem is that often a note may be put into more than one file category. As a practical matter, there is no complete answer to this (unless the researcher has a staff of helpers, or is pursuing one of the relatively rare subjects little affected by the problem). The following are procedures of some value: (*a*) duplicate (or multiple) notes may be made, but researchers will not want to accept the labor or expense involved in large-scale application of this "solution"; (*b*) cross reference notes may be made, and put in appropriate research note file categories, referring the researcher to a note in another category; (*c*) many schemes are used that involve coding with numbers, letters, or colors. Thus, a note found in file bin A–1 may bear (most usefully at the top of the note sheet) codes directing its use in other categories also. At the proper time, therefore, notes with a given code may be plucked out of all file bins and combined with those notes in the file category in question.

2. Preliminary analysis[6]

All note taking that is not mere copying involves analysis, some of it simple, some sophisticated. Analysis is involved in

---

[6] We have found it useful to emphasize that the instructor will look at and

the simplest process of selection. A student investigating the
relations between church and state in a country where and
when church and state were to some degree united will, of
course, read the church's records; and in making notes, he will
have to decide which subjects dealt with in the records were of
merely ecclesiastical interest and which were relevant to the
state as well as the church. The processes of condensation and
paraphrase also involve selection, comparison of data (from
the memory), reformulation, even judgment. Sometimes all this
is implicit rather than explicit in the note; but sometimes there
is explicit commentary. Nearly all note taking should involve
implicit analysis (i.e., simply copying merely postpones the
process of analysis, and involves some duplication of effort);
some will involve explicit analysis. Not all materials require the
latter. The purpose of the research and the nature of the material dictate what is taken down. It is, however, a good general
rule to perform as much analysis as possible when the original
note is made (of course, much later analysis involves the use
of many notes on the same subject or complex of subjects).

The following suggestions will be helpful:

a) Summarization and paraphrasing are highly necessary
skills. Train yourself to avoid taking many materials down verbatim. Beginning researchers woefully overestimate the use
they will have for direct quotations. It will be found that often
a page, even a chapter, occasionally a book, may be summed
up in a few lines for the researcher's purposes.

b) Inevitably, the criteria for selection of data change in
the course of a research task. In the early stages of the task
selection is bound to be especially difficult. Again using the
example of investigation into the relations between church and
state in a country with an established church, the student might
begin by ignoring church worship on the assumption that this
subject would concern the church alone. Later in his investiga-

---

discuss some of the student's research notes, and that all of the notes will be
turned in with the completed paper. This helps to force analysis of materials
from the beginning of the process of note taking.

tion, however, he might find that changes of ceremonial in worship aroused public feeling to such a pitch that state intervention was demanded; the student would then have to begin taking notes on church worship.

c) The "corroborative note" often is a special breed. Sometimes it will state that the data in one source virtually or strongly supports that in another, and is of about the same value (i.e., the data and/or argument may not have to be repeated in the corroborative note). Use of this device depends both on the correspondence between the sources involved, and on the value to the research in the given case of small variations in testimony or other evidence in corroboration of evidence. For example, the diaries of men who attended a secret meeting could be used in this corroborative manner in an attempt to establish what took place.

d) Some "negative" notes are likely to be taken—for example, notes stating that no evidence on a given subject appeared in such-and-such a place, where it might have been expected that such evidence might appear. Interpretation of this absence of evidence depends on the particular circumstances in each case.

e) It is important to recognize that often it is not sufficient to take down summaries of statements found either in the accounts of witnesses or in studies. In many cases the note, at the time it is taken, should also include discussion of the cited sources of the study being used (or the fact that no sources were cited, if that is the case), or discussion of the argument used by the historian, or indication of what it is that the witness bases his statements on (visual observation, from what distance, under what circumstances; etc.).

An essential set of procedures—mechanical and mental—is here disposed of in few words out of our conviction that the skill required to take research notes competently can only be taught by a tutorial method—i.e., by practice guided by comment. Figure 4 consists of examples of research notes, illustrating both the forms involved and examples of the process of preliminary analysis.

Figure 4. Examples of research notes

The following examples of research notes are illustrative, and do not cover all the variations to be found in a large research note file. Research notes all will be on sheets or cards of one size. The examples below, however, divided by lines, do not show the blank spaces that would occur on many note sheets. Brackets [ ], often used to indicate interpolated material, may be indicated in research notes by double parentheses (( )) when a typewriter lacks brackets; this cannot be done in finished manuscripts. Of course, many research notes will be handwritten, in which case brackets can be drawn.

```
P Notte, C Eur & Asia, II, 63                    Graustark threat China aid

Says no doubt Graustk made the threat ((cites only Madrid Noticias Graficas
5 nov 82)); but consid doubt if had any notn really tryg get Chinese aid
((cites no evid, and does not give reasong)).

II, 78 cites letter (Archives Nat., Paris), Count Marko, Fgn Min Graustk to
Ch. Clouvier, Grstk Amb to Paris, suggestg possib threat such a connecn ((but
no more analysis than on p63; & no indictn effort find corrob or contradictg
evid elsewhere)).
```

```
NYT editl 4 nov                          Winkler's tariff speech 3 nov 82

Says Pres W good on econ issue, but "less than candid" on moral issue. On
whole creates strong suspicion W playg politics rather than searching for
best solutn fr pt v USA.

        ((NYT doesnt say why less than candid; & remember NYT havg feud with
        admin on other issues at this time))
```

```
NYT 5 nov 82  datelind Graustark 4 nov       Graustark govt reacn W's tariff
                                                    speech 3 nov 82

Graustark Fgn Mintr today in speech to Natl Assoc of Manuf dinner stated W's
speech "demagogic," lackg in desire find real solutn.  Main interest speech
was Fgn Min hint that Graustark might turn to China for assistance.

        ((corresp not at dinner; says no handouts text; got data fr "friendly
        guest" at dinner; corrsp pts out govt often uses this method express
        "unofficial" displeasure))
```

```
Vaughan, Intl Rels in XIX, II 78

I ((sic)) 142:  Says Marko in letter to son Jules, sept 82 ((no day given, and
no collecn or repository cited)) asserted that "he was convinced that the
activities of anarchists 'require me to recommend the use of a Chinese threat'".
```

No diacritical marks are included in these notes. For comment see introduction to Figure 3, page 91.

Figure 4—*Continued*

```
Cong. Rec,105th cong,2d sess,1892,CI,Part 5,9553-9674        Cong debate on W's
                                                                   3 nov speech

These pp contain speech 18 senators on issue.  5 suppt speech without reservn;
5 suppt W, but not enthused over speech; 3 rail vs speech; 5 vs W, but not
hydrophobic in criticizing speech....The 10 fav are Dams; other 8 Repubs; so
reactns ff strictly party lines.
   The 3 rabid critics incl Smythers, the Alaskan ultrareactry; Clark of Ohio,
asusual vs any tariff reducn, flagwavg, etc; and Simms of Idaho, who simply
seems to distrust W.
   On whole speeches concentrate on econ issues, tho all allude to moral
questns, and two make big fuss ca moral issue (altho they disagree with each
other on definitn).  Everyone claims be vs appeasement, but define it diff.
   Very clear that most wld vote for some tariff reducn, but far apart on amt.
   16 mention Graustark threat to turn to China; 3 say it empty threat; several
others simply vaguely worried; a few pt out that no official threat; clear
majority think it possib serious; 3 couple with US need maintain milit str.
   Most remarkable thing ca debate as whole is restrained, responsible tone
as compd with debate in jan 82 over the Constantinople incident.  ((Of course
the only thing that cld restrain Smythers wld be a muzzle.))
```

```
K Botsch, US & Graustark 2d ed          cong reactn to Graustark threat on China

69:  says cong up in arms ca the threat ((cites cong record 105th cong 2d sess,
1892,CI, Pt 5, 9553-9674, but gives no analysis or reasoning)); does not pursue
the subject, except to say that this "no doubt" one of reasons for increase in
naval approps only two months later ((no evid adduced)).
```

```
Amb Carl V Platt, US Emby London, to Secy        Graustark feeler to China for
State,10 jan 85 (in Docs Fgn Aff, XX,86-88)  aid in re crisis with US on tariff

Amb states that got hands on ((doesnt tell how)) fr reliable source copy of
apparent message Graustark Fgn Min to its Min to China, dtd 8 nov 82.  US Amb
pts out message hints at Graustark milit aid in return China econ concessns
if internatl tensions dev as at present.
   Text Graus. message printd.  Is, indeed, merely hint.  And no direct
indicatn that US involved in internatl tensions mentnd.
   Editors of vol state ((88 n)) that it is however a fair presumptn, given
date of message, and reptd speech of Fgn Min a few days bef in wch threatnd
agreement with China in retaliatn US tariff changes, that Graustark made the
feeler with US in mind.  Editors pt out however that since no word of the
message leaked out till Amb Platt got copy over 2 yrs later, Graustark
didnt push the threat very far.
```

```
U Gotlieb, Kans & Intl Politics             Kans business & Graustark tariff issue

29:  says no quesn but that Kans business much arousd, esp over packagd pro-
ducts issue, and put massive pressure on public offcls ((citing J Dousel,
"Kans and the tariff," Am Hist Rev, Jan 1910 -- but without discussg the
char of Dousel's evid))
76:  says Chambers of Commerce very active in puttg pressure on pub offcls
((citg N Rutt, "Tariff Issues in West," Ec Rev, Feb 1949, and statg that
Rutt's view is solidly fded on exam offcl records 18 Chambers of Commerce in
Kans))
101:  says "public opinion in Kans was arousd by this threat to US sovgnty
by Graustark" ((citg Kans C Star 7 nov 82--pretty dubious way showing all
Kans arousd))
```

Figure 4—*Continued*

```
Memoirs J Cloud                          reason for Winkler's 3 nov 82 speech

19:  says he present as W's Secy Interior 28 oct, 3 pm White House when
P House of Dem Natl Comm presented analysis reactn tariff policy and urged
nec speech.  Cloud claims argument that seemed to impress W most was dissatis-
fcn in orgzd labor.
49:  prints excerpt of letter fr P House to J Cloud, 7 jun 84, alludg to
meetg of 28 oct 82 at White House, mentiong that both present at that meetg,
and statg "President Winkler was moved to make the famous speech of nov 3
primarily by my rept on agricultural unrest on the West Coast."
49-51:  Cloud rambles on at gt length refuting House's statements, ptly on
grds Cloud has better memory, ptly on grds West Coast agric in good shape
at that time, and cites statistics to prove latter ((fr Dept Agric Statistical
Bull, 12 jan 83, pp 72-79, 111-115))
             ((check on this))
```

```
Martinez, Docs Mex, IV, 190-195          influence sheepherders on 98 tariff

     See note filed under AGRIC & 98 TARIFF
```

```
Sandy, "Calif and 98 tariff"             mining interests and 98 tariff

     Material on this in article.  I only took notes on Calif agric
     and the tariff fr it.  See if expand study.
```

```
Rept F Pizarro to crown 5 nov 1537       amt gold div at Sacsahuaman
  (in Doc Ineds, III, 234-246)

     Doc reprinted fr orig in Arch de Indias.
     Rept written nearly 2 yrs ff events.
     Says total 11,345 lbs (ie pesos) gold, wch he saw weighed, and certificate
to that effect signd by him, by Friar Montesinos, by Assessor Guzman, the
Treasurer Calderon.  He incl copy certificate, and notes it sent with his
orig rept of nearly 2 yrs bef, tho Crown now claims it cant find it.
     He incl affidavits by Montesinos and Guzman that 11,345 was amt, & that they
signd certif.
     Claims story was another 5,000 lbs. gold in another bldg he didnt have
weighed, but kept himself, a lie.  Says 1 of 2 men claimg this, Urquiza,
was not at Sacsahuaman at time weight taken, but near Arequipa, 200 miles
over mts.  Incl affid signd by 8 impt conquistadores to this effect....Says
another accuser, Pi y Margall, was present at weighg, but known trouble-
maker, and his (F Piz's) personal foe, due fact Piz had to discipline him
once for cruelty to Indians ((a laugh, coming fr F Piz))....Rest of rept is
self-praise of gt services of Piz to crown.

     ((about all can tell fr this is that Crown suspicious of Piz; and that Piz
can get people to testify for him...and that even this early a conquistador
notd for cruelty to Indians considerd it politic to indicate to crown that
he was careful of Indians--ie knew crown concernd))
```

```
Oviedo, Hist nat III                     relatns bet Pedrarias and Balboa

98, 182 et seq:  Number of incidents described by Oviedo, claiming he
witnessd them, in wch Pedrarias actd arbitrarily, & contrary to royal
orders, persecuting old settlers who were there bef his arrival.  Three of
these involvd Balboa.  One of them involved Oviedo.  Says (182)"Here the
orders of His Maj are interpreted by only one man, Pedrarias Davila"....The
language thruout indicates strong dislike of Pedr.  On other hand, Oviedo
is proud of his task as historiographer, seems to have consid affecn for objec-
tive reptg, so that I doubt he inventd all these incidents, or even Pedrarias'
genly arbitrary character....Further, Oviedo shows no animus vs Balboa, nor
any affecn for him, and finds little to criticize (or praise) in his actns.
     ((copy this note also filed under ADMIN JUSTICE COLONIAL ERA))
```

Figure 4—*Concluded*

```
V. C. Smith, "Diary," Univ Wisc Archives        corroboration deal on 1882 tariff

    Under entry for 8 oct 1882 he gives an approx 2500 word summary of speech
Winkler at White House dinner Democ state chairmen, 7 oct 82, wch Smith
attended.  ((His acct almost exactly agrees with that in Robinson Memoirs.
I had fotostat of latter & compared them.  The differences are of no imptce.))
```

```
Walker, My Exper in Politics            no evid on Dem Natl Comm activ on 1882
                                                                         tariff

    Nothing herein of value on subject, altho several historians hint that
there is.  Actly, they make unwarranted inferences.  Is useful testimony
on several allied subjects ((and I have separate notes)).  Fact is, Walker
in Europe for 3 wks bef the critical Dem Natl Comm meetg until a wk
thereafter ((see his ltr to daughter in Natl Arch, 9 sept 82, filed under
MISC my files)).
```

V

Using evidence:
External criticism

Using evidence requires knowledge of (a) external criticism, which determines the authenticity of evidence; (b) internal criticism, which determines the credibility of evidence; (c) the grouping of evidence in relationships of various sorts; (d) the interpretation of evidence in the light of many factors and in the absence of others; and (e) exposition or the communication of evidence to others. These subjects are treated in Chapters V–VIII. Although external criticism, subject of the present chapter, is a process relatively little pursued by beginning researchers, it is important for them to develop the habit of thinking in terms of the critical approach developed in this chapter. They should look at all evidence in this critical manner. And the specific problems and techniques of external criticism will be most useful to an understanding of the pitfalls of internal criticism and synthesis. The techniques of external criticism are modern; they have been developed in the Occident since the Renaissance.

A. External criticism

1. Its aim

The aim of external criticism is to get evidence ready for use in the examination of human affairs: That is, to prepare it for internal criticism. External criticism authenticates evidence and establishes texts in the most accurate possible form. It sometimes is said that its function is negative, merely saving us from using false evidence; whereas internal criticism has the positive function of telling us how to use authenticated evidence. We repeat the assertion because it helps differentiation, not because it tells us anything about the relative usefulness of the two. For the same reason we note that external criticism sometimes is referred to as "lower" and internal as "higher" criticism. Another way of putting the matter is to say that external criticism deals with the document, and internal with the statement or meaning of the document. The types of problems attacked by external criticism include forgeries, garbled documents, partial texts, plagiarism, ghost writers, interpolations. External criticism deals with both intentional and accidental errors in texts.

External criticism especially means determination of the authorship and date of evidence, which may prove or disprove the authenticity of the evidence, and almost certainly will aid in its examination by the processes of internal criticism. As a concept, external criticism is not difficult; as a process, it can be frustratingly complex. The phrase—but not the process—sometimes is criticized, but it has the values of traditional use, brevity, and some semantic content. Let us remember then that there is nothing mysterious about the difference between external and internal criticism; at the heart of it is the difference between authenticity and credibility. Remember this, and there should be no confusion because we look *inside* a document in engaging in external criticism, and of course we use other (outside, external) materials when engaging in internal criticism.[1]

Beginning researchers engage relatively little in external criticism, because: (*a*) they have enough other problems to occupy them; (*b*) they usually lack materials requiring external criticism, or do not realize that they require it; (*c*) they usually lack the skills to engage in such activity; and (*d*) much material has been authenticated for them. An enormous amount of ex-

---

[1] There are many "overlaps" between external and internal; e.g., although information on author and date are the essence of external criticism, they also are needed for internal criticism.

ternal criticism has been done by specialists.[2] Millions of pages of documents have been authenticated and published, sometimes with elaborate notes and commentary;[3] uncounted physical remains have been similarly proved, cataloged, indexed, stored, often put on display. Many unpublished manuscripts in archives have been at least partially or tentatively authenticated.

Many professional historians seldom or never engage in external criticism. If the need arises (and it varies considerably from field to field), they either can apply to reference books and manuals for aid in doing their own authentication or restoration of texts, or refer the material to a specialist, who may devote all his time to external criticism, usually in a relatively narrow field. Some of these specialists are discussed in V (B), where their work is entitled "auxiliary disciplines."

2. Determination of author and date

The author is wanted because: (a) there is a suspicion that the document is wholly or partially false; or (b) it is needed for internal criticism. The document may proclaim an individual as author, or a class of author (priest, lawyer, soldier) may be indicated, explicitly or implicitly. If it turns out that the asserted author (individual or class) surely did not compose the document, the next step is to determine the sort of falsehood involved. For example, if the forgery is a 16th-century Spanish document claiming to be a letter by an English admiral, we may at least learn what sorts of lies Spaniards thought it worthwhile to tell about Englishmen at that time.

The date is wanted because it can (a) show whether the

---

[2] The student is cautioned that the textual purity (in toto and in detail) of many documents in important sets is open to doubt. Sometimes editors tell us little or nothing about the methods they used in authenticating documents. A well-known example is the *Colección de documentos inéditos relativos al descubrimiento, conquista y organización* . . . , on the Spanish colonies overseas, published in 67 volumes, in two series, by the Spanish Academy of History, in 1864–1932.

[3] In many elaborate sets of published documents, not only is material furnished on authentication, but also analyses that result from internal criticism. A famous example is the *Monumenta Germaniae Historica,* in 125 volumes, begun in the early 19th century and finished in 1925.

asserted or implied date of composition can be correct, (*b*) show whether the indicated author can indeed have been involved, and (*c*) orient the researcher for the processes of internal criticism. The date is that at which the document was composed or the object made, not the date of the material treated in words or the date at which artifacts of a given type ordinarily were constructed. Sometimes a year, or week, or even a day or hour is needed; for some purposes, a century will suffice reasonably well. There are cases in which the date can be closely determined without much material on authorship being available (e.g., a Latin list of household objects, reliably dated from papyrus type, ink, structure of language as Latin of the third century A.D., but conceivably prepared by various sorts of persons for any one of several purposes, and in one of a thousand places).

Determination of authorship and date involves one or all of the following: (*a*) content analysis, (*b*) comparison with the content of other evidence, (*c*) tests of the physical properties of evidence. Division might also be made between the social and the physical properties of the evidence. Content analysis is, then, examination of the social content of the evidence. Comparison with the content of other documents either means direct comparison by the researcher, or the consultation of reference works, which are, in the end, founded upon many comparisons and classifications of pieces of evidence. Such reference works now exist in profusion, and include many types of information: inscriptions, signatures, seals, letters, various types of governmental papers, church materials, the records of such institutions as universities and craft guilds, and many more. Often they have been prepared with great care by specialists, and may be of the greatest assistance in establishing the authorship and date of newly discovered or studied documents. The availability of this mass of carefully prepared material, often with extensive commentaries, as we have said before, constitutes a major difference between the historical method of the last century and a half and earlier times.

The language of the document may in itself provide useful general indications of where and when it was composed. The

Latin of Roman times changed considerably over the centuries, as has English since the Norman Conquest. Specialists can assign dates to certain constructions and vocabulary, and even in some cases pinpoint regional usages that provide a clue to place of authorship, or to the place of origin of the author. The content of the document may provide data to permit general classification of the author: e.g., a man with a good but unspecialized education, or an ecclesiastic, or a lawyer. Sometimes yet more data exist, permitting judgment that it was composed by a member of the United States Congress in the years just before the Civil War, with an indication that he was a good friend of Henry Clay. That would lead to research on Clay's acquaintances.

a. Content analysis.

(i) Anachronisms of many sorts may be useful in establishing (or invalidating) authorship and in fixing (or loosening) the date. This includes anachronisms of spelling, in the use of words in certain senses, in the structure of language, in types of scripts, in references to objects or events or persons who have been (or can be) reliably dated and fixed in place. Simple examples would be an asserted author of the first half of the 15th century using the word "America," or an asserted 17th-century letter writer using the expression "didn't get to first base."

(ii) Dating may be suggested by mention of dates that are or can be reliably fixed: religious beliefs, astral events, domesticated animals, floods, battles, construction projects, elections, all may be revealing.

(iii) Script may be compared with known samples of an individual's hand. There are reference books containing samples of the writing of important individuals.

(iv) Tests of consistency would include consistency of sentiment with the known predispositions of a culture, consistency of an individual's statement with his presumed cultural, general, or occupational background. As to the internal consistency of the document, one should question whether it seems to be of a piece, or whether there are indications of multiple authorship, and if the latter of what sort, and how divided in time.

b. Comparison of pieces of evidence.

By comparison of pieces of evidence contemporary with that under consideration, we may learn what have been the usual styles of composition and forms of documents in given places, offices, times, for given purposes. In some cases, we may find other documents with identified authors, and so similar to that under study that the latter may be ascribed either to that author or to one of that class. In even happier cases, an authenticated document by a known author states that he wrote another document that clearly can be identified as the one under study.

c. Physical properties of evidence.

Most of the tests for the physical—as opposed to the semantic or cultural or social—properties of evidence are of modern origin; many of them were devised only in recent decades. Since the 17th century we have had systematic treatises on some of the physical properties and appearance of paper, parchment, vellum, inks, seals. These include such things as color, weight, gloss, grain, watermarks. Much more recently this sort of material has been subjected to chemical and spectroscopic analysis. Measurement of the age of materials now is possible through analysis of the decay of radioactive carbon, used spectacularly several times to push back the time of anthropoid origins, as well as the time of the arrival of man in the New World. Tree rings have a use in dating. On a humbler level, parts of documents have been matched by the shapes of stains going through the pages, or the paths of wormholes.

3. Forgeries

Forgeries include complete documents (or artifacts) or forged interpolations into documents. Plagiarism (unacknowledged use of another's words) is a special form of forgery. Documents garbled because of either forged interpolations, or accident (e.g., bad copying), or the merging of documents are treated later in this chapter under restoration of texts.

Monetary gain is one motive for forgery. Fraudulent wills are by no means rare. Many historical, literary, and government documents are forged for sale. Fabricators of this type of material are sensitive to the market. In our day, it is known that Americans yearn for love letters exchanged by the young Abraham Lincoln and Ann Rutledge, so forgers supply them. Visitors to Mexico today lust (illegally) for ancient artifacts of the Mexica, Olmecs, Maya, so the descendants of those peoples make replicas and "authenticate" them.

Other forgeries are committed for political profit or in support of causes. Many a modern electoral contest has been livened by the appearance of fake documents that cast a sickly light on a candidate. Governments sometimes manufacture documents to "prove" claims. The history of religion is thick with proven forgeries, and with documents and holy artifacts of dubious origin.

Some forgeries are made in pursuit of fame (e.g., by a scholar, or an explorer). For example, in 1648, Kircher published some music which he alleged was the lost accompaniment for the first "Pythian Ode" of Pindar. Some fabrications have been at least in part the result of esthetic pride, satisfaction in work well and cleverly done. There have been forgers who enjoyed making mischief. Yet other forgers seem to have been driven by frenzy, but this sometimes is difficult to distinguish from devotion to a cause.

Determining authenticity thus means whether a letter offered by a bookseller on Fifth Avenue for $25,000 as from an ardent Napoleon to Josephine, is in fact the manufacture of a Parisian penman of today. Or whether the baseball-sized shrunken head offered a museum collector at Iquitos, on the headwaters of the Amazon, is a Jíbaro tribal masterpiece, or the uncle of a Chinese entrepreneur of Lima, who smokes such delicacies for the market. Is the cobbler's bench an 18th-century occupational artifact, or a Hoboken-made approximation for the split-level trade? Is a postage stamp genuine, a forgery, or a facsimile (an ac-

knowledged forgery)?[4] "Historical evidence" has been and is
being fabricated in appalling amounts.

In the early 17th century, C. Barth wrote some poems in
Latin which he falsely claimed were from the pen of Vestricius
Spurinna, a Roman soldier and very minor poet of the first century A.D. More recently, a good many alleged ancient statues
and other works of art have been manufactured, occasionally
with great success, like the over-life-size Etruscan warrior which
was considered genuine for some 60 years by authorities of the
Metropolitan Museum of Art in New York. Detection of bogus
statues is made by minute study of the style of modeling and
painting, the methods of manufacture, and microscopic examination of both the surface and interior of the material in the
object.

4. Restoration of texts

Documents sometimes contain "corrupt" passages, which
may be the result of a variety of causes. Some may be produced
by the conscious interpolation of forged sections, others may be
simply the result of poor copying and transmission of the text.
Diarists sometimes alter the entries in their own journals through
insertions or changes long after the event. Sometimes this is done
in the sincere (though possibly mistaken) belief that accuracy
is improved. Sometimes changes are made to make the diarist
appear more clever, a better prophet, or less harsh-minded. For
later publication as pamphlets, Cicero, we are told, so altered
the texts of speeches he had delivered. As a result of this, Caesar
promulgated an official daily gazette which contained reports of
the gist of speeches made in the Roman Senate. Ghost writing is
a modern phenomenon that presents us with problems of establishing the authorship of certain books and articles, problems
which are sometimes beyond solution. Barry Goldwater once
said that over the years he had employed a very large number

---

[4] There are even cases of fake facsimiles; e.g., the supply on order of an
asserted facsimile of an authentic title page which is in fact simple an invention of the seller.

of "ghosts," with the result that, unhappily for him, extant Gold-waterian documents do not always present the actual Goldwater-ian point of view. Hence, ghosted sources must be used with extreme caution.

Plagiarism offers the difficulty of finding the source from which something has been lifted. Discovery of the original is not always made quickly, owing to the flood of books, articles, and newspapers which flows from our presses. Plagiarism, it should be noted, was an acceptable practice in Greece and Rome. A special kind of nonauthentic documentation is found in the speeches inserted by Greek and Roman historians in their narratives. Thucydides, for example, included long orations delivered by Pericles and the other protagonists of the Peloponnesian War. He clearly said, however, that he was giving only some parts of them word-for-word, and that, as a rule, he reported no more than the general drift of a speaker's language. Study of the content of these speeches makes it certain that we do not have verbatim accounts, since all orators speak in a style which is unique—it can only be called "Thucydidean" Attic. Spartans and Corinthians never spoke in Doric. Classical writers used this convention to make their histories more varied, lively, and realistic.

Detection of interpolations and multiple authorship is sometimes hard and sometimes easy. In general, it is done by finding anachronisms or inconsistencies of style. In the book of Genesis, God is sometimes called Yahweh and sometimes Elohim. Since proper names were vitally important to the ancient Hebrews, not only for naming a thing or being, but also for defining its nature, such differences probably mean that at least two authors have been at work. This becomes certainty when there are doublets in Genesis—that is, recounting the same event twice—doublets which are consistent in that one set always uses Yahweh, and the other always calls God Elohim. It must be that early traditions of the origin of the world, or of the flood, were put together in ancient times to make the version of Genesis which has come down to us.

In dealing with corrupt passages, most of the work of scholars is not concerned with detecting forgeries, but with dealing with phrases, sentences, or paragraphs which make no sense. A great deal of such textual criticism has been made by Biblical scholars, since the exact text of the Old and New Testaments is of extreme importance from the religious point of view. Biblical scholars have to work from manuscripts which are copies of copies; the originals are lost. In the case of the Old Testament, the books or parts of the books were written down between the eleventh and second centuries B.C. Until fairly recently, the oldest surviving manuscripts were those made by the Jewish Masoretes in the ninth and tenth centuries of the Christian era. The discovery of the Dead Sea Scrolls in 1947 was a windfall for Hebraists, because among the scrolls were some made in the first century B.C. These much older documents are less likely to have suffered from the mistakes of copyists than the later ones. Another version of the Old Testament is the Septuagint, a translation into Greek made in the third and second centuries B.C. It shows what the Hebrew text was like at that time. It is not always to be preferred to the Masoretic text, however, since not all the translators were equally proficient, and also since the translation was made from texts brought to Egypt from Judeah some centuries earlier. Fourth, there is the Samaritan Pentateuch, which was (and is) used in northern Palestine, whereas the Masoretic text was derived from the version used in the south around Jerusalem. The method of Biblical scholars is to collate these four versions, that is, to bring them together for line-by-line comparison, so that the original text of which these four versions are descendants, may be reestablished as closely as possible.

Study of these texts of the Old Testament shows that most corrupt passages were caused by carelessness of copyists, and that little or no effort was made to deceive. Most mistakes, moreover, are simple and understandable ones, although endlessly and mindlessly repeated by generations of scribes. There is the copying of a line or phrase or word twice, the repetition coming right after the first appearance sometimes, but sometimes much later by a sort of curious mental lapse. There is, in reverse, the omission of a word, phrase, or line. There are simple mistakes in spelling. There is also the mistaking of one word for another which looks like or sounds like the correct one. Biblical scholarship has convincingly shown, incidentally, that the transmission of the text of the Bible has been, on the whole, amazingly accurate.

The same method of collating manuscripts is also used in establishing the texts of classical authors. This technique was already known to Greek scholars at the Alexandrian Museum in the third century B.C. In some cases, ancient works have come down to us, not in four main versions, as with the Old Testament, but as a single manuscript or papyrus. In this case there can be no collation. Textual criticism then becomes a complicated (and somewhat chancy) business, and requires a good knowledge of the language of the document, as well as, in some instances, of dialectical variants. It also requires a knowledge of the culture, both secular and religious, of the author or authors, and, what is more, of the milieu in which the copyists lived during the centuries when the manuscript was being carried forward. The spellings and meanings of many Greek and Latin words changed between the classical period when the ancient literature was written down, and the middle ages during which it was copied. When there is a single manuscript, then, difficulties arise. Lines in poems can sometimes be restored by study of the meter. Words which do not fit in or are foreign to the poet's dialect can be excised, and similar-sounding words which fit the poet's meter, dialect, and style inserted. Such emendations are not always right. It is known that the texts of the plays of the great Athenian playwrights have been contaminated by interpolations inserted by actors who imagined that they had hit upon some particularly happy line. Detection of these is very difficult—sometimes impossible—and depends upon deciding whether a suspect line really represents the thought and language of an Aeschylus or whether it sounds more like the poesy of some ancient Kirk Douglas.

Broken Greek (or Latin) inscriptions can often be restored with some accuracy; first, by determining, where possible, the original length of the line. From the fifth century B.C. on, Athenian inscriptions were almost always written in *Stoichedon* style; that is, with the letters engraved rigidly in both horizontal and vertical rows and without spaces between words and (usually) sentences. Public decrees almost always begin with the set formula, "Decreed by the Council and People, (the tribe) So-and-So was in Prytany, So-and-So was First Secretary of the Council, So-and-So was Archon, So-and-So was Chairman (of the Assembly), So-and-So moved (as follows). . . ." If a part of this opening is preserved, the rest of it can often be filled in, establishing the number of letters in each mutilated line below. The language of official Greek inscriptions (or the acts of medieval kings) tends to run in set phrases, vocabulary, and style, and the study of bureaucratic usage of any period is an important help in restoring damaged texts. Furthermore, the subject matter of public acts also restricts the possibilities for restoration. Decrees, for example, authorizing naval expeditions will have nothing to say about the sacrificial calendar of Athens. The same principles may be applied to the restoration of partially destroyed papyri or parchments.

Some words and phrases can never be recovered. Numbers are especially subject to error, because they are unique terms whose correctness is not controlled by the surrounding context, as in the phrase, "the wooden frigates put out to sea." (All 18th-century frigates were of wood, and there was no place for them to "put" but to sea). Plutarch says that around 445 B.C. the Athenians kept "60" triremes in commission every year in peacetime for training purposes. This number is impossibly high, because 60 ships would have cost Athens more than half her annual income. Since we know that more than half her budget was in fact spent on other things than the navy, Plutarch's text must be corrupt. All manuscripts, however, read "60" so that we are compelled to use our wits. The easiest emendation, the one that would most probably correct a copyist's mistake, would be to change "60" to "16" since these numbers are as similar in Greek as in English. We get probable confirmation that this is right from Thucydides, who remarks that at a moment of extreme danger in 440 B.C. when the Athenians had to use their warships in commission as rapidly as possible, to call for urgent reinforcements from their allies and to find a reported enemy, they sent out 16 ships in advance of their main body.

The tasks of detecting forgeries and interpolations, and of emending corrupt passages, demand of the young textual critic that he must be, above all, *erudite*. He cannot know too much about the period in which he is working, and, most of all, about its language.

B. Auxiliary disciplines

"Auxiliary" here merely means that in an age of specialization, a historian may need consultants in fields other than his own. Physicians and scientists have the same need and follow the same practice. For historians, such specialties may be useful either for external or for internal criticism. The historian today has available a huge mass of accumulated, classified, interpreted data, and specialists to help with it, such as previous ages never dreamed.

Most of the auxiliary disciplines of interest to historians have been developed in Western Europe since the Renaissance. Much of the work in these fields has been done in the last two or three centuries. Some of it is wholly the work of the 20th century.

Some modern historians underplay the change that has occurred in method, partly through the development of the auxiliary disciplines, partly through conceptual changes. These modern partisans of the past found their views on four sentiments. First, the classical Greek historian Thucydides was so obviously intelligent, and was so "modern" in some of his points of view, that it seems unbearably condescending to assert that we have the advantage of him in other than insignificant details. It would be an exaggeration to contend that this is the equivalent of refusing to concede that Einstein had tools not available to Aristotle; but there is some truth in the analogy. Second, and well-illustrated by the Aristotle-Einstein analogy, historians quite properly insist that from many points of view men must be judged by the standards of their own time. This is a staple of modern methodology. The problem here is to decide *which* points of view or purposes require such judgment. Thucydides possibly did as much with what he had available as any subsequent historian. This assertion does not, however, dispose of the question whether later historians accomplished more because they had more useful concepts and tools.

Third, the argument sometimes proceeds from the claim that if an early scholar anticipated a concept or technique that was only worked out in detail and institutionalized (i.e., used regularly) many years (even centuries) later, nevertheless he must be celebrated as the inventor. Even worse, the historian may leave us with the suggestion that the inventor's culture possessed his discovery. In fact, in such cases his posterity paid no attention to the anticipation. Students of the history of method should concern themselves chiefly with "effective" firsts. Fourth, a few students are overly impressed by declarations by classical historians that they are much concerned with their method.

Modern methodology, much of it developed by the auxiliary disciplines, at least has increased the area of historical knowledge about which there is relatively little controversy, thus freeing inquiry to some extent to concentrate on the more difficult aspects of investigation. The latter may still be handled largely by "common sense," as many historians aver, but even in connection with such problems as bias and causation the level of sophistication, and the understanding of the problems—even their insolubility—is improved.

The auxiliary disciplines were developed in Europe, and so have tended to be somewhat culture-bound. This was especially true in earlier generations, but some of the bias still remains. This is merely to say that the specialists first focused their attention on European and related Near Eastern antiquity. Such specialization not only was a reflection of ethnocentrism; we now see it as a necessity. In most of these specialties it is not possible for an individual to function well in more than one or a few cultures. To take an example, it is enough to be an expert in the authentication, decipherment, and interpretation of Greek (conceivably Latin also) inscriptions. There is no such thing as a universal epigrapher, who flits from Greek to Egyptian to Mayan to Chinese.

European ethnocentrism did lead to some such asssumptions as that epigraphy meant the study only of Greek and Latin inscriptions; or that diplomatics meant medieval European official documents; or that philology meant study of ancient European languages. But the great pioneers in these specialties in Europe were not only compiling materials in their relatively narrow range of interest, and constructing rules for authentication, dating, and the like; they also were laying the foundation for construction of similar systems of organized knowledge for all societies that had similar cultural phenomena. So, in later years, the term philology has fallen from use, replaced by the term linguistics, which all understand to be universal in its interest. So, too, it is clear now that Mayan inscriptions are as worthy of study as Cretan. And archeology, as a science or art devoted to the material remains of cultures, embraces all the human experience. But within the field of archeology scholars are Egyptologists, Assyriologists, Sinologists, and the like. The universal digger can only be an amateur.

Some of the traditional specialties are listed here, with comment. We will refer later to some of the newer techniques, largely scientific or technological. These last are much less culture-bound.

Specialties dealing with language and writing

Linguistics. This is the study of language. It is a modern term, and signifies a discipline that is both humanistic and scientific. It has tended to drive from use such older terms as philology, associated in the past especially with the study of the Greek and Latin languages and literatures. The rhetorical and analytical study of language was developed by the Greeks in the fifth century B.C. The subject was pursued independently in India as early as 400 B.C. Renaissance European scholars tried to apply classical linguistic modes to modern European languages, with limited success. With Europe's introduction to Sanskrit in the 17th century, comparative linguistic study broadened its scope. But scientific linguistics did not begin until the 19th century, when the recovery of the lost languages of Babylonia and Egypt became monuments of European scholarship. The decipherment of the old Greek script of the Mycenean period is a triumph of the 20th century. Maya writing has been subjected to an increasing weight of scholarly attention in the last century. Only the most sophisticated analysis can hope to penetrate its mystery.

Paleography. While paleography means the study of "ancient" handwriting, by extension the term can be applied to the study of all handwriting and to the materials involved therein. As developed in Europe it meant ancient and medieval European writing, and the forms of the manuscript book (i.e., bound handwritten book or scroll). The discipline deals with the decipherment or reading of handwriting, dating, and determination of location where prepared. Both external and internal evidence are used in the process. The discipline was built up by finding examples that clearly could be deciphered and identified, dated, located, in order to compare them with others not so easily interpreted. Thus, the subject is inescapably culture-bound. Research involves the forms in which letters were put down, the use of abbreviations and punctuation, the material on which written, the instrument used, the ink-like substance employed. It requires knowledge of the practices of authors, scribes, booksellers, and many other aspects of specific cultural practice. Huge amounts of Greek, Latin, and medieval European scripts have been printed for the guidance of scholars. Much modern European manuscript material cannot be read by scholars without some paleographic training.[5]

Epigraphy. This is the study of inscriptions, which are in some part studied as a specialty, and in some part inextricably a part of the work of scholars interested in other things as well.

---

[5] *Papyrology* is a branch of paleography which deals with writing on papyrus. Extant papyri are largely from Greco-Roman Egypt.

Actually, it is the paleography of inscriptions, which are documents incised on a hard (as opposed to a paper-like) substance. The specialty was developed in early modern times in Europe, beginning with Greek and Latin inscriptions, then extending to Egyptian and Near and Middle Eastern cultures, and finally to the Far Orient and America. There is no reason to consider inscriptions as special sorts of documents. Clearly, their study presents special problems. There is the physical difficulty of moving or copying many of the inscriptions. Also, in recent times, there has been nationalistic objection to their movement. Sometimes the resistant nature of the material required extreme brevity and much abbreviation, which has impeded decipherment. One of the great achievements of the specialists has been the copying and publication in great series of volumes of all known classical inscriptions. Presumably the same will some day be done for other cultures. Inscriptions have been left on stone, metal, clay, wood, ivory. They exist in Mexico, China, India, and elsewhere. Many are quite short, some less than a sentence; some are long. They were prepared for religious, political, and social reasons; to promote public or private business; to memorialize kings, fathers, wives, and sons.

Diplomatics. Diplomatics is the critical study of official or business (rather than literary) documents. It sometimes is considered a branch of paleography. Jean Mabillon in 1681 published the first important treatise on the subject, founded on his study of medieval European documents. All later work has followed from his excellent beginning. The documents with which this specialty deals are both public and private. The public documents are issued by public authority and include legislative, administrative, judicial, and diplomatic documents. The private documents are issued either by individuals or by corporations (e.g., municipal or monastic organizations), and include many sorts of materials, including huge numbers of conveyances of real property. Mabillon systematized the examination of the different forms and parts of official documents by some of the public offices of medieval Europe. The same sort of examination has subsequently been made of such materials in other places and times.

Seals. These have long been used in both Occident and Orient. They were used in ancient Greece and in China. The study of seals sometimes is termed sigillography (from Latin for seal). The most intense European effort to rationalize this field has been devoted to medieval seals, and especially those put on public documents. The subject thus has been a part of diplomatics. In medieval Europe seals were used for the business of monarchs, and by bishops, municipalities, monastic houses, and private individuals. Some agencies or great personages used both a great seal and lesser seals for minor business. The subject of study is mostly of the impressions (usually in wax) made by the seals on documents. The specialist is concerned with the materials, the legend, and the way the seal was put on (or tied to in many cases) the document.

Heraldry

Heraldry (also termed *armory*) is a system of symbols on shields that identifies a person or family or organization. The practice arose among the medieval European nobility. It has long been a complex matter, requiring specialists, and sometimes involving legal interpretation. Some arms or heraldic devices came to be signs of authority. Family and corporative and military service and ecclesiastical devices are used in the modern world. Specialists in medieval European heraldry help in the identification of a variety of artifacts that carry such devices as their only "signature," and in following the intricate marriage alliances of the nobility which were so important in both public and private affairs, and were reflected in heraldry.

Genealogy

Genealogy, the study of human pedigrees, is related to heraldry. A number of aristocratic societies in both East and West have from ancient times paid much attention to genealogy. The study draws on other specialties—e.g., paleography and chronology. Preliterate peoples often kept oral records of genealogies, both of public leaders and of private families. Christians and Jews are familiar with the "begats" of the Old Testament. Ancient Greek aristocrats delighted in claiming descent from the gods or larger-than-life heroes. But as with all these specialties, genealogy was only put on a soundly organized and scholarly basis in recent times. Much professional—and possibly even more amateur—genealogical work is being done today. Vast amounts of material have been published on the subject.

Numismatics

Numismatics (from the Greek for "coin") is the study of coins and medals. Coins are important sources of historical information, not only for the data they offer, but because they are durable, and often were hidden, so that many have been preserved. Coins are pieces of metal (the most important ones gold or silver) marked by public authority with an official sign which guaranteed (supposedly) their weight and purity. Coins were invented by the Lydians of Asia Minor at the end of the eighth century B.C., about the same time by the Chinese, and independently in India about four centuries later. This means that much of ancient civilization knew no coinage. The locations of hoards of ancient coins give us data on the circulation of coins struck at different mints, and therefore an idea of the routes and volume of trade. The debasement of coinage—as common in China as in the West—is good evidence of financial or economic troubles. The artistic and technological levels of cultures may be judged from coins. Sometimes data of aid to chronology is on coins. All sorts of cultural information is contained on coins— religious, political, economic. The vast amount of work that has gone into this field in modern times gives us a tool unavailable to earlier historians.

Chronology

Chronology, the measurement of time and the placing of events in time, has been known in a number of cultures. It was not, however, likely to have been an activity of prehistoric man; and our records of civilization show that the fixation of events in time sequence arose long after urban life developed. Much of the earlier material that we have relates events in terms of regnal dates ("in the fourth year of the reign of King Phool, the city was rebuilt"), or lists of monarchs or other royal or ecclesiastical officials. This is the case with much of the early written record of China, Egypt, India. Thucydides had such materials, and noted the difficulties involved in relating them to each other, i.e., in achieving and being confident of the accuracy of an uninterrupted sequence of events from the past to the present. None of these peoples had a reliable original referent from which to reckon time. Romans ultimately adopted the notion of dating things A.U.C. (which meant from the year of the foundation of Rome in what we call 753 B.C.). Some of them knew then, as we know now, that the events and dates asserted often were legendary.

A Christian monk in the sixth century invented the Christian era, positing that Christ was born in 754 A.U.C. Even if this was nearly correct (as it was) in terms of events calculated since that time, it did nothing to overcome the legendary nature of the earlier dates asserted for the A.U.C. system. Furthermore, the Christian era was adopted even in Europe only over a long period of time. It was not general in Europe until the 11th century, and some areas of the continent did not accept it even then. In addition, there was disagreement as to when the Christian year should start, and for many centuries December 25, January 1, March 25, and Easter all were used for the purpose. This only hints at the imposing difficulties presented by the systems of dating used in medieval European documents.

Another, and often baffling, problem is how to correlate dates between the systems of different cultures. Possibly the most difficulty is presented modern scholars by the Maya system. There were no cultural relationships between the Maya and the civilizations of the old world. The Maya had a year of 365 days, but in counting between dates they used the *tun* of 360 days because the other five days were so unspeakably unlucky as to be literally nameless. Many Middle American peoples used a "calendar-round," which repeated itself each 52 years. The Maya also used a "long-count" that indicated time elapsed since a date in their chronological system that now is thought to correspond to about 3000 B.C. This presumably was the date of some mythologic event, as were the Maya calculations that reached a hundred million years into the past, The specialists can read the Maya calendric symbols, and relate one Maya date to another; the problem is to relate the Maya system to Christian era dates, so that developments of the European past can be related in time with developments in Maya history. The oldest date in Amerindian glyphs yet found comes from the Olmec culture, and is thought to correspond to 31 B.C.

Some new scientific techniques

In addition to these traditional specialties, historians recently have been getting new help from science and technology. Computers are used to examine problems. This was done in a study of Stonehenge in Britain. It long had been supposed that this pattern of stones must represent a religious symbol for a prehistoric group. As early as the 16th century it was guessed that the pattern was related to some type of astronomical measurement or event. The exact relationship eluded scholars. Then very recently an astronomer, using the research of others on the period when Stonehenge was constructed, programmed the important astronomical dates and eclipses, combined with the pattern of stones, to see if Stonehenge was built in a sophisticated way so as to be aligned to certain important astronomical events, such as the equinoxes. The computer enabled him to demonstrate conclusively that the locations of all of the stones could be accounted for if the structure had been reared in 1500 B.C. The astronomer was careful, however, to limit the interpretation of his findings. He surmised that the uses of Stonehenge probably were religious and agricultural.[6]

---

[6] Gerald S. Hawkins, *Stonehenge Decoded* (New York, 1965).

Many of the new techniques are used for the dating of artifacts or the remains of flora and fauna. The carbon dating
system has been widely used. Charcoal remains are examined
to determine how much a certain radioactive isotope of the
element carbon has disintegrated since the charcoal was created. This is possible because the "half-life" of the radioactive
isotope has been determined. This gives information on the age
of the material burnt, which in turn sometimes permits a presumption that other materials associated with the burnt material
—for example, chipping stones—are of about the same age.[7]

A recent method dates stone artifacts from their thermo-
luminescence—the light they emit when heated. It requires that
the object have been subjected to fire (e.g., in the making of a
vase or to help shape flints, or accidentally). What is measured
is the radiation the artifact has received since being subjected to
the fire. It is subject to a plus-or-minus error of 150 years from
the date. More troublesome is that if the artifact was subjected
to fire again after its creation, the test would only show results
from the second heating, and thus could give a highly misleading result. It is the only reliable technique for dating sites older
than 50,000 years (beyond the range of radiocarbon dating) or
younger than 500,000 years (too recent for potassium-argon
dating). Thermoluminescent testing also is used for interpreting
the technique of making artifacts, and for determination of faked
objects.

A number of other techniques are being used. Electron-
microscope pictures of obsidian found in Greece showed when
it was formed by volcanic eruption, proving it the same age as
the obsidian of Melos, and ruling out some other possible
sources of supply. Valuable work also is done in the spectro-
chemical analysis of glass artifacts. It may be done by burning
samples in a spectrograph, and projecting the vapors through a
grating to identify the components by the different wave lengths

---

[7] Difficulties and disagreements exist with regard to the interpretation and
reliability of radio carbon dating, as well as in connection with some other
new scientific methods of measurement as applied to historical problems.
Many of the reported conclusions must be accepted only tentatively.

of light from the elements. Or X-ray fluorescent equipment can be used to analyze an entire glass object, with counters to read the characteristic radiations of elements in the specimen. Or the artifact can be subjected to neutron bombardment in a nuclear reactor, which changes the structure of a fraction of the atoms of many elements in the sample. The new forms, radioisotopes, lose radioactivity on an individual timetable of decay, which can be measured. This permits calculation of the rare earth ingredients of glass. Many samples, analyzed in these ways, possibly combined with archeological evidence, then may be classified, so as to establish the supposition that certain types of glass are associated with certain places and times. This bears some general relationship to the ways in which some of the traditional auxiliary disciplines built up bodies of evidence to serve as norms. But the scientific techniques were not available until day-before-yesterday.

VI

Using evidence: Internal criticism

An authentic piece of evidence may lie or mislead, intentionally or unintentionally. The letters of Cortés to the King of Spain on the conquest of Mexico misled both out of the intention of Cortés to glorify his deeds and out of his inability to understand much of American Indian culture. The authentic outpourings of Adolf Hitler teem with misunderstanding, exaggeration, misconception, and lies. The historian is interested in lies as well as truth, but he must be able to distinguish between them. It is the task of internal criticism to determine the credibility of evidence. It thus deals, in the case of documents, with statements about specific things or ideas or customs. The beginning researcher will spend much of his effort on internal criticism. He should be aware that this process, as described in this chapter, will in fact overlap with the processes of synthesis and exposition dealt with in later chapters. It is the details dealt with by internal criticism that later will be fitted into patterns or relationships. Of course, relationships and tentative hypotheses will be generated in the course of internal criticism.

The division of subject matter in this chapter has proved

141

workable; it is, however, no more logical than many other schemes for internal criticism. At this point, the student should consult in other chapters: IIA, "Facts as values, ideas, objects, events"; IIB, "Probability, plausibility, certainty"; VIIC, "Bias and subjectivity." It should be noted that although many materials in those sections are directed to clarification of the mind of the *investigator,* they also are applied in internal criticism to the mind of the *witness* (i.e., the source of the evidence).

A. Literal meaning and real meaning[1]

The process of internal criticism must begin with an understanding of the words of the document in their literal sense. In many documents this is complicated by language foreign to the reader, or by obsolete or technical terms, or by odd spelling or a lack of punctuation or the use of abbreviations. Much time and care, and the use of specialized reference books, may be involved in this process. And at its end, it remains to be certain that the literal and real meaning are identical. The author may have been using words in some oblique sense—for example, ironically or allegorically.

Place and time influence the meaning of words. The English spoken in London differs from the English spoken in New York; the English spoken in New Orleans differs from that spoken in Boston. Even more significant for the historian are the changes in language over the course of the years. Suppose he is studying the Fundamental Orders of Connecticut of 1639, often called the first written constitution in America. The first sentence of the document states that "we the Inhabitants and Residents of Windsor, Harteford and Wethersfield are now cohabiting and dwelling in and uppon the River of Conectecotte and the Lands thereunto adioyneing . . . ." What does "cohabiting" mean? A modern dictionary defines "cohabit" as follows: "to

---

[1] Langlois and Seignobos, op. cit., 148ff., call this determination "positive criticism," which is succeeded by the "negative" internal criticism of the good faith and accuracy of authors. This illustrates the apparently unavoidable ambiguity of many of the tags used in discussion of historical method.

live together as husband and wife: the word usually implies sexual intercourse, and is applied especially to those not legally married." Is this the meaning of the statement in the document? Were the Puritans engaged in an experiment in free love? Our bewilderment is solved when we discover that "cohabit" has as its archaic meaning simply "to live together."

A more serious question occurs later in the document when the right to vote is awarded to all "freemen." The first dictionary definition of "freeman" is "a person not in slavery or bondage." Is this the meaning of the statement in the document? Were all men and women not held in servitude allowed to vote? A familiarity with 17th century usages will rule this out. Freeman is unquestionably to be defined in its second dictionary sense: "a citizen; person who has all civil and political rights in a city or state." This means that the right to vote in Connecticut was restricted to those inhabitants who ranked as "freemen."

The investigator must follow "the rule of context"—that is, he must interpret the meaning of any particular statement in view of what precedes and follows it. He must not isolate particular phrases and sentences from the rest of the document. The more famous the document, the greater the danger of tearing its statements out of context. American isolationists have always found a wealth of slogans in President George Washington's Farewell Address of 1796. For example: "Europe has a set of primary interests which to us have none or a very remote relation . . . . Hence, therefore, it must be unwise in us to implicate ourselves by artificial ties in the ordinary vicissitudes of her politics or the ordinary combinations and collisions of her friendships or enmities." Or: "Why quit our own to stand on foreign ground? Why, by interweaving our destiny with that of any part of Europe, entangle our peace and prosperity in the toils of European ambition, rivalship, interest, humor, or caprice?" These statements have often been quoted as meaning that Washington opposed foreign commitments for the United States under any and all circumstances. But a reading of the whole message will show that he qualified his meaning very carefully. He said: "It is our true policy to steer clear of *permanent* alliances with any portion of the foreign world, so far, I mean *as we are now at liberty to do it;* for let me not be understood as capable of patronizing infidelity to *existing engagements"* (italics added). Or again, he said: "Taking care always to keep ourselves by suitable establishments on a respectable defensive posture, we may safely trust to *temporary alliances* for *extraordinary emergencies"* (italics added).

When documents are produced under unusual circumstances such as wartime censorship or totalitarian control, they may contain statements which have a larger or different meaning than a literal reading would reveal. In broadcasting radio reports to America from Nazi Germany during the early months of World War II, William L. Shirer tried to outwit the censors. He describes his tactics thus: "For the last few months I've been trying to get by on my wits, such as they are; to indicate a truth or an official lie by the tone and inflexion of the voice, by a pause held longer than is natural, by the use of an Americanism which most Germans, who've learned their English in England, will not fully grasp, and by drawing from a word, a phrase, a sentence, a paragraph, or their juxtaposition, all the benefit I can."[2]

B. Other sources of error in internal criticism

1. A catalog

We will not set down all the numerous but rarely encountered sources of error in evidence. Among the most common are: ignorance, in its many degrees and guises; bias, an ever-welling fount of human error; falsification, of wholes and of parts; failure of the senses, with men too apt to suppose that they cannot see and hear awry; cultural difference, within or between cultures; self-delusion and mental unbalance; mutilation of evidence; and the misuse of evidence by adherence to a dubious scheme of interpretation. Two or more of these, or other, sources

---

[2] William L. Shirer, *Berlin Diary: The Journal of a Foreign Correspondent, 1934–1941* (New York, 1941), p. 511.

of error may be present at the same time. Most of these sources of error may affect either the author of the evidence or the researcher using the evidence. Put in another way, error may exist in the evidence, or it may arise from the use made of it by the historian. Bear in mind, also, that error may be either willful or inadvertent, and that it may be either total or partial—that is, the piece of evidence may be a mixture of the true and the false.

The motives for deliberate falsification run the gamut of human drives and social thrusts: lust, greed, political ambition, jealousy, timidity, levity, and the like. Error is intruded into the record unintentionally in more ways than can be listed here: ignorance (e.g., inability to understand what was witnessed), failure of the senses, or mistakes in spelling or transcription or translation. It is difficult to know whether bias and mental unbalance led to deliberate or unintentional error; possibly the question in many cases has no meaning. We know that the limits of human credulity are wide, indeed, corresponding to such needs as ego-bolstering and fear-reduction. Knowledge of modern psychological concepts has increased the depth of our understanding of this sort of error.

2. Observation of the detail

A good part of historical research is concerned with determination of the accuracy and value of observations of details left to us by witnesses of events. The analysis of stubborn problems and the construction of grand generalizations comes only after large numbers of details have been gathered, often corroborative testimony on the same small subject. These little building blocks of knowledge are best cast into the form of the loose-leaf notes recommended in Chapter IV, each as nearly as possible confined to one subject or detail. This is where knowledge of human history begins, and much of it is dependent upon the testimony of witnesses of events or things. The ability of the witness to observe thus becomes a matter of prime importance. There are physical and social aspects to this ability.

a. Physical ability to observe

This includes the condition of the witness, and external conditions that affect his observational powers. The sight and hearing of the witness may be either naturally good or defective, and may be affected by illness, drugs, age, or by noise, or by intervening objects. Also, sight and hearing may be affected by the distance of the reporting witness from the event or object: Was he at the top of a big stadium, or at the lower edge of the arena? Beside the thing observed, or across a broad and crowded square? Next to the jury box, or in the back of the courtroom? Also, witnesses may be weary or bored; attention may be sharp during part of an observation, lax during another part. When no information is available as to the physical ability of the witness to observe, the investigator can only hope for the best, fear the worst, search for corroboration, and use the data with caution.

b. Social ability to observe

Social ability to observe concerns the familiarity of the witness with the subject matter, and his willingness to observe to the best of his ability. He should understand the language spoken, and not have to guess at many of the meanings. Imperfect knowledge of languages is productive of much dubious testimony. A report of a battle by a man unfamiliar with military affairs may be worse than useless—positively misleading. An account of a court trial by an observer with little knowledge of the substantive or procedural law in use may be sadly deficient. A man of one culture reporting on another may be ludicrously wide of the mark. The accounts of Amerind actions and culture by Spanish conquerors often were sadly in error. Also, willingness to observe may be inhibited by social conditions. A witness under the eye of secret policemen may be unwilling to peer too intently at events. A member of a Chamber of Commerce or of a social club may find himself under severe pressure to conform. Finally, we must be aware that observation often is affected by prejudice, so that the eye apparently beholds and the ear apprehends what the mind wishes them to report.

3. Reporting the detail

This concerns the fashion and frame of mind in which the document was composed. For this purpose the document may be classified in terms of (*a*) the ability of the composer to report, (*b*) time of composition in relation to the observation of the events or objects reported on, and (*c*) the intent with which the account was set down.

a. Ability to report

This is much like the ability to observe. Bias (personal and cultural), pride, ambition, and other mental states play a similar role in both processes. Additional factors here are facility with language, access to recording materials, and the conditions under which the record was set down or recited. The presence of secret policemen, censors, enemies, or others might inhibit reporting. Ability to report may also be affected by literary, religious, legal or other cultural conventions.

Controlling or recognizing bias, as we have stated, is a part of the elements of method. This means control of the researcher's biases and recognition of those of the witness, for everyone has the bias of his interest and culture, skills, temperament. The historian must remember that he is looking at the evidence through the prism of his own culture and time. This is why history so often is reinterpreted: different things and patterns are seen, partly because new generations of historians are looking for new things, partly because they are not interested in seeing others. In the end, possibly three rules should be followed: (*a*) the problem should be actively recognized, (*b*) efforts should be made to identify one's own biases, (*c*) it should be realized that biases often are unacknowledged or unrecognized, and influence us willy-nilly.

In terms of the witness, it must be remembered that much of historical research deals with biased people under stress. The ways of looking for biases in witnesses are many. Crude methods may suffice, or it may require subtlety. Bias may be covert or overt. Bias may be indicated by an institutional connection.

What are we to do about an author with a "point of view?"
All have some. Is he aware of his tendencies of thought?

b. Time of composition

It is obvious that with the lapse of time even highly accurate
observations by a witness may become lost or confused. This is
the factor that distinguishes journals or diaries, kept more or
less as events occur, from memoirs composed long after events.
Of course, the former may be used for the composition of the
latter.[3]

c. Intent of composition

Many documents can be described usefully in terms of the
purpose of their composition. The question is: did the composer
wish to report as nearly truly as he could, both in terms of accuracy and of coverage? So we observe classes of documents in
terms of degrees of probability that the composer would not
purposefully distort what he had observed. Quite often the intended and accidental distortions go hand-in-hand. For example, Bismarck's memoirs, *Thoughts and Reminiscences,*
written after he left office in 1890, provide a very unreliable
account of the German statesman's involvement in the Revolution of 1848. In part, this is a result of Bismarck's desire to hide
his earlier lack of interest in German unification; in addition,
the account suffers from simple lapses of memory. Bismarck
could not remember the details of his actions some 40 years
earlier, and he was too vain to check the records.

d. Types of distortion in reporting

This includes lies of commission and of omission, partial
truths, twistings, favorable interpretations—the vocabulary is
rich in phrases in this area. The motives for deliberate distortion
in reporting are as varied as human hope, fear, and hate. Special

---

[2] An unrelated matter, often confused with the time witnesses set down
their observations relates to the time nonwitnesses record their views. It is clear
that if the composer was not a witness, and consulted no witnesses, it matters
little whether he wrote 50 or 500 years after the event.

attention must be directed to reporting distortions introduced by the nature of the audience for which the document is intended. There is a presumption that the views which a man confides to paper for his own eyes only may be more accurate than those he prepares for other eyes. This may be accepted as a probability only. The account may be so sketchy as to invite misinterpretation; it may appear to be private, but in fact have been meant to be read, immediately or later; and some men are so constituted that they must lie even to themselves. When a document is composed for an audience, some conscious or unconscious editing occurs. It might be thought that the greater the size and/or the heterogeneity of the audience, the more editing would occur in order to communicate clearly the heart of the matter to people with various capacities and knowledge. This rule must be used carefully; it is pretty clearly applicable at its extreme limits (e.g., the family group and the total national population), but it is more difficult to apply as a rule to groups of moderate size.

In any event, we might expect that a chemist might report an experiment one way to a lovely but not scientifically-trained young lady, another way to a college faculty, another to a Chamber of Commerce, and yet another to a television audience. The author's expectation about his audience will have affected differently a letter from Benjamin Franklin to a French lady, a White Paper issued by the government of the United Arab Republic while at war with Israel, and a public report by a tobacco company celebrating the non-toxic quality of its cigarettes. It matters whether the audience is friendly (one's own foreign ministry) or unfriendly (an enemy nation's government), educated or uneducated, rich or poor, young or old, interested or not, and how interested (e.g., as legislators listening to a report on a pending bill, or physicians hearing a speech on foreign policy).

e. Additional possible clues to intended veracity

A good reputation and no apparent motive for distortion incline us to consider an author a good risk in terms of reporting.

Downright indifference to the subject on the part of the reporting witness seems especially encouraging to some investigators.
Indifference can, of course, be feigned. Researchers are happy
to find witnesses making statements damaging to themselves,
on the supposition that this will not be done unless an unavoidable truth must be displayed. But men may so testify inad-
vertently, or in fright or hysteria, or in order to distract attention from other matters. It may seem encouraging to credibility
to find detail in an account on matters unconnected with the
main line of testimony, on the supposition that there could not
be a motive for distorting testimony on such incidental matter.
A moment's reflection will indicate that here again we have only
a probability.

Some of the difficulty involved in judging veracity may be
seen in the case of Joseph Goebbels' two accounts of Nazi Party
life in Berlin in the 1920's. *Kampf um Berlin* (1930) and *Vom
Kaiserhof zur Reichskanzlei* (1934), although written by a
master propagandist and political liar, are, on the whole, re-
markably honest and objective works. The reason is not that
Goebbels suddenly developed a passion for truth, but that the
truth served his political purpose at the time of writing. Since
the Nazi Party had outgrown its miserable beginnings, he could
afford to be honest about—indeed, glory in—the time of political inconsequence and financial difficulties, as well as the repeated setbacks suffered in its struggle for power.

C. Some illustrations of error and distortion

1. A fictional scenario

Strikers at the Star Textile Company's Worcester, Mass.,
factory, were being addressed in 1922 at the plant gates by a
member of the leftist Industrial Workers of the World. The
"Wobbly," in the Italian language, told the pickets to leave their
union and join the IWW and fight for a classless society. About
30 uniformed company guards, pistols in their hands, moved
through the crowd of pickets toward the speaker. Men in the

crowd shoved and kicked the guards, and a few brandished knives and clubs and lengths of pipe. A guard shot a striker. Strikers then knocked down a number of guards, and the latter fired into the crowd, which retreated. In the space that opened between guards and strikers lay some figures, some still, some writhing. It turned out that eleven guards had been injured, six seriously, and that one would die of his injuries. Three strikers had been killed outright by gun shots, and twelve others wounded, two of whom eventually would die of their wounds.

Public opinion throughout the United States was aroused by the newspaper accounts. Headlines shouted "Worcester Massacre," "Anarchist Riot at Worcester," "IWW Battles Police," "Working Men Slain in the Streets." This sampling indicates editorial polarization. Much of the reporting was equally slanted. At that time newspaper operations were heavily influenced by their publishers, mostly conservative. Early accounts in pro-company papers featured an announcement by a Star Textile Company vice president, based on his observation of the affair from the second story of a building near the gate where it occurred:

I saw it all. A radical agitator had infiltrated the union pickets, and urged them to attack our plant. He was screaming and gesturing like a crazy Bolshevik. At any moment the mob would have stormed our gates. When our guards, under orders, tried to remove the anarchist from our property (We own the access road to the gate.) the mob attacked them with knives and clubs. The guards fired to save their lives.

It turned out, after investigation, that the company official was not reporting the Wobbly speaker's remarks as of his own hearing; he probably was too far away to distinguish words, and in any event the official did not know Italian. In one of the trials resulting from the affair, the official admitted that he had the words of the Wobbly speaker indirectly from Italian speaking strikers. What the official did observe were the gestures and facial expression of the IWW speaker, and he probably could hear what he described as his "emotional" voice. It also turned out that the official's fear of labor violence had been heightened by the fact that his uncle, president of a New York bank, had been killed in the Wall Street bombing of September, 1920. The company official was opposed to labor unionism, and convinced that it necessarily had strong links with communism and anarchism. Obviously, both his physical and his social ability to observe and to report objectively were dubious. All this could be brought out in the 1920s in the United States through investigative reporting and court proceedings. The same sort of difficulties exist, of course, with older testimony that never was subjected to query by reporters and attorneys.

The labor press and its sympathizers among the commercial papers at first featured the testimony of a supposedly unbiased casual passerby:

I saw the whole thing. I was walking about a block away from the factory gate when I saw company guards march up to the pickets, who were standing there peaceful like. The guards walked right up to the pickets and began to fire without anyone having offered them any hurt.

It turned out that the observer, although not an employee of the Star Textile Company (hence, supposedly objective), had two brothers who were. Also, the observer was 5 feet 3 inches tall, and could not see or hear the Wobbly addressing the workers, because he could not see over the crowd, because he was too far away, and because it turned out that a line of heavy horse-drawn construction carts was rumbling down the unevenly paved street where he was walking. But before this had been brought out, he had told the newspapers:

That speaker was just telling the pickets that all labor groups ought to cooperate, that that was the only way they could beat the millionaires and trusts, and that they should be careful not to use violence, because that was what the crooked newspapers and courts wanted.

During one of the trials that followed the Worcester Massacre, the following exchange occurred:

Labor Lawyer, to Company Official on witness stand: Why does your company have so many Italian immigrants in its employ?

Company Lawyer: Objection.

Judge: Sustained.

Labor Lawyer: You have a training program. I assume it is conducted in Italian.

Company Official: Yes.

Labor Lawyer: Do any company officials speak Italian?

Company Lawyer: Objection. This line of questioning is irrelevant and immaterial to the issues in this murder trial.

Labor Lawyer: Your honor, we contend it is highly germane to show the labor policies of the Star Textile Company.

Judge: Objection sustained.

Labor Lawyer, to Company Official: You have asserted that you consider that most of your employees are loyal, though occasionally led astray by radical agitators.

Company Official: Yes.

Labor Lawyer: Given the language difficulty, how do you arrive at that conclusion?

Company Official: Some of our people are bilingual.

Labor Lawyer: And they spy for you?

Company Lawyer: Objection.

Labor Lawyer: I'll change the question. They report to you?

Company Official: Yes.

This is enough to give an idea of the fundamental difference of view between the union leadership and company officials, and to hint at the great gap in understanding between management and labor. The company hired immigrants because they would work for low wages, and were difficult to organize into unions, both because of the language problem, and because they were happy to have escaped even lower wages in Italy and fearful of getting in trouble in America. The opinions and actions of Americans on the issue of this fictional Worcester Massacre clearly would be bitterly divided, as in the actual Sacco and Vanzetti case of the 1920s. Opinion inevitably would suffer from almost every imaginable form of bias, mutilation of evidence, cultural misunderstanding, rival views of society, political passion, cries for revenge and punishment, and the like. Many somewhat comparable earlier affairs have suffered similar errors and distortions, without leaving so comprehensive a rec-

ord as the Worcester Massacre surely would have left, and as
the Sacco and Vanzetti case did in fact leave. And the Sacco
and Vanzetti case is not yet "settled" to everyone's satisfaction.

2. A case of peculiar interpretation

The investigator must be constantly on guard against authentic documents which use undoubted facts, but interpret
them in unacceptable ways. For example, United States Senator
James Eastland of Mississippi a few years ago made a speech in
the Senate in which he cited "evidence" and statistics (often so
convincing to the uncritical) to give the impression that judges
of the Supreme Court under Earl Warren were pro-communist.[4]
Eastland based his charge on voting behavior in 1953–62,
which he asserted showed that Warren voted "pro" communist
in 62 of 65 decisions, that Justice Black "supported" the position of the Communist Party in all (102) of his decisions, and
that Justice Douglas "reached a conclusion favorable to" the
Communist Party in 97 of 100 cases. Eastland's speech offered
no real basis for such assertions. Also, it ignored the complicated questions of jurisprudence involved in the cases before
the court, reducing everything to a simplistic and unreal division into "for" and "against" communism. The latter was not
the issue in the cases, and Eastland ignored the great constitutional issues that were involved. Unfortunately, the Eastland
speech was widely reprinted by critics of the Warren Court.[5]

3. A case of bowdlerization

Evidence is suppressed or otherwise distorted for many reasons. It is not just panic-stricken or malicious liars who cause
trouble for historians. Bowdlerization is a modern form of deliberate distortion of reality designed to protect morals or fur-
bish images according to selected namby-pamby patterns. It is

---

[4] *Cong. Rec.,* 87 Cong., 2 Sess., May 2, 1962.

[5] E.g., *Is the Supreme Court Pro-Communist? Here Are the Facts* (Richmond, Va.: Patrick Henry Group, n.d.).

seldom helpful to the historian, always is irritating upon detection, and occasionally can result in serious misunderstanding.

Ex-Governor Leland Stanford of California commissioned a painting of the "wedding of the rails," the joining of the sections of the transcontinental railway near Ogden, Utah, in 1869. The painter worked from a photograph of the event, but he eliminated two things that it showed—liquor bottles, and ladies of questionable virtue—and added prominent citizens who were not in fact present at the ceremony. The absence of the latter is scarcely interesting, since the ceremony itself was of small consequence, but to show the West without strong drink and strumpets is to distort social history rather sizably.[6]

4. Cross-cultural error

Error due to cultural differences is common, and often difficult to detect. Of course, it may be simple to find error in the reporting of a poorly educated person testifying on something in his own environment. It may be more difficult to discern the distortions and complete misunderstandings consequent upon an effort to report on an alien culture. Historians long have been aware of this problem of cultural difference; they talked of combatting it with "historical-mindedness." This sometimes meant what anthropologists later called cultural empathy. Such cultural or historical empathy comes only with effort. Voltaire, a man of genius, did not make the effort, and so misunderstood the culture of medieval Europe, which he decided was shameful and of no importance to modern times.

How enormous and socially crippling over the centuries were the errors made by Europeans about the black slaves they carried from Africa to America, and about the Indians they found in the New World. It was not simply a matter of clashing interest and European determination to dominate. Europeans, being technologically superior in some critical areas, assumed that all

---

[6] Cf. Thomas A. Bailey, "The Mythmakers of American History," *Journal of American History,* LV (June, 1968), 5–21.

aspects of their culture must be "superior"—morally, esthetically, psychologically—to those of black Africans or red Indians. The result was the creation of ideas of innate Indian and black inferiority, which can only rather slowly be eradicated by revisionist studies by historians, anthropologists, psychologists, and others.

Cultural empathy or historical-mindedness must be cultivated both as a technical necessity and as an obligation of interpretation. It is necessary for the understanding of many aspects of a culture, and many of the motivations and actions of individuals. Neither the examination of individual pieces of evidence nor the synthesis of bodies of evidence can be pursued with confidence without this quality of sympathy founded upon study. This does not mean that the researcher abandons his own values in his own world, or that he never applies them to the historical scene he is studying. It does mean that he must first try to think and believe like his subjects, discover how they performed in their own eyes, inform the reader from this point of view; then he may, with identification of his purpose, venture a comparison—a judgment, if he must—involving other value systems, even his own.

It is well to close this section by asserting that a modest amount of reflection will enable the student to smother the notion that nothing is knowable. In the early stages of the career as researcher it is enough to believe that there are degrees of probability regarding the errors in the record and our perception of them. We may be confident that Napoleon lived and did numerous things that we know something about (consider the contrary supposition with regard to Bonaparte, Lincoln, and Julius Caesar), and we have a fair idea of the effects of the American Civil War on the economy of the Confederate states.

D. Checklist for internal criticism

Beginning researchers often get lost in the verbiage of discussions of internal criticism. This minimum (far from exhaustive) list of questions or steps to use in connection with a piece of evidence provides an easy first entry into the critical examination of statements. The amount of evidence being checked may be a sentence, a paragraph, or more. The investigator must decide on the proper unit. Not all these suggestions will apply to all pieces of evidence; others that are not on the checklist often will be needed.

1. Is the real meaning of the statement different from its literal meaning? Are words used in senses not employed today? Is the statement meant to be ironic (i.e., mean other than it says)?

2. How well could the author *observe* the thing he reports? Were his senses equal to the observation? Was his physical location suitable to sight, hearing, touch? Did he have the proper social ability to observe: did he understand the language, have other expertise required (e.g., law, military); was he not being intimidated by his wife or the secret police?

3. *How* did the author report?, and what was his *ability* to do so?

a. Regarding his *ability* to report, was he biased? Did he have proper time for reporting? Proper place for reporting? Adequate recording instruments?

b. When did he report in relation to his observation? Soon? Much later?

c. What was the author's *intention* in reporting? For *whom* did he report? Would that audience be likely to require or suggest distortion to the author?

d. Are there additional clues to intended veracity? Was he indifferent on the subject reported, thus probably not intending distortion? Did he make statements damaging to himself, thus probably not seeking to distort? Did he give incidental or casual information, almost certainly not intended to mislead?

4. Do his statements seem inherently improbable: e.g., contrary to human nature, or in conflict with what we know?

5. Remember that some types of information are easier to observe and report on than others.

6. Are there inner contradictions in the document?

7. Are your own biases or preconceptions distorting your view of the document or the exact statement in it?

8. Consult reference works as required to resolve doubts.

9. Does the statement leave you sufficiently confident of your knowledge of that detail so that no corroboration is required?

E. Corroboration, contradiction, and measurement

When we come to the problems of corroboration and contradiction, we have passed beyond the simple internal criticism of the individual document or the specific statement therein. We now are comparing evidence. It is proper to think of this either as a more complex type of analysis than that involved in the single document, or as a low level of synthesis. A major part of historical method relates to efforts to find corroborative evidence and weigh its quality, or to resolve problems arising from contradictory evidence, by corroboration for one explanation or another.

Difficult as this process can be, it occasions less doubt than the problem of the single source, where we have neither corroboration nor contradiction. In such a case we are truly in complete doubt, unless (as is seldom the case) the single source is almost unarguably credible and sufficiently weighty. It should be pointed out that, on the other hand, much of recent history presents us with the opposite problem of almost too much potentially or partially corroborative material.

How much corroboration is required to make us feel comfortable in our interpretation? The answer is that it depends on (*a*) the problem (i.e., on what is being investigated—an entire culture, the location of a ford over a stream, a man's motives), and (*b*) what evidence is available (a three-line diary, 6,000 pages of legislation, no eyewitness reports, or the observations of 3,000 witnesses). It is foolish and simplistic to fix a number of corroborators, even of stated quality: e.g., two or more reliable and independent witnesses. We are not in a court of law.

Reliability and independence are highly desirable in evidence, but two witnesses may give us no more of either than one witness. It depends both on the types of witnesses and on the types of problems.

We have commented in Chapter III on the qualities in authors or witnesses that create a supposition of reliability. They relate to ability and willingness to observe and report accurately. The reliability of the corroborative witness is an important element in determining the amount of corroboration required.

Some historical problems are more difficult to handle than others. Sufficient corroboration for a description of Lincoln's assassination is a very different thing from sufficient corroboration of the assertion that class antagonism in France so seriously weakened national morale that it was a critical element in her quick military defeat in World War II. In general, we may say that the corroboration of relatively small events ought to be easier than corroboration of large complex events; that accounts of physical actions are generally easier to feel confident of than descriptions of states of mind; that it is easier to corroborate testimony on commonplace matters than on things people care enough about to lie and to torture their observations; that some matters scarcely can be reliably corroborated, because almost everyone either avoids testimony or feels no obligation to tell the truth (e.g., crime, espionage, illicit sexual activity, treason).

The quantity of corroboration available, as opposed to the quality of an individual piece of corroboration, may seem critical in handling some problems. Corroboration by sampling given portions and types of population groups often seems appropriate for public opinion questions.[7]

Indirect or negative corroboration is better than none, but sometimes not much better. The absence of contradiction in other sources is especially chancy. There are circumstances when we may feel fairly sure that it would have appeared in

---

[7] Cf. Chapter III (C), on oral testimony.

other sources (e.g., large newspapers in countries with a free press in modern times), but many others when we cannot be sure. Similarly, it is difficult to feel secure with such "corroboration" as the reputation of the author, internal consistency of the document, or lack of anachronism, conformity with the formulations of physical science, or by the lack of bias or the possession of expert knowledge by the witness in place of a multiplication of witnesses. All these have value, but must be used with caution.

Analysis of the problem of corroboration may be furthered by thinking of it in terms of methods of "measurement" (or weighting). We tend to think of this in terms of *physical* measurement—i.e., comparison with a fixed physical standard, as the inch, or kilogram, or dollar (which is at least more or less fixed at any given time, and a bit less subject to varying interpretation than the standards of "virtue" or "truth"). This is, indeed, one type of measurement available at times to historians: quantitative method. Two others of value are definition or delimitation, and comparison or analogy.

The quantitative method of today is new. It bears no relationship of consequence to methods employed before modern times by historians. It was not that earlier historians could not do arithmetic, but that (*a*) the statistical sources did not exist to permit them to gather good quantitative data, (*b*) they had much less notion of what sorts of quantitative data might be useful than do scholars today, (*c*) they had much less interest in quantification *per se,* being more simply concerned with qualitative or moral or ethical or personalistic issues, and (*d*) if the foregoing had not been the case, they would have been unable to handle the materials well. Records simply are kept better today than in the past. Methods of manipulating quantitative data to permit new understanding have been much changed in recent years. This is partly because of conceptual advances, partly because new instruments, especially computers, have permitted activity never before practicable.

Although some important subjects (e.g., virtue) do not lend themselves readily to quantitative analysis, and presumably never will, many others do. It is, therefore, a reasonable expectation that modern scholars will identify the quantifiable portions of their subjects, and try to supply the quantitative data, or explain why it is lacking or deficient. Immensely valuable economic and social and political history has been written in the last century by attention to quantification.

To turn to the second "measure," one virtue of the definition and delimitation of ideas is that it often improves measurement of the value even of qualitative evidence. Merely because definition in this sense does not deal in ergs or decibels does not mean that it does not improve accuracy. The frequency with which we encounter waters muddied by the sloppy definition of concepts justifies calling definition a measurement. Even virtue can be defined against some standard or set of presuppositions or propositions; yet how often the writer merely tosses in the judgment without that definition. The definition of terms and concepts is one of the essential and operating members of the body of scholarly method.

Comparison or analogy is yet another sort of intellectual operation that either partakes of the nature of measurement or produces insights or clarifications or definitions that assist in measurement. Comparison means the matching or contrasting of small items or notions (vases, the word for dog in two languages, the view of incest in several cultures), or of great aggregations of objects, institutions, and ideas (ancient Cretan and Egyptian cultures). Quantification and definition in comparative studies have been found to lead to insights that permit of altered quantification and definition and judgment of the individual "cases" (little dogs, or Chambers of Commerce, or entire civilizations) involved in the comparison. Transnational comparative studies of political history on carefully quantified and defined bases are barely in their infancy today.

VII

Using evidence:
Synthetic operations

Synthetic operations involve such mental processes as comparison, combination, and selection. Strictly speaking, almost everything in research involves some mental activity of this sort. The scope of synthetic activity is, however, greatest in connection with the processes discussed here. Although much of this activity occurs in the later stages of research, *it may occur whenever sufficient evidence is available to require it.* Scholarly use of such terms as analysis, interpretation, generalization, explanation, and synthesis often is imprecise and contradictory. Some of this is unavoidable; some of the ambiguity can be avoided. Researchers should at least be aware of the difficulties of discussing such matters.

It is emphasized again, as in Chapter I, that at the very beginning of a research effort the investigator needs to develop questions or hypotheses to apply to his material. If he does not, it will be impossible to know which facts to collect. In practice, what happens if no preliminary hypotheses or questions are adopted is that the researcher makes selections either helter-skelter and with little discrimination, or he uses poorly defined

163

or even unacknowledged criteria. It is much better to adopt tentative hypotheses and let them shape the search for a time, being alert to modify or abandon them at need. Such tentative hypotheses having been adopted from the beginning, the researcher necessarily frequently tests them against the views of other scholars and against contemporary evidence as he uncovers it. In short, "synthetic" research activity goes on at various levels almost from the beginning of the research effort.

A. Analysis and synthesis

We must not—to repeat in slightly different words—suppose that all consideration of evidence prior to the *final* synthesis is "analysis," untouched by synthesis. We did, indeed, choose to speak of external and internal criticism in terms of analysis. But some of this, and especially in internal criticism, was quite complex, and did in fact involve synthesis.

Analysis is a systematic attempt to learn about a subject or problem by looking at its elements, that is, by breaking it down into components or parts. Deciding what are the components into which to break a question for analysis often requires considerable thought, and the set of components may be much altered in the course of investigation. The part in some cases may consist of one or a few pieces of evidence bearing on one aspect of the total subject under study. To these elements or components are brought to bear all the resources of the mind, the research files, concepts and techniques of special disciplines, and such added research as may be necessary.

We do this sort of thing in everyday life. Suppose the problem is to go from point A to point B. We analyze it by a series of questions. Where is B in relation to A (direction? distance?), and what forms of transportation are available? Which will be quickest, cheapest, or otherwise best suited to our purpose? The questions have the effect of separating the major problem of getting from A to B into smaller, more manageable problems— but observe what happens next. Having developed what we consider sufficiently good answers to the smaller problems, we must next synthesize an answer to the original problem.

In the same way, in investigating a large historical subject, we analyze bits of evidence, compare them with other bits, combine bits into groups in a less than total synthesis of the subject, and finally combine all the groupings of evidence into the final interpretation or account. Thus, the answer to the question of at what point does analysis cease and synthesis begin is: at many points. What many writers mean when they discuss synthesis is the final synthesis in whatever research task is undertaken.

It may help the student to think of historical analysis and synthesis as being transactional, like the relations of buyer and seller, each affecting the other. On the basis of initial acquaintance with and analysis of his material, the historian formulates a tentative, working hypothesis. This may be at a low level; not all hypotheses need involve the fate of nations. It may be done by interrogation ("Is this a formal agreement or a tacit understanding?"), or by postulating a theory to be tested ("It seems likely, given this situation, that there was no formal agreement."). The hypothesis may also be reflected in the types of analyses employed, and these in turn affect the next hypothesis. Analysis and synthesis thus proceed together, often overlapping or merging; it is, however, generally true that emphasis will shift from analysis in the early and middle stages to synthesis in the final stages of work.

An example from the research experience of an author of this *Guide* will illustrate the relationship between analysis and synthesis. The project was to describe and explain when, how, and why certain international organizations for mutual help in scientific research came into being and developed. One of these groups finally emerged as the European Space Research Organization (ESRO). The initial analytical questions included the following: Where did the idea originate? What persons took the initiative in forming ESRO? Were governments originally involved, or did they become involved later? How did the involvement come about? What organizational procedures and institutional forms were used?

Such questions guided the search for data which, upon analysis, proved incomplete and contradictory. Renewed collection and more sophisticated analyses established certain points as being generally agreed upon, others as still disputed in part, and a few entirely unproved. Moving from the more to the less certain, relationships were explored. It was established that the idea first came into the open (it being impossible to know when it first entered someone's mind) at an informal meeting of several European scientists.

From that starting point it was possible to establish a chronological and, less certainly, a causal sequence of events. Finally, it became possible to trace the story from that first meeting through informal and formal exchanges among scientists, and, later, political leaders, to international negotiations and formal agreements. Particular attention was paid to trying to identify those happenings or situations except for which matters would not have developed as they did. Some of these situations were in the strictest sense outside the immediate subject. The Western European scientists and others concerned would probably not have considered joint action except that none of their countries by themselves could hope to match American or Soviet efforts in space research. Synthesis therefore meant not only putting together the internal story of ESRO, but also relating this to larger situations and problems, and interpreting the whole in the light of such ideas, principles, or philosophies as the mood of international competition, attitudes toward the aims of scientific research, and reigning ideas on war and peace.

Although the history—at which we have barely hinted—of ESRO is complex, it is but a part of the modern history of Europe and the world, and modern history is in turn but a part of yet larger histories. Thus, synthesis is a process in historical method which occurs at many levels, from wee generalizations based on bits of evidence, to brave assertions about the total life of man upon the planet.

B. The working hypothesis

The hypothesis is a natural and useful device. Natural in this context means that the researcher cannot avoid thinking of hypotheses. According to an older methodology, premature hypothesis might prejudice interpretation, so should be avoided. Actually, no one with imagination can deal with even a single piece of interesting evidence without having tentative hypotheses flicker through the mind. As we collect more than one piece of evidence, we see analogies, and something similar to an hypothesis exists whether we will it or not. Analogy is important in the formulation of hypotheses; that is, seeing fundamental similarities between things that apparently are different. A working hypothesis probably will include a preliminary supposition regarding causation, which we discussed in Chapter II. Assignment of a tentative cause or causes is a guess at an explanation. These, obviously, are processes requiring imagination; but it is imagination arising out of evidence, for a useful working hypothesis can only begin with some facts. A hypothesis should be: (*a*) founded on all the available facts and contradict none; (*b*) plausible, and not contradict the laws of nature; (*c*) capable of disproof or verification (historians scarcely can grapple with miracles); (*d*) as simple as possible.[1]

The problem is to not let hypotheses become straitjackets; they must be abandoned at need. This is what we mean by "working" hypothesis. It helps our labors. It is tentative, but it must be clear that even the most tentative of hypotheses is apt to guide research to some extent, to serve as a standard of relevance, to affect our selection of material, or our degree of attention to evidence. The only defense against such dangers is the consciousness that they exist. Finally, it is clear that in the adoption of working hypotheses the researcher must be conscious of

---

[1] After Wilson Gee, *Social Science Research Methods* (New York: Appleton-Century-Crofts, 1950), 197, citing D. Luther Evans and Walter S. Gamertsfelder, *Logic, Theoretical and Applied* (1937), pp. 315–16.

the dangers of bias, ethnocentrism, and over-simplification, as in all his research activity.

As an illustration let us proceed a short distance into the use of working hypotheses in connection with the subject "The Spanish Conquest of the Aztecs." Probably we will tell ourselves that we want to be able to describe the process in terms of the following five areas of interest: (*a*) why was it undertaken? (*b*) how well did it succeed? (*c*) why was it accomplished so quickly and easily? (*d*) what were the results for the Spaniards and for the Aztecs? (*e*) what did the conquest mean to the rest of mankind? Each of these is a large and complex subject in itself. Here we will deal, for illustrative purposes, only with (*c*), why was the conquest so easy? We assume that it is beyond argument that the conquest of millions of Amerinds by a few hundred Spaniards in two or three years may be considered easy.

Examination of the testimony indicates that the following factors were explicitly asserted by contemporary Spaniards as contributing to the rapid victory: superior weapons, good leadership, Spanish alliance with Amerind groups, Amerind superstitious fear of Europeans, Amerind military ineptitude of various sorts. There is considerable evidence in Spanish and Amerind sources to make it seem that the probability is very great that these factors had something to do with the matter. We also quickly discover that the contemporaries of the conquerors, and later historians also, do not entirely agree on the *why* of these factors, and that some of the historians suggest weaknesses in the Amerind social structure as also contributory. So our initial hypothesis is that a combination of factors was responsible for the rapid and easy conquest of the Aztecs by the Spaniards.

The researcher at this point discovers that he is not satisfied. More research is required, and different sorts of consideration of both old and new evidence seem to be indicated as a means of trying to identify better the importance of the ingredients in this historical process. The activities sketched above involved location and criticism or analysis of pieces of evidence, and much combination or synthesis of evidence. The synthesis was not, however, final synthesis in this investigation. We will return to synthesis in this research task later in this chapter.

C. Bias and subjectivity

Common usage interchanges "bias" and "subjectivity" (or "subjectivism") as if they were synonymous. They are not. Every person is subjective in the sense that he is aware of and seeks to understand that which has meaning in terms of his personal values. Many values are shared with others, so that groups have common interests and similar responses to certain stimuli, but each individual develops his own reality world in the process of living. This is the psychological matrix from which his purposeful behavior stems. "As he thinketh in his heart, so is he." Thus runs the biblical proverb, and modern scholarship adds, "He is, in large measure, as he feels."[2] Subjectivity is, therefore, an inescapable human quality. It cannot be willed or wished away.

Bias may mean a judgment reached without examination or without consideration of the evidence in full. It may also mean a commitment to a particular belief, position, or cause held so strongly that it precludes consideration, or even awareness, of contrary evidence and opposing views. Few scholars would claim to be free of all bias, and probably none would be justified in making such a claim. We cannot eradicate all bias, but we can do much to minimize it. "The safeguard against bias in the writing of history, as in the natural sciences, is not to indulge in useless resolutions to be free of bias but rather to explore one's preconceptions, to make them explicit, to consider their alternatives. . . ."[3]

Students who wonder (and many of them do) if they may

---

[2] For a brief discussion of this by an eminent social psychologist see Handley Cantril, *"Sentio, ergo sum:* 'Motivation' Reconsidered," *The Journal of Psychology,* 65 (1967), 91–107.

[3] Cohen, *The Meaning of Human History* (1946 ed.), 80. Note that Professor Cohen included natural sciences as well as history.

properly express opinions in their research papers, or who fear
to do so lest they be charged with subjectivity, are worrying
about the wrong things. The proper question is not, "Is this an
opinion?" but "What are the bases for this opinion?" And the
proper follow-up questions are: what evidence was sought? what
evidence was found? what was selected for use? what was actually used and for what purpose? It is proper to demand that an
historian be thorough, fair, and impartial in seeking and using
all the evidence, not just evidence which accords with his preconceptions or supports his thesis. It is not proper to demand
that he be an unperson with no standards, judgments, or
opinions.

The historian often has to deal with multiple variables; as
he examines them, his conception of their interaction and individual importance alters. This makes absolute precision and
certainty impossible, but it in no way excuses lack of intellectual
rigor. Because we have to deal with approximations, it is important to make sure that they are as exact as possible. The same
reasoning and obligations apply to bias and subjectivity. We
must try to identify and correct for biases in ourselves, as well
as in the evidence. We must accept the subjectivity of our per-
ceptions and be prepared to recognize that what is valid for one
may often appear invalid to another. There is every reason for
an historian to be humble about his performance, but no reason
for him to be humble about the scholarly craft he professes and
practices.

Bias may take the form of uncontrollable attachment to a
church or religious ideas, or to a political party or political
views or a social class, or a distaste for certain occupations or
for men with beards. It also can be a much larger and pervasive
thing, as the cultural patterns of the ancient Maya, so different
from those of their European conquerors as to make communication on many subjects nearly impossible. Or how much communication could exist between Polynesians and early New
England missionaries on the "duty" of work, the sin of naked-
ness, or the beauties of sexual abstinence? We have mentioned
earlier the problems of error due to ethnocentrism.

Bias or prejudice may be thought of as exaggerated points of view. The point of view, the experience, the beliefs, the attitudes of the historian must affect his interpretation of history. What is important is that he should be aware of this, and be willing to discuss opposing points of view.

An excellent example of how changing experience and point of view affected the work of an historian concerns the role of Hernán Cortés in the conquest of Mexico. A Spanish historian wrote in 1935 in praise of the chronicle of Bernal Díaz, one of Cortés' soldiers, who criticized the great captain as having received exaggerated credit for the achievements of his men. Immediately after this, the historian took part in the bloody Spanish Civil War of 1936–39. This gave him a different understanding of the problems of military leadership, and he wrote a new discussion in which he defended Cortés against what he now called the jealousy, greed, and ambition of Bernal Díaz. He also developed a new explanation of some of Cortés' more devious actions, as being dictated by the need of manipulating his soldiers into accepting intelligent direction by pretending that ideas and decisions came from the ranks.[4] Although we would call this a change in point of view rather than in biases, the similarity in kind if not in degree is apparent. The fact is that huge amounts of military history have been written by men with no military experience and sometimes with little appreciation of military problems. All this without reference to the fact that some modern scholars so dislike military institutions that they are unable to analyze them with approximate impartiality.

It is difficult to guess whether bias or self-delusion is the more prominent in the following example, and possibly it does not matter. The Haymarket Affair of 1886 in Chicago involved an isolated act of terrorism by a lone anarchist. Some conservatives in the United States insisted on viewing it as part of a wave of radicalism threatening to destroy American institutions. The

---

[4] Ramón Iglesia, "Two Articles on the Same Topic: Bernal Díaz del Castillo and Popularism in Spanish Historiography and Bernal Díaz del Castillo's Criticisms of the *History of the Conquest of Mexico* by Francisco López de Gomara," *Hispanic American Historical Review,* XX (1940), 517–50.

opposite self-delusion or political bias was that of the left, as when the French revolutionary periodical *Le Révolté,* declared of the Haymarket Affair:[5]

Blood flows in the United States. Tired of leading a life which is not even a mere existence, the worker makes a final effort to struggle against the beast of prey which is devouring him. . . . And this beast of prey . . . turns its slaves [soldiers and police] loose upon the worker. . . . It is open war.

This document is good evidence for one thing only: leftist hope of revolution.

Bias in the form of adherence to Marxist doctrine led to a dubious system of interpretation of evidence in Herbert Aptheker's *American Negro Slave Revolts* (New York, 1943). Aptheker uncovered numerous slave disturbances in the antebellum South, but, in the view of most historians, exaggerated their significance in terms of militant slave resistance. He concluded that black militance and overt examples of revolt were common, critics contend, in order to advance a Marxian interpretation of slavery in the United States. It is entirely understandable that with the recent growth of black consciousness in the United States, interest in the degree of slave resistance has increased.

In using bias as an important element in the assignment of error or falsification, probability often is all we can achieve. But this may be a considerable gain. For years a famous quotation was attributed to Woodrow Wilson by virtually every major historian dealing with his presidency or with American intervention in World War I:

Once lead this people into war, and they'll forget there was ever such a thing as tolerance. To fight you must be brutal and ruthless, and the spirit of ruthless brutality will enter into the very fiber of our national life, infecting Congress, the courts, the policeman on the beat, the man in the street.

Recently it has been argued that Wilson either never made the statement or that it might have been made in a different form.

---

[5] Quoted in Henry David, *The History of the Haymarket Affair* (2d ed., New York, 1963).

The quotation originally was cited in J. L. Heaton, *Cobb of the World* (New York, 1924), as coming directly from Editor Frank Cobb, who had it from the lips of Wilson. Now it has been shown that Heaton had it only at third hand, from Maxwell Anderson and Laurence Stallings, as purportedly repeated to them by Cobb at the time of the incident, then given by them to Heaton many years later. It is pointed out that Stallings and Anderson were such fanatical pacifists, with considerable literary ability, that this argues—with some other evidence—for a verdict of possible fabrication. Their motive assertedly was to endow Wilson with prophetic powers regarding the effects of warfare. The issue is by no means settled to the satisfaction of historians, but some doubt has settled upon the quotation.[6]

Objectivity is, of course, the goal at which the scholar aims. And in this connection the reader may well be troubled by the assumption that history writing involves the principle of *selection*. The historian selects both the facts that he will include and the causes that he will assign to events. Does this condemn history to the mere whim and prejudice of historians? Is there no objective history? That is the view of some of the new left revisionist historians in the United States. They assert that the work of all historians is inescapably subjective, and that the pertinent question is what cause they will favor. A positive aspect of this has been bold reinterpretation of old and possibly ossified views; a negative side of it has been insufficient interest in accuracy and proof in terms of probability, and some glorification of irrationality and intuition at the expense of reason.

In any event, even in the case of the historian who believes in the possibility of maximizing objectivity, and in the necessity of identifying and sometimes minimizing subjectivity, the danger is real that there will be lapses. The honest historian guards against this as best he can. He remembers that he is involved in the process that he is describing and tries to rise above his own biases and limited point of view. If he suggests an hypothesis, he attempts to subject it to rigorous testing, weighing both the

---

[6] Cf. Jerold S. Auerback, "Woodrow Wilson's 'Prediction' to Frank Cobb: Words Historians Should Doubt Ever Got Spoken," *Journal of American History*, LIV (December 1967), 608–17.

supporting and the conflicting evidence. He tries to give a well-rounded account that will include all the *significant* and *relevant* evidence. These last are difficult principles that we deal with later in this chapter. To give way completely to despair of any control over subjectivity in historical studies surely compels adoption of such attitudes as that public servants cannot rise above their personal biases, and that we sanction their refusal to try to do so. To the ordinary person of common sense, both propositions are rather childish.

D. Relevance and selection[7]

The impossibility in a large research task of using all evidence remotely touching the subject indicates the need for selection. Obviously, what is desired is selection of relevant data. The function of the test of relevance, therefore, is to help in the selection of data. Nothing is more important in historical investigation, and few things are as difficult. Sometimes, for one thing, it is not at all clear whether a piece of evidence is relevant. Also, one's notion of relevance often shifts during a research task, making some evidence already selected either totally or partially irrelevant, and making some evidence that has been discarded now clearly relevant.

One approach is to cast aside "insignificant" evidence—that is, evidence too picayune or too tangential to be very helpful. In discussing the development of the blast furnace we might well decide that the connection with man's original conquest of fire was irrelevant. Often it helps to ask whether the need in a specific case is to establish facts or to interpret them or to find causes. If we are simply counting barrels of flour, our needs are different from the case where we wish to know why congressmen voted taxes on flour elevators, or in the case where we are in-

---

[7] The positioning of a discussion of relevance in this part of the guide must not be taken to mean that the process of determining relevance occurs only during the later stages of research and composition. Decisions regarding relevance are made from the beginning of research. Cf. Chapter VII (A), on hypotheses in the determination of relevance.

terested in the role American grain played in sustaining the Allies in World War I. It may help to look at parts or aspects of the question under study, and decide what is needed for understanding of each aspect; then, finally, one may know what is relevant to study of the entire subject.

The test of relevance is most easily applied to studies devoted to narrowly defined topics. Suppose the problem is child labor in English factories during the early 19th century. Many facts are clearly relevant: legislation, statistical data, evidence of conditions, etc. But other data may be of questionable relevance: working conditions for adults, general economic conditions, educational institutions. Some of these may help to illuminate the chosen topic, others may not. In any case, there is a danger that the historian will digress more and more from his main concern to the bafflement of his readers.

How can the historian keep on the main path? One useful device is to think of his topic as a proposition, or a hypothesis, to be proved or refuted. The proposition might be: English factories during the early 19th century seriously jeopardized the health and welfare of children. Then the test for inclusion would be whether the data supported or refuted this proposition. The hypothesis is a useful device, but only if its testing is fair and rigorous. Almost any historical thesis can be proved, if only supporting evidence is selected. The historian should be especially conscientious in considering the contradictory evidence and be prepared to abandon or modify his working hypothesis accordingly. Insofar as possible, the researcher must examine *all* the evidence that relates to his problem. In the light of all the evidence, he then selects for inclusion in his account those facts that are important and are representative of the total body of the evidence—that is, they set forth the pros and cons in true proportion.

Another procedure for maintaining relevance is to think of the topic as either a single question, or a series of questions. To what extent did English factories at different periods employ children? How is child to be defined? Under what legal safeguards were children employed? How long were their hours?

How were they treated? For many topics, analysis by key questions is more rewarding than procedure by hypothesis. It avoids the artificiality of debate, with the historian inclined to take one side or the other, and makes the researcher's task the exciting one of asking the right questions and searching for the answers. If the questions are properly framed, there will be little temptation to diversion into unrewarding irrelevancies.

For longer historical works, the problem of relevance is more complex. Yet analogous methods will be helpful. Certain general hypotheses, or a series of hypotheses, may be set up and tested. Or a series of questions may be asked and answered.

There is a broader question of relevance that we have referred to in several sections of this guide: the changing views of historians as to the general relevance of certain aspects of human activity to their scholarly craft. Medieval chronicles are replete with miraculous occurrences and prodigious feats of arms. They are singularly devoid of information on life among the lower and middle classes. Clearly the monkish scholars placed highest value on evidence of divine intervention and knightly valor. In contrast to this, 19th-century British and American historians tended to ignore miracles, minimize battles, and emphasize constitutional and legal growth. They placed their highest value on what they liked to call "ordered liberty." In the 20th century, historians have placed increasing stress on economic and social developments and have related political development to these factors.

At least, in each period of historical writing, certain generally-held standards of values provided the historian with a guide as to what was considered important. The process, moreover, may be regarded as an evolutionary one. The earlier selection of events seems to us not so much erroneous as fragmentary. As men have raised their sights and enlarged their aspirations, their view of the past has widened. For this reason, the astute historian will not select his data solely on today's values but upon those which he believes will come into increasing recognition tomorrow. For example, if in the future scientists are going to play an increasingly important role in human affairs, today's historian will be wise to increase the attention that he is giving to the scientific advances of the past. And in so doing, he will help to advance the values that he recognizes. The historian's role is by no means merely passive. By his explanation of the past, he helps to shape the future.

E. Final synthesis[8]

The final synthesis, and its expression, are the terminal processes of the historical endeavor. The operative word here is "final." Other syntheses, as we have observed, will be made in the course of the research task.

1. Important preliminary observations

There are three preliminary observations to make about synthesis in general before moving to final synthesis in particular.

a. Digestion of evidence

Adequate synthesis of evidence at any level will not be attained without proper *digestion* of the evidence. This means sufficient reflection on and manipulation of the evidence to permit its meaningful synthesis. This requires poring over the evidence, reading and re-reading it, making preliminary generalizations and combinations and re-combinations. If this seems obvious, let it be clearly understood that our many years of experience in teaching historical methods shows that all too often beginning researchers do not familiarize themselves sufficiently with what they have collected, either for purposes of internal criticism or analysis or for synthesis at all levels. These beginning researchers have evidence on notes, in files, but they do not *possess* it mentally. They cannot see interconnections and contradictions simply because they do not know well enough what they have. They think pieces and small groupings of evi-

---

[8] We have dealt elsewhere with such matters important to the final synthesis as causation, motivation, contingency, values, ideas, relevance, laws, hypotheses.

dence will reveal larger meanings. Not so. The evidence, or facts, do not speak for themselves. The collector must become thinker and puzzle out meanings for himself. Much digestion may be done during the processes of collecting, evaluating, analyzing pieces and groups of evidence; even so, some final digestion will be necessary. If little digestion has occurred during the process of collection and preliminary analysis, toward the end a great deal of digestion will be necessary. It is impossible to overemphasize the importance of this process of digestion, as a necessary preliminary (or accompanying step) to synthesis. We could mention modern nations whose historical output is distinguished by zeal in collection and publication, and by distaste for the hard work of digesting evidence, with really lamentable results.

b. Using other syntheses

Synthesis requires the use of the work (including the syntheses) of other scholars. This is true of all but the smallest research tasks.[9] The investigator will, of course, have been doing much of this since the beginning of his inquiry; now, however, we are speaking specifically of the conclusions (explicit, or implicit in the structure of synthesis) of other scholars. Thus, successful synthesis involves the capacity to judge the quality of work of other scholars. This is, to be sure, a requirement of analysis in external and internal criticism, as well as at all levels of synthesis; at all these stages the investigator will be making use of the work of other scholars. Now, finally, you will be, in a manner of speaking, synthesizing your research with that of others. It is essential to learn to use the work of others well, in order not only to avoid repeating what has been done adequately by others, but to incorporate into your own research and interpretation everything worthwhile that has been done before you. This is not an easy task. Nor is it so obvious a requirement to the beginning as to the experienced researcher. The beginning researcher too often thinks that all his work must be with "sources"

---

[9] There are few subjects so new that no literature touching them exists.

—i.e., evidence. Maximum use must be made of what others have done with evidence.[10] One of the many great talents of the eighteenth century historian Edward Gibbon was his skill in blending the scholarship of others into his own work with evidence.

c. Synthesis as generalization

Some historians affect to be leery of generalization. All historians practice generalization, willy-nilly. It changes nothing to call generalizations explanations. The problem, of course, is finding sufficient evidence for the specific generalization. This means not certainty, as we have emphasized, but sufficient evidence for the assertion of degrees of probability. Few generalizations about large-scale human affairs should speak of certainty. Generalizations usually require qualification: nearly always, usually, almost, in the majority of cases, most likely, perhaps. The term "always" must be used with precision; if there could be exceptions, so far as the researcher knows, the word cannot be used. If all the causation of an event cannot surely be assigned to one source or influence, multiple causation must be admitted as a possibility. Finally, improper use of analogy is a special form of generalization from insufficient evidence. It may not properly be asserted that the creation, development, and disappearance of human cultures involves a natural process akin to the birth, growth, and death of biological organisms, or the fixed procession of the seasons on earth.

The above points having been made, we now discuss final synthesis under four headings: interpretation, emphasis, arrangement, and inference. These processes are interacting and overlapping, but to promote communication they must be con-

---

[10] Cf. Langlois and Seignbos, op. cit., 229–31: that "the operations of history are so numerous" that no man can do it alone; history, with its need for millions of facts, should have a proper division of labor, but has never enforced sufficiently rigorous and accepted standards so that such division exists, thus it is difficult to be sure of the quality of scholarly works; but the latter must be used, although "with the same critical precautions" that are given to contemporary evidence. See Chapter IV (D), on preliminary analysis in note taking.

sidered separately, The first two require little attention. For one thing, they are in fact included under other labels (e.g., generalization, relevance, arrangement), and have been or will be discussed there. But the terms are so often used as to require a word of explanation, and there are some minor points to make.

2. Interpretation

Some scholars consider it useful to insist that all of final synthesis is interpretation. And there is value in the claim that most of interpretation is either (*a*) the finding of causal relations that permit explanations of human events, or (*b*) assertions of value judgments by the researcher or author. To say that these are the same thing is a counsel of despair; we must assume that there are some things that most (possibly all?) complex human cultures will interpret the same: e.g., some causal relation between loss of nine-tenths of the population by plague and a decline in economic production. To be sure, cause of the plague may be assigned to virus, an angry God, emanations from comets, or noxious airs. In any event, interpretation often is in fact synonymous with the usage of explanation, or causation, or generalization.[11]

3. Emphasis

Interpretation, generalization, arrangement all result in emphasis; the process cannot work in reverse. There are, however, two things to say about emphasis in the final synthesis: (*a*) Remember that the *amount* of the account devoted to the subject may give emphasis, as may the *intensity* or skill devoted to a part of the treatment, and even the very order in which matters are discussed. (*b*) The historian should at least try to define his intended emphases, and struggle to see that they are in fact executed as he wished. The last injunction relates as much to composition as to the mental operations of synthesis.

---

[11] Cf. Chapter III (A), on a similar terminological morass involving classifications of evidence as sources, secondary, etc.

4. Arrangement: chronologic, geographic, topical

Arrangement, or the grouping of evidence, is interpretation, although it may be said to be necessary also in the more narrow sense of communication. Certainly there will be little communication if historical evidence is simply printed in sequential blobs of words selected by a blindfolded man groping in a bin of notes. So any arrangement involves some sort of interpretation or judgment, although a simple listing of dates, in the manner of primitive annals, does little to promote communication, and less to promote understanding through interpretation.[12]

The commonest ways of arranging historical evidence in the final synthesis are chronological, geographical (usually meaning by the territories of political units), or topically. In a large synthesis, it is common to combine two or all three of these schemes. The easy advice is to suit the arrangement to the evidence and to the principles of interpretation adopted. What is most suitable is not, alas, always clear. Sometimes, indeed, two or more types of arrangement might be equally meaningful.

It is at least clear that all historical arrangements are to some extent *time oriented*. Even if the major divisions are political jurisdictions, and the next level of arrangement is by topics, within each of these the treatment or arrangement will be chronological. The major problem usually is whether the primary divisions should be chronological or something else.

It should be noted that following chronological treatment within a geographical, topical, or chronological order, is not the same thing as determining the time period in the first instance. This last, the process of *periodization,* can scarcely be done purely on the basis of time: e.g., a history of the 19th century makes no sense as a group of years from 1800 to 1900, since human affairs do not begin, end, or undergo significant changes in such arbitrary 100-year periods. The regnal dates of monarchs, or the years of presidential administrations, make some sense from certain limited points of view. These must, however,

---

[12] See Chapter VIII (B), on the outline; and Chapter VII (C), on bias and subjectivity, which are likely to affect arrangement.

be carefully specified. Much of the life of a nation begins long
before the reign or administration commences, is little changed
during it, and endures long after it. The value of such "periods"
as "The Age of the Enlightenment" or "The Progressive Era" is
that they permit emphasis on certain aspects of life during the
period stated. The danger is that the impression may be given
that all was either enlightenment or progressivism in such
periods.

In connection with periodization, the modern tendency is to
determine what important developments occurred, in selected
realms (e.g., Europe since the fall of Rome, France in the first
decades of the industrial revolution, Hispanic America in the
colonial period, or the suffrage in England from the Great Revolution to the present), and declare the periodical divisions to fit
the results of such inquiry. Thus James Shotwell put it tersely
that, since facts can be arranged in various ways, "arrangement
is argument."[13]

5. Inference

Inference is the process of reasoning from facts that are not
entirely connected. It is used to fill gaps in the record or to
supply connections between bits or classes of evidence. To call
it "informed invention" is possibly overly-pessimistic. At any
rate, it should be done tentatively, provisionally, even modestly.
Although this type of reasoning or interpretation is as chancy
as the assignment of causes, in most investigations it must be
used. Remember, that all inferences are probabilistic. An inference may even be thought of as an hypothesis; that is, a suggestion as to relationships between facts.

The process is to some extent intuitive, undemonstrable,
partially free of fact; but it should cling to whatever facts are
available. It is not mechanical, but a creative process. It is not,
however, inventive in the sense that fiction is contrived. The
historian may not move the first voyage of Columbus to 1516

---

[13] *The History of History,* 198.

to suit his whim. He must "create" attitudes toward facts by the processes of selection and combination, and by his ascription of motivation and causation. The possible errors to be avoided are numerous, and only a few are mentioned here. It is erroneous to suppose that the ideas, life-styles, etc., of an upper class, or a specialized group (e.g., intellectuals) represent a total society, and therefore to infer connections between "elitist" facts and others that probably have at least some of their grounding in the common folk of the society. It also is dangerous to base inferences involving large groups of people upon what is known of an individual.

Common sense suggests that the more inference is involved in a synthesis, the greater the likelihood of error. The greater the inference, the further removed the interpretation is from the evidence. Common sense also suggests the probability that the larger the synthesis the smaller its relation to reasonably demonstrable fact or what we must call probability. Such meta-historians as Spengler and Toynbee necessarily deal largely in inferences. This does not mean that the largest possible synthesis should not be attempted. It does suggest that modesty might be appropriate in the presentation of grand syntheses.

6. Checklist for synthesis

At this point, some beginning scholars might do best to proceed with the suggestion made above that synthesis is combination, comparison, arrangement of evidence, with connectives provided by inference, and explanations provided by assignment of cause. Other beginning researchers will benefit from further attention to the elements of synthesis, and the approximate order in which they occur. This will assist understanding of a process that is intrinsically difficult both to use and to explain.

We can list at least 15 elements considered in this guide that are important in the process of synthesis. There is no single, always best, answer to the questions of in what order or in what intensity these elements are to be used. In addition, we cannot expect always to be conscious of their use. Practitioners of the

craft do not proceed on such a basis. Their synthesis or correlations often are instantaneous (after a lot of preparation); and
may be intuitive in the sense that correlation sometimes leaps
to the mind apparently without an effort to create it. But researchers do need *sometimes* to be conscious of the elements of
synthesis. In any event, in order to discuss synthesis at all, we
must specify the elements of the process.

The 15 elements in synthesis are here numbered and grouped
into five categories.[14] The roman capitals in parentheses indicate the chapters of this guide in which the primary discussion
of each element occurs.

Category one. We may think of the elements in this category as being essentially preliminary to synthesis: (1) literal
and real meaning (VI); (2–3) observation and reporting of the
detail (VI); (4) bias and subjectivity (VII).

Category two. We will call this initial synthesis: (5) corroboration, contradiction, and measurement (VI); (6) probability, plausibility, and certainty (II); (7) working hypothesis
(VII).

Category three. We will label this secondary synthesis: (8)
causation (II); (9) motivation (II); (10) individuals and institutions (II); (11) contingency (II); (12) facts as values, ideas,
objects (II).

Category four. Final synthesis: (13) inference (VII),
which supplies the ultimate speculative connectives.

Category five. Which is really the implementation of synthesis: (14) relevance (VII), often used earlier in the process
also, but now operating at the highest or final level of synthesis;
and (15) arrangement (VII).

7. An example of synthesis

In illustration of the process of synthesis, we here continue
discussion of "why was the conquest of the Aztecs so easy?",

---

[14] There is some overlap—unavoidable and useful—with the nine operations in the "Checklist for internal criticism" in Chapter VI (D).

which we began earlier in this chapter in connection with working hypothesis. This is not a perfect illustration, for the good reason that there is no such thing. Nor will we grapple in a perfectly balanced and consistent way with all the 15 elements of synthesis listed above (some of which are not even synthetic). The reason is simple: all discussions of synthesis are distortions, artifices. We merely intend to help the beginning researcher understand the complex process which he, hopefully, will be able to discuss with a seasoned scholar in terms of the beginner's own efforts to synthesize evidence.

We left the problem of the conquest of the Aztecs with the working, or tentative, hypothesis that a combination of factors was responsible for the easy victory of the Spaniards. We were not certain, however, that we had identified all the factors involved; even less satisfied that we knew the relative weights of the elements in the mix, or how the mix itself operated; nor were we sure that the factors operated just the same in all combat engagements and other decision-making actions involving the Aztecs and the Spaniards and the Amerind allies of the latter. And we had begun to wonder whether the Spanish conquests of other Amerind groups were replicas of the Aztec conquest, or similar, or very different; and whether other cases would help illuminate the Aztec case, possibly by reinforcing our impressions of the former. Further, we were increasingly aware that explanation of the Aztec conquest is chiefly interesting as it helps explain the larger question of the Spanish conquest of the Amerinds generally.

So the next step is to look at the Spanish conquests of the Incas and the Mayas. These turn out to have been accomplished rapidly by small bands of Spaniards, and for the same reasons operating in the Aztec case. We become convinced that the Amerinds simply could not resist the Spaniards. We put to one side for the moment some of the special difficulties in the Maya area, and decide that it is clear that the most advanced cultures and largest concentrations of population succumbed quickly to small forces because of certain identifiable factors in some sort of combination.

The next step must be an examination of the relations between the Spaniards and the lower Amerind cultures. Immediately upon entering this subject we are in trouble. The Spaniards found great difficulty in conquering many Amerinds of simple culture. We have much data to interpret on clashes between Spaniards and Amerinds in the first century of relations after Columbus' initial voyage. The texts are difficult, and we may not avoid all errors due to mistaking literal for real meaning; but probably this is a minor factor. Great doubts remain in some cases about the observation and reporting of details of negotiations, agreements, battles. But so many cases have been investigated, and so much corroborative evidence has been found, that at least the gross physical events seem more or less clear—i.e., we believe that we know *what* happened with a high degree of probability, who fought when and where and with what casualities and with what physical results.

We now have the generalization that the highest Amerind cultures succumbed more easily than many of the lower cultures. This raises the questions: (*a*) why did not *all* of the lower resist with about equal success? and (*b*) why did *many* of the lower resist more successfully than the higher? As for the former, we find that sometimes the location (e.g., on islands) of the Amerinds made it difficult for them to resist, because they had few remote redoubts into which to retreat and from which to sally forth to the attack. We find, also, that some Amerind groups—e.g., the island Arawaks—were less accustomed to warfare than others.

The next question might be: Of those who resisted rather successfully, were some more successful than others? The answer is yes. We find some groups that put up serious resistance for centuries—e.g., in Costa Rica, Chile, Argentina, northern Mexico. Why? Terrain? Leadership? Strength and persistence of Spanish effort? We inquire: Were the Spanish trying as hard in the case of the lower culture groups? How do we measure this? By the number of Spaniards? By the number of Spaniards in proportion to Amerinds? By weapons (e.g., number of firearms)? By persistent effort over the years? By the intensity of

Spanish effort? And how do we measure? A possible approach to the question of intensity can be made by coupling it with statistics on the size and direction of Spanish efforts and with indications of the nature of Spanish interest in their efforts.

The size of Spanish efforts presents difficulties, but fairly good results can be obtained. The nature of Spanish interest is quite clear: it was economic (understanding that a desire for status and authority depended upon the acquisition of wealth). Wealth in the conquest period meant either precious metals or access to large numbers of Amerinds who were accustomed to working regularly under direction. We find that there was some correspondence between the size of Spanish efforts and the presence of one or both of these factors; and we speculate (with considerable confidence) that the intensity of Spanish effort varied in proportion to the presence of these two possible rewards.

We are further encouraged by the observation that the patterns of early Spainsh settlement tended to coincide with the presence of precious metals or of the Amerind concentrations mentioned. We accept this as a working hypothesis, but soon must temper it with the observation that Spaniards also settled in places without these characteristics, so that the generalization is: early Spaniards *often* settled in areas offering precious metals or concentrations of Amerinds accustomed to working regularly under direction.

Does there seem to have been some relationship between the order (schedule) of Spanish operations, their size, their intensity, and their interrupted duration, on the one hand; and on the other the presence of either precious minerals or concentrations of Amerinds accustomed to working regularly under direction? The answer is that there is some correspondence, but some at least partial exceptions. Possibly the most conspicuous exception was to the north of the Valley of Mexico, where a series of silver discoveries led to rushes of Spaniards to the areas, with consequent clashes with Amerinds of a lower cultural condition than the Aztecs and their allied and tributary peoples. The Spaniards found the warfare in the northern silver areas troublesome in much the way it was in Chile. This made mining camp life, supply, and travel, sufficiently precarious so that some of the more distant and difficult to defend mining areas were long unworked. On the other hand, a mineral belt north of Mexico City was defended. What we can state with confidence is that there were special difficulties in conquering the Amerinds of the lower cultures north of Mexico, but that they could be overcome if the incentive was great enough.

We have not yet grappled with the possibility that variations in Amerind culture affected the ability of the indigenous population to resist conquest. (We may have begun by now to consider the possibility of limiting research to specified aspects of a problem frequently sprouting new ramifications.)[15] It does not take long to discover that there were important cultural differences between Amerind groups. It is more difficult to demonstrate that they were pertinent to the question of easy conquest. Some cultural characteristics we feel were not relevant to this issue, some we cannot know about, and some apparently had some relevance (considerable inference is involved here). Aside from the high population concentrations and regular patterns of labor under direction, there were in higher and quickly conquered cultures rigid class systems with little social mobility, high differentiation of labor, elaborate political structures, religious legends involving white gods, systems of tribute between dominant and inferior states, military mobilization systems and armies of considerable size with hierarchic organization, and governmental jurisdiction over wide territories. We find some high cultures paying tribute to others, even warring with them. The Spaniards allied themselves with one group against another. We hypothesize that the lack of political unity among Amerind groups, and the lack of a sense of "Amerind nationalism or culture unity" were major factors in conquest everywhere. But where the largest political jurisdictions existed (Inca, Aztec)

---

[15] This problem of confining the subject is introduced to warn the beginning researcher of a problem he surely will encounter. See Chapter VIII (A).

conquest was most rapid because the defeat of the "national" armies found much of the entire population ready to accept the result without much further resistance. Indeed, the loss of a single important leader of the military hordes of the higher cultures tended to lead to panic.

Things were far otherwise with the lower culture groups. Conquest of a group in the field often resulted in tribal retreat into the forest, plains, or mountains, continuing the struggle as what we would call guerrillas. Further, the fate of one small tribal group might have almost no influence on decisions of another small group. There was no winning a war at one fell swoop. There was no war, but unending skirmishing.

We will not pursue the problem of interpretation or synthesis of this large, important, and difficult subject of the character of the Spanish conquest of the Amerinds, to say nothing of the even more important question of the results of that conquest for the Spanish, the Amerinds, and the rest of humanity.[16] Let us consider, instead, two possible ways, with variations, of arranging the materials on the subject.

The large mass of evidence on the conquest, it finally becomes clear, might usefully be arranged into three categories: (1) activities before battle, including negotiations, treachery, acquisition by the Spanish of Amerind allies against other Amerinds, and the benefit the Spanish received from Amerind fears of Spanish animals (horses, war dogs) or weapons (especially firearms) or supposed supernatural origins; (2) the evidence of the battlefields; and (3) post-battle activity, which sometimes included astounding surrenders by huge populations. This arrangement would permit a form of comparison of critical elements that might be quite illuminating. A variation of the

---

16 It is likely, of course, that the historian would have developed interest in other important matters also; e.g., whether the differing ease of conquest with reference to culture groups related to crown impatience with the actions of *conquistadores,* cruelty to Amerinds by Spaniards, ease of christianization, introduction of new labor systems among the Amerinds by the conquerors, introduction of African slaves, or the incidence of race mixture involving Spanish men and Amerind women.

arrangement might be to use the three divisions, but group the cases being analyzed into lower cultures on the one hand, and higher on the other.

Another attractive, because potentially useful, arrangement would be in terms of two classes of Spanish advantages over the Amerinds: (1) physical advantages; and (2) psychological or social advantages. Or the latter might be divided into two classes. The entire arrangement could be under these headings, or there could be subheadings under the pre-battle, battle, and post-battle arrangement suggested in the preceding paragraph.

Physical advantages included such things as acquisition of Amerind allies (psychological and social factors also were involved here), horses, iron or steel swords and lances, firearms, war dogs, sometimes ships. The psychological and social advantages of the Spanish may be said possibly to have had their basis in human nature, and they clearly related to the Amerind cultural condition. Panic in the Amerind ranks sometimes resulted from relatively minor events. It seems that if the Amerinds had possessed the fierce individualism of the Europeans, they might have resisted better, both in battle and thereafter. Thus, among the higher cultures, great populations and territories fell into Spanish hands after a few battles. Fighting the lesser groups was different because all territorial jurisdictions were small; no event in a tribal area much affected another area; no grand conquest was possible because no grand culture existed, with a rigidly compartmentalized social structure and an authoritarian and hierarchic governing system.

We thus have ended with the beginnings of a multiple-causation explanation of the ease with which a few Spaniards conquered millions of Amerinds. We have considered several possibilities for the arrangement of materials, both for final synthesis and interpretation and for communication or exposition. Synthesis and communication are closely related but not identical subjects; the latter is considered in the next chapter.

VIII

Using evidence:
Communication

Communication of what he has decided is probable fact and most plausible interpretation is the end of the researcher's endeavor. If he can communicate with clarity, strength, and grace he will have achieved all that can be hoped for from craftsmanship and style. The materials of this chapter will aid in the development of that craftsmanship necessary to clarity in communication, and hopefully may lead beyond that to strength and grace in expression.

A. Selecting and refining subjects

As stated above in the Preface, we supply students with subjects in order to plunge them as rapidly as possible into research. Some instructors, however, prefer that students find their own subjects, so we offer a few suggestions. Although students often have great difficulty locating and properly refining a research subject, even at the M.A. or Ph.D. levels there is no mystery about the process. A proper subject is anything you and your audience find satisfactory—that is, there are no "natural" subjects. The following suggestions will be helpful:

191

1. Be sure that sufficient evidence is available for study of the subject. (We guarantee this by issuing lists of subjects.)

2. Definition of the subject will be affected by the audience for which the research product is intended. (Our students are required to assume an audience of scholars.)

3. The frequently printed admonition to select a subject that is interesting and important merely means that it should seem so to the researcher and to a fair part of his audience. There is no other measure available.

4. The subject for this training purpose should be narrow enough to permit examination in some depth. Nothing will be learned by producing so generalized a descriptive paper that it might have been copied from a single account. One of the consequences of this requirement is that the original subject often is narrowed—or refined—to cover or emphasize only a segment thereof. Do not feel that this means that you are neglecting part of the subject; consider, rather, that you have a "new" subject.

5. Do not choose a subject that is beyond your skills—for example, in languages, mathematics, geographic techniques, economic concepts.

6. You are not looking for a subject that will permit you to make a contribution to knowledge, but merely for one that will permit the development of research skills, a large enough task.

7. The subject should have *unity* in the sense that it is possible to discuss it more or less in isolation from the other subjects that surround it. (No easily imaginable subject is so large that it is not surrounded by yet other subjects.) This means that each of the following would be a suitable subject: (*a*) the Civil War; (*b*) the artillery in the Civil War; (*c*) the Union artillery in the Civil War; (*d*) Union artillery ammunition in the Civil War; (*e*) manufacture of Union artillery ammunition in the Civil War; (*f*) labor problems and the manufacture of Union artillery ammunition in the Civil War; (*g*) shortages of skilled labor and the manufacture of Union artillery ammunition in the Civil War.

8. As a final caution it should be remembered that some types of subjects are inherently difficult to study: for example,

those involving activities that the participants therein try to hide (e.g., illegal or immoral actions), or activities of so commonplace a character that they seldom occasion comment (e.g., the household activities of an illiterate peasantry in a society dominated by a small upper class), or subjects concentrated on the beliefs and attitudes of common folk (e.g., in Baltimore in 1850) who did not write books or answer questionnaires. On the other hand, certain types of subject are apt to offer considerable evidence to the researcher: for example, a subject arousing large public interest on the part of a modern representative governmental system, and the concern of organized interest groups, and the press. Thus, the Spanish-American War, or Medicare, offer floods of documentation to the researcher.

B. The outline

An outline is merely a device for helping in the organization of materials and thoughts, a subject we have discussed in Chapter VII. Outlining involves: (*a*) a decision as to the primary categorization and presentation of materials; (*b*) subdivision of the primary categories; (*c*) the use of sketch or telegraphic style rather than sentences; (*d*) some effort to create a general correspondence between the number of the outline entries and the length of the sections of the manuscript that will be based on them; (*e*) an understanding that no level in an outline can have only one unit (e.g., if there is an "A," there must be at least a "B"; if a "1," at least a "2"; etc.). Finally, remember that outlines are working devices, and should be changed as often and as much as seems required by altering conceptions of the research task.

Although the simple mechanics of the device are of some consequence, it must be remembered that the purpose of the exercise is the effective organization of materials, both for improvement of the researcher's understanding, and in consideration of the needs of communicating findings to the audience.

If a student has properly considered the organization of his study, using the outline device, he will have anticipated many of his audience's (instructor's) queries—partly by perceiving deficiencies in his own knowledge and/or thinking.

It is a convenience to the instructor for all students to use the same system, so we suggest:

    I. _____
       A. _____
       B. _____
         1. _____
         2. _____
           a. _____
           b. _____
             i. _____
             ii. _____
   II. Etc. _____

The primary organization of the study is usually chronological or topical; a geographical organization is rarer for historical or social science studies; other types of primary organizations (e.g., biographical) are rarer yet. Even when a primary chronological or topical categorization is elected, the major sections probably will be arranged internally in the other manner (i.e., a chronological section may be developed topically and vice-versa). Of course, no paper will follow strictly chronological order. Most historical studies might be described as being the chronological arrangement of topics, or the topical development of periods of time. Overlap, or repetition, must be kept from boring multiplicity—but sufficient repetition of vital elements must occur in each section of the paper.

C. Drafts

Writing is hard work, and the excuses authors find for postponing it are legendary. Force yourself to begin, regardless of mood; there should be no waiting for "inspiration." A poor beginning can be changed later. If the outline properly reflects the material you have collected and your decisions as to its arrangement, the direction of writing should be fairly clear. Of course, work on the first draft often discloses defects in the tentative organization of the paper as set down in the outline. It is common to find that the material will not sustain a separate section that had been planned, and it will in the draft have to be combined with something else. Working with a typewriter is better than handwriting, especially because errors are more evident in typescript. It is not necessary to defer writing until all the research is finished. You may prepare drafts of sections as soon as the evidence seems adequate for a coherent account. Researchers differ, of course, as to how much they require before preparing a first draft.

A good paper or book almost always goes through two or more drafts, at least of parts of the manuscript. At the first try, thorny matters of evidence and emphasis will not always be well arranged, to say nothing of well expressed. The second or later drafts will result in tightened language. First drafts inevitably are wordy, hence the saying, "I could have made it shorter if I'd had more time." In revising drafts, scissors and paste sometimes will save time, but beware of scrambling the sense and especially of mixing up the citations. In all drafts attention should be paid to having sufficient evidence, examples when they are required for clarification, clearly reasoned interpretations, no excess data or language, no irrelevancies, and an organization that is clear, that carries the argument logically from beginning to end, and that provides strong and clear linkages between the parts of the investigation.

Writing should be directed to a specific audience. The audience for these papers is the scholar, which means that the exposition probably will also be suitable for the audiences of many public and private report-writing agencies. Clarity—in organization and statement—is the first aim. Whatever the audience, put yourself in the place of the reader as a means of making sure that you state exactly what you have in mind, and leave no room for ambiguity or misinterpretation.

There are many workable methods for putting citations into

the first draft. They can be put in brackets in the text; in the margin; at the bottom; on filler sheets of a different color inserted between sheets of the text. Also, it is possible to use short footnote references in the first draft, if it is clear that they will lead to the proper research notes when completed footnotes must be made later. Some scholars use a code (letters or numbers) in the manuscript and on research notes to refer to materials that will be used later for footnotes at the designated places in the draft. Some scholars turn on edge in the files the research notes to be used for footnotes later; some separate them entirely from the general files. Occasionally, it is possible to clip research notes to the proper pages of the draft for later composition of footnotes at designated points; but in a large research task this seldom is feasible, except when working with small sections at a time. This last offers one method of reducing the difficulties. If the investigation is well enough arranged, and is of the proper character for such procedure, you may be able to write a draft of a small section of the subject, with indications of places for footnotes; then immediately do the section over, improving style and organization as required, and making the footnotes from the small research note file being used for the section. Some writers do not put citations in the first draft; others put only some of the major items; others only feel comfortable when fully documenting as they go along. The only requirements are that the final draft be adequately documented, and that the method used for that purpose be the result of thought and planning, and as efficient and accurate as can be contrived.

How long should the paper be? In our experience most good papers resulting from one semester of work and following our procedures and requirements are between 25 and 30 pages, including footnotes and bibliography. Most longer papers would benefit from tightening of the exposition and especially from strengthening of the supporting evidentiary base.

A few other suggestions may be made. Avoid crowding pages, so as to leave room for insertions and other changes. Sometimes gaps may be left (properly labeled) for material that clearly is required. When inserting extra pages, be careful not to get the citations scrambled. The draft need not be pretty, so long as it can be puzzled out from deletions, insertions, and other changes.[1] Avoid excessive quotations. Yes, give your own "opinions" (i.e., views founded on stated evidence). Do not hesitate long over style and polish at this stage.

D. Form and use of footnotes[2]

There are three common types of footnotes, and they may be combined. One cites the source of the statement made in the text. The second is a cross-reference to another part of the paper. The third elaborates or explains the text. This last may be done when the material is not critical to the point being made in the text or would unnecessarily interrupt the argument. Beware of abuse of this third type. The types of material that may properly appear in footnotes are numerous: e.g., comments on translations, discussions of foreign or obsolete measures or weights, explanations of variant spellings, examination of chronological questions, comments on the reliability of witnesses or scholars.

Footnote styles and conventions are numerous—too numerous. A standard guide is Turabian's *Manual,* cited in our Preface, above.[3] Students subject to the fiat and whims of professors, graduate schools, and editors must, of course, accept their footnote rules. When they seek to publish the results of their research, they will find that most scholarly journals and publishers have style sheets of their own. It is wise to acquire the style manual of the publisher to whom a manuscript is to be sent, and to alter the manuscript accordingly before submission. The most radical changes will be in footnotes, but date forms, capitalization, and (for British publications) spelling

---

[1] We often require the student to show the instructor a page or two of his draft, with at least one footnote of some complexity.

[2] We make it a practice to examine samples of footnotes before the student's paper is finished.

[3] University of Chicago Press, and based on the *Manual of Style* of that press.

are areas in which mandatory changes are apt to be required.
Footnotes may actually be at the foot of the page, or at the ends
of chapters or of the paper or book, or inserted into the text
where they occur (but separated by lines drawn across the
page above and below the text), or interleaved on separate
sheets of paper for each page of text. Instructors will indicate
their preferences.

Although we depend on Turabian for instruction on the
form of footnotes, we here emphasize the following: (1) A
printed item (e.g., title of book, name of journal) is italicized
(accomplished by an underline in the typescript). (2) Articles
in journals and magazines are in quotes and not italicized. (3)
The author's name is put first, and in regular (not inverted)
word order: e.g., John Henry Smith, *History of York* (New
York, 1966), p. 12. (4) Be careful to state if there is an editor
or compiler instead of an author. (5) Give the number of volumes in a multiple volume work on the first citation, but not
thereafter. (6) Always indicate the volume cited when a multiple-volume work is involved. (7) Do not use "p." before the
number of a page cited unless confusion might result (*History
of France,* II, 66; but *Paris in 1916,* p. 122). (8) Put the
place of publication at the first citation, but not later.[4] (9) Put
the name of the publisher at first citation if it serves a purpose.
Most modern commercial publishers in countries with a reasonably free press can be omitted.[5] (10) The order of citation is
author (or ed. or comp.), title, edition (if other than first),
number of volumes (if more than one), place of publication,
publisher (if appropriate), date (or dates) of publication. (11) ·

---

[4] Some scholars prefer not to put the number of volumes, or place and
date of publication, even in first citation, if there is a bibliography appended to
the work.

[5] It is easy to locate such publishers if they are wanted. The citation should
include publishers if they are apt to be strongly biased (Communist publishers,
many church publishers, Fascist houses, etc.). The publishers of older works
sometimes are put down as part of the means of identification. For underdeveloped countries, even though the press may be relatively free, the name of
the press often is an aid to finding the materials, and sometimes to the quality.
N.B.: Many style systems are strongly insistent that publishers always be supplied at first mention in a footnote, and/or in bibliography listings.

Do not repeat in the footnote material that is in the text (e.g., if you name the author and title in text, give only the other bibliographic data in the footnote). (12) When citing newspapers give name and date, but not pages, and do indicate (in text or note) whether it is an editorial, news dispatch, cartoon, or signed column. (13) Volume numbers of magazines and journals are put in capital romans, without "vol." (*Magazine of History*, XV, No. 1, Oct., 1922, pp. 66–69). (14) Abbreviate bibliographic data and dates as much as possible without creating communication problems, and without worrying about purists who find this a dizzying liberty. Many style systems insist that in footnotes the names of months be spelled out. (15) Any material you supply in quotations or bibliographic citations is put in brackets in both text and footnotes.

The above is to be learned as useful, even necessary, but scarcely difficult, interesting, or directly related to critical methodology, and it is this last we are striving for. It will not always do simply to give a bare citation of source. All too many scholars follow this practice in circumstances when it will not do. At least in some important cases there must be comment on, even discussion of, the character and value of the data cited (either in the text or the footnote or in both). The citation Henry Adams, *History of the United States,* II, 33, 67–69, means nothing by itself except that Adams was willing to make some statements (and was a talented, diligent, and responsible scholar); what sometimes is needed is some indication of what he based his statements on (e.g., Adams, II, 33, citing a letter of Jefferson to Gallatin recounting his own observation of the affair at the wharf, and in 67–69, citing a convincing number of other accounts by 12 different witnesses, most of them members of Congress). We cannot overemphasize the importance of the critical appraisal of evidence.

Such critical analysis tends to be most complex when a number of sources—hence a number of citations—is involved. Thus, we use the *multiple citation footnote* as a training device; not, of course, in footnoting per se, but in the bringing together of substantial bodies of analyzed evidence in support of findings.

Of course, much of the discussion of corroboration and contradiction may occur in the text rather than in the footnotes. As a
minor matter, a complicated multiple citation footnote can be
confusing; therefore, the technique of putting together the citations and argument is of some consequence. Nevertheless, the
important element is the critical effort, the weighing of evidence,
the estimate of probability, the description of the boundaries of
doubt, the enunciation of the question, "What do I *know,* for
sure, and how?" In short, what is important is the struggle with
uncertainty, contradiction, and corroboration. Clearly, not all
aspects of a research task require or permit such elaborate
analysis. A few cases suffice for training purposes.[6]

Figure 5. Illustrative multiple citation footnotes
N.B.: Some of these sample footnotes were invented to illustrate
points, others were taken from historical works.
Number 1. This contrasts the evidence for differing interpretations, thereby implicitly criticizing previous work and supporting the
present author's viewpoint.

---

27 John Chasuble, "Intellectual Origins of Swinners," GHST,
XVIII, No. 3 (April, 1947), pp. 58-97, insists that the
sect permitted essential freedom of expression, but supports
his view only with a few examples of open heterodoxy in a
period of 157 years; Pi y Margall, Justificación, 101,
suggests that since "everyone" supported control of publication and expression, it was not oppressive, and dismisses
imprisonment for heresy as having political rather than
intellectual or religious aims, but he cites no evidence for
this view; F. T. View, The Swinner Controversy (New York,
1951), 16, 76, 144-56, argues that censorship was unimpor-
tant, on the basis of some 1,000 copies of works on the
Index that he found in library lists for the relevant period.
Cf. W. Blackton, "How to Count," Lancer, X, No. 1 (November,
1959), 90-103, demolishes the View thesis, pointing out that
the 1,000 copies of condemned books represented only one
percent of the volumes View himself found listed, and
probably represented no more than one-tenth of one percent
of all the books in the country, even at a modest estimation
of the contents of the known libraries of the country at the
time.

---

   [6] Appendix A, on assignments, shows how we work the multiple citation
footnote into our instructional schedule so as to try to force attention to the
critical examination of evidence.

Figure 5—*Continued*

Number 2. Having cited the essential evidence on the issue, this note suggests that an assumption made by well-known scholars may be unwarranted. In this, as in the previous example, the author expresses opinions which are not important enough to include in the body of his text.

27 Numura Cable No. 277, May 8, 1941 (Foreign Office Archives). Statements in Hull, Memoirs, II, 996, and Langer and Gleason, Undeclared War, 470, to the effect that Nomura sent Hull's four principles to Tokyo in April, together with the "Draft Understanding," represent what would normally have been a logical assumption in the circumstances.

Number 3. Here is detailed the nature of the evidence which underlies the accepted position, but citation of a dissenting opinion demonstrates that the author has not uncritically adopted the argument presented in the text.

18 George Paisley, "Graustark Grain Trade," History Magazine, XV, No. 3 (March, 1913), 22-56, assigns the policy almost exclusively to the royal family's interest in the condition of its estates, founding his view on extensive examination of the personal correspondence of the royal family, and on the printed record of the debates in the parliament. Only Maffick, Diplomatic History, II, 77-78, disputes this thesis, on the basis of three letters by Duke Elmer, and without commenting on Paisley's massive collection of evidence.

Number 4. The assumption of other scholars is noted here in support of the opinion in the text which, as this note makes clear, nevertheless remains merely an assumption.

18 Some leading scholars believe that this was the main purpose of Lincoln's question. See Benjamin P. Thomas, Abraham Lincoln (New York, 1952), 189; Baringer, Lincoln's Rise to Power, 24.

Figure 5—*Continued*

Number 5. In addition to citing the basic document, the author adds to the opinion of contemporaries the evidence he has himself uncovered, evidence which supports their opinion of events and justifies his using that opinion in his text.

112 Ravidavia's manifesto of 1821, Ravignani, "El Congreso
Nacional, in "Levene (ed.). <u>Historia de la nación argentina</u>,
VII, Part I, 28. See also Ignacio Nuñez to Woodbine Parrish,
July 15, 1824, Alberdi, "Derecho público provincial
argentina," <u>Obras selectas</u>, XI, 101-102; Ravignani, <u>Historia</u>
constitucional, II, 179-183, 186-191. In advocating free
trade between the provinces, Ravadavia undoubtedly had in
mind conditions on the Paraná River. Entre Ríos detained
ships engaged in the trade between Buenos Aires, Santa Fé,
and Paraguay, and taxed them heavily. Agreement between
Buenos Aires and Santa Fé, August 22, 1821, Ravignani,
<u>Asambleas constituyentes</u>, VI, Part II, 150.

Number 6. This is a minimal footnote. It gives an original source for the narrative presented in the text and adds an important interpretation which challenges a part of that source.

43 For Botha's speech and an account of this stormy meeting,
see Lloyd George, <u>Memoirs</u>, I, 359-63. Paul Birdsall,
<u>Versailles Twenty Years After</u> (New York, 1941), comments on
Wilson's position, arguing that the President won a considerable victory.

Figure 5—*Continued*

Numbers 7 and 8. These two notes summarize the contrasting views of scholars on controversial issues discussed in the text, a technique which informs the reader of the author's ability to weigh the evidence as well as naming the authorities on the questions.

1 For good examples of the "conventional" treatment of the ideas of the Avenir movement, see Alec R. Vidler, Prophecy and Papacy (London, 1954), 163-83; Charles Boutard, Lammennais, sa vie et ses doctrines (3 vols., Paris, 1905-13), II, 137-69; and, more briefly, Adrain Dansette, Histoire religieuse de la France contemporaine (2 vols., Paris,1948-51), I, 300-302. A far more perceptive treatment may be found in André Trannoy, Le Romanticisme politique de Montalembert avant 1843 (Paris, 1942), 170-94.

14 William B. Hesseltine, Ulysses S. Grant, Politician (New York, 1935), 77-79; Stanton to W. P. Fessenden, Oct. 25, 1866, Huntington Library. Including Stanton as a popular figure may surprise some, but see a contemporary attestation to Stanton's general prominence in Miscellaneous Writings of the Late Honorable Joseph P. Bradley, ed. Charles Bradley (Newark, N. J., 1901). Such evidence is strikingly different from recent commentaries on Stanton in Otto Eisenschiml, Why Was Lincoln Murdered? (Boston, 1937), and Theodore Roscoe, The Web of Conspiracy (Englewood Cliffs, N. J., 1959), which should be measured against James G. Randall's plea for a realistic appraisal of Stanton, in "Civil War Restudied," Journal of Southern History, VI (Nov. 1940), 455-56.

Figure 5—*Concluded*

Number 9. This is a good example of a footnote that contains material that some scholars would prefer to put in the text. The decision depends both on the purpose of the study, and on the judgment of the author as to the relative importance of the data.

35 Consulting numerous files of southern newspapers for 1858, I found that Douglas' Chicago speech had a much greater effect upon editorial opinion than did the Freeport doctrine. Denunciation of the latter was confined almost entirely to newspapers already bitterly inimical toward him like the Washington <u>Union</u>, <u>North Carolina Standard</u>, Charleston <u>Mercury</u>, Mobile <u>Register</u>, and Jackson <u>Mississippian</u>. A few journals which had either condoned or only mildly reproved Douglas' anti-Lecompton stand actually defended the Freeport doctrine. Among them were the Louisville <u>Democrat</u>, Richmond <u>Enquirer</u>, and Augusta <u>Constitutionalist</u>. A surprising number of southern newspapers, furthermore, took little or no notice of the doctrine in the weeks after its denunciation, and some, like the Memphis <u>Appeal</u> and Montgomery <u>Confederation</u>, even became more friendly toward Douglas after the debates began. Thus southern press opinion concerning Douglas in 1858 was both varied and variable, but one conclusion appears to be sound: The Freeport doctrine produced no significant change.

E. The formal, annotated bibliography

The list of materials at the end of the paper, after the bibliographic essay, must include everything cited in the paper. In addition, the following materials often are listed: materials that made a contribution to the paper but were not cited, or materials probably of some importance to the subject but which were not used (either because not available or because time did not allow), or materials consulted but found of no use (especially if readers would be likely to suppose they might be useful, a not uncommon circumstance). Do not list all items looked at; the padding of bibliographies with trivial and irrelevant items is a squalid practice.

Listing styles vary somewhat; if the information is clear, the style is satisfactory. The style in the Turabian *Manual* is acceptable. An entry is much like the first mention of an item in a footnote, except that the last name of the author is given first. The following rules are useful:

1. Arrange items alphabetically by authors (by title if there is no author or editor or compiler).

2. Listings begin at the left margin, and continuation lines also go to the margin.

In the case of multiple-volume items, *do* give total volumes, but not the volumes and pages used (footnotes will show that, where necessary) in most cases.

4. With newspapers, lump the dates of issues used, when feasible: e.g., (i) 1939–42; (ii) Aug., 1927–Sept., 1928; (iii) scattered issues in 1950–57, 1959, 1960, and all of July, 1961–Sept., 1962; (iv) March 3–14, 1860, April, 1861, scattered issues in 1862.

5. With magazines (e.g., *Saturday Evening Post, The Atlantic Monthly*), as opposed to scholarly journals (e.g., *American Historical Review*), you may sometimes want to list the dates of issues used (e.g., *Review of Reviews,* May, 1910–April, 1912), if your chief purpose was to survey public opinion insofar as indicated in the press, rather than to list the names of authors and articles. Your footnotes, however, may often show the names of articles and authors (or editorials or cartoons) from such magazines.

6. Listings may be grouped or categorized. Nearly always materials should be divided between materials contemporary with the period of the study, and more recent studies of the period (sometimes labeled primary and secondary materials). Often the contemporary materials should be subdivided into manuscript and printed materials, government documents, newspapers, diaries, etc. Either the contemporary materials or the studies may require division into topical, geographic, or chronologic subsections.

7. Whether bibliographic aids are included depends on the subject and/or individual preference. Generally, for the sort of task we are discussing, they should not appear in the formal bibliography.

8. The extent of annotation varies according to the topic

and the item under review. In the case of manuscripts prepared for publication, annotation often is kept to a minimum to cut printing costs. For the beginning researcher, it is wise to over- rather than under-annotate, because the process is valuable in developing a critical attitude. Even if an item is so nearly value- less as scarcely to merit annotation, the fact may well be stated in a single sentence, with a clause indicating why that is the case. The following suggestions usually will be helpful:

a) Indent the first line of the annotation considerably, but carry continuation lines to the left margin.

b) Few items require more than two or three lines of annotation.

c) Annotate: (i) the most useful items; (ii) well-known works (if only to say they were useless); (iii) those you list but did not cite in the paper.

d) Observe the ways in which the annotations in the formal bibliography differ from those on the working bibliography cards: e.g., abbreviations, language, data of interest to the re- searcher but not to the audience.

e) Do not abbreviate, but be as succinct as possible.

f) In the case of multi-volume works, usually it is not neces- sary to identify the volumes used (footnotes will show that where necessary). Just indicate what the set contains that is important to your subject, and your judgment of the value of that data.

g) The content of the annotation will depend to a consid- erable extent on the subject under investigation. Therefore the annotation remarks on the portions of the item relevant to this specific research paper. It is not a book review for the general reader, so coverage, style, and "interest" are irrele- vant.

h) Strive for meaningfulness in annotation: e.g., a most common failure in this regard is to say that an item is "good" or "definitive" or "indispensable," without adding a phrase or two to indicate why. The examples in Figure 6 illustrate some of the suggestions made above.

Figure 6. Bibliography entries, with annotations

N.B.: These entries generally follow the University of Chicago style and the Turabian *Manual* based on it. We do, however, omit publishers. On this question see footnote 5 to this chapter.

Example 1. This annotation describes, but does not comment on, the content of a multi-volume work.

Chalkley, Lyman. <u>Chronicles of the Scottish-Irish Settle-</u>
<u>ment in Virginia</u>. <u>Extracted from the Original Court Records</u>
<u>of Augusta County, 1745-1800</u>. 3 vols. Rosslyn, Va., 1912.
    Abstracts of will books, muster rolls, deed books, fee
books, vestry books; lists of bonds given; reprints of
letters. Contains information on Lewis' surveying operations
west of the Valley of Virginia, and his land-holding in the
same area.

Examples 2 and 3. These annotations explain both the usefulness and the bias of two modern studies.

Justice, Arthur Z. <u>The Patriot Party and the Industrializa-</u>
<u>tion Program</u>. Zion City, 1935.
    Useful for the party point of view, by a partisan.

Meneńdez y Pelayo, Marcelino. <u>Historia de los ortodoxos</u>
<u>españoles</u>. 2d ed. 7 vols. Madrid, 1911-32.
    A great deal of comment on the Economic Societies, by
an advocate of Roman Catholic orthodoxy, who considered the
Societies instruments of materialistic philosophy. Undocu-
mented, biased, repetitious, sometimes absurd, it has had
great influence.

Example 4. Here, a brief explanation is necessary to describe what an unedifying title does not.

"The Preston Register," <u>Virginia Magazine of History and</u>
<u>Biography</u>, II, No. 4 (April, 1895), pp. 399-404.
    A contemporary document listing the people killed,
wounded, or captured by Indians in Augusta County from
autumn, 1754, to May, 1758.

Figure 6—*Continued*

Examples 5 through 9. These annotations briefly record those
characteristics of items which are important to the author's study.

Arcila Farías, Eduardo. <u>Comercio entre Venezuela y México</u>
<u>en los siglos XVI y XVII</u>. Mexico, 1950.
    A valuable and challenging scholarly work, emphasizing
the great problems Spain faced in contriving an economic
policy for the entire empire, and demanding a re-evaluation
of interprovincial trade, especially that centering on New
Spain.

Basterra, Ramón de. <u>Una empresa del siglo XVIII: los</u>
<u>navíos de la Ilustración. Real Compañía Guipuzcoana de</u>
<u>Caracas y su influencia en los destinos de América. Caracas,</u>
<u>1925</u>.
    A mass of assertion without demonstration.

Bunkley, James N.   <u>History of the Province of Catawba</u>.
4 vols. Boston, 1920-24.
    A much-quoted and much-condemned economic interpreta-
tion of history. It is difficult to determine the basis for
most of his sweeping generalizations.

Calvo, Carlos. <u>Anales históricos de la revolución de la</u>
<u>América latina</u>, acompañados de los documentos en apoyo.....
5 vols. Paris, 1864-67.
    The Introduction (I, pp. V-CXXXVII) has many statistics
(not always well certified) on colonial economic life,
especially overseas trade, mining, and government revenues.

Cappa, Ricardo. <u>Estudios críticos acerca de la dominación</u>
<u>española en America</u>. 26 vols. Madrid, 1889-97.
    Father Cappa's work is pro-Spanish, and literary rather
than scientific, but contains some interesting information
and views on the colonial economy, largely that of Peru, and
emphasizing the 16th century.

Figure 6—*Concluded*

Example 10. An extensive, general, important or "standard" work is assessed and its general line of interpretation outlined in this long annotation.

```
Carrera Pujal, Jaime.  Historia de la economía española. 5
vols.  Barcelona, 1943-47.
          Covering 1500-1808, emphasizing economic literature
rather than economic life, it is an excellent account of
Spanish views of the country's economic woes, but less satis-
factory as a description of the economy itself.  Carrera is
critical of scholars (e.g., Colmeiro) who oversimplify
economic history, but he does believe that the weakness of
manufacturing was the critical element in Spain's economic
thought and action from the 17th century to the 18th, and
notes that the revisionists of the latter were not invariably
sound in their proposals.  Fairly extensive use was made of
the publications of Spanish Economic Societies.  The study
is primarily based, however, upon writings on economic sub-
jects, rather than on government, business, or other types
of records.
```

F. The bibliographic essay

In the finished paper, the bibliographic essay precedes the annotated list of materials consulted. Because it summarizes the nature and adequacy of those materials, however, it is written after the student masters these problems by completing the annotated bibliography. The bibliographic essay is valuable to the user of a scholarly work in giving a succinct estimate of the adequacy of the evidence available for study of the subject, and the quality of previous studies touching the matter. All too few scholarly works contain adequate bibliographic essays. Such discussion may, of course, be put in the preface, or scattered throughout the text and footnotes. It is, however, especially valuable when associated with the bibliographic list.

Preparation of the bibliographic essay has great value in the training of the researcher: it forces him to discuss the adequacy of the evidence as a whole, and it compels consideration of the entire body of relevant scholarly studies. Beginning researchers often will not do these things if permitted simply to comment individually on studies and bits of contemporary evidence.

Although there is no standard form or length for the bibli-

ographic essay (most guides do not even discuss it), it is suggested that in most cases it will be helpful to consider that the
essay should:

1. Be short—usually not more than two pages.

2. Deal in a general way with the source problem (i.e., contemporary materials) on the one hand, and with studies of the
subject on the other hand. These should occupy clearly distinct
sections of the essay; two large paragraphs should be sufficient.
The discussion should emphasize special difficulties, schools of
thought, or prejudices affecting workers in the field.

3. Deal with broad *classes* of sources and/or studies (e.g.,
manuscripts, public opinion materials, government documents,
biographies), rather than repeat the annotations to individual
items in the bibliographic list that follows the essay.

4. Enlighten the reader as to the researcher's grasp both of
the subject and of the research problems involved in dealing
with the subject.

5. Give the reader immediate understanding of the adequacy of the materials consulted, and the precise merits and/or
deficiencies thereof for the study of the subject.

6. Be keyed to the subject studied. Remember, you are engaged in a scholarly investigation of a specific subject, not writing book reviews for the heterogeneous audience of the *New
York Times*.

7. Do not give full bibliographic data (e.g., author's first
name, number of volumes, date of publication), since they are
in the list that follows the essay.

The examples of bibliographic essays in Figure 7 are meant
only to be suggestive; they should not be followed slavishly.

Figure 7. Bibliographic essays
  *Example 1: From a graduate paper on "The Censorship
  Struggle in Guatemala, 1800–1821."*

  The actual legal provisions of the Spanish censorship may
be found in the *Novísima recopilación de las leyes de España,*
and were of course applicable to all portions of the Spanish
realm. This is the best source, and makes unnecessary an ex-

amination of the *Recopilación de leyes de los reynos de las Indias.* On the prohibitions of the Inquisition the best source is the *Indice Ultimo* of 1790. The material therein covers many years; and the supplement for 1805, and the manuscript additions reaching to 1819 in one of the copies in the Los Angeles Public Library, carry the picture well up to the end of the period under investigation.

The operation of the Inquisition in Guatemala may be derived from Mérida's *Historia crítica de la Inquisición en Guatemala,* which while less complete for its purpose than are the sources mentioned above for theirs, is very useful, and all we have. The reprinting of various documents is a valuable feature of Mérida, as is the rather extensive catalogue of the material confiscated by the Inquisition in Guatemala. There is, in short, about as much primary as secondary material in Mérida; of course, there is no way of checking on his methods of selection, since the documents of the Guatemala Inquisition have since disappeared.

Information regarding publication in Guatemala can be drawn from no source superior to Medina's *Imprenta en Guatemala.* The thoroughness of his work is demonstrated by the few additions made 23 years later by Valenzuela's *Imprenta en Guatemala.* The listings in Medina, Valenzuela, and in the *Historia de la imprenta en Guatemala* of Díaz, and in Beteta's "Nuestra bibliografía colonial," are for the purposes of this investigation about as nearly complete as we can expect.

In the catalogue of documents in the Archivo general de Indias de Sevilla, entitled *Independencia de América,* and in the *Documentos acerca de la cooperación de Guatemala en la independencia de Centro América* is a considerable body of primary material dealing with the censorship as applied to Guatemala, and particularly with the attitude of the colonials towards this censorship.

This paper has been written largely from the eight or nine primary sources noted previously. The historians, as Marure, Montúfar y Coronado, and Montúfar y Rivera Maestre, give little information directly pertinent to the subject. The general literary studies, as Henriques Ureña or Quesada, treat these matters very loosely. A fair amount of scholarly work has been done on small aspects of the censorship and publication subjects; much of it has been published in the *Anales de la Sociedad de Geografía e Historia de Guatemala.*

Example 2: From a study of "The Policy of President Winkler on Graustarkian Watches."

The official policies and statements of the two governments are well covered in the U.S. Department of State's blue book, *The Graustarkian Tariff Controversy,* and the Graustark Foreign Ministry's *American Economic Imperialism.* While the considerations that entered into the American policy remain obscured in the classified files of the State Department, an excellent survey of the elements involved is the article in *Foreign Affairs,* "American Choices in the Current Tariff War," by "N," generally believed to be a high official in the State Department. The *Congressional Record* reflects the opinions of various interests on the issue, which was widely discussed in the United States. Since the Graustark legislature possesses little authority, and engages in no debate, the few proclamations issuing from that body are merely reflections of the views of the executive power. These proclamations were printed in the officially-controlled newspaper *Verity.* The attitudes of other governments toward this controversy are well summed up in the report of the United Nations Committee on Current Trade Barriers.

President Winkler's rather tortuous course through the dangers of this crisis may be followed by way of the newspaper reports of his public speeches and press conference statements. Of some relevance, also, is the statement of the Democratic National Committee on the issue on the occasion of the first meeting of the platform committee at the last national convention, since it gives exactly the justification of Winkler's twistings and turnings that he himself usually gave.

Public opinion in the United States was badly divided on the matter, partly because of the technical intricacies of the tariff, partly because of Winkler's habit of obscuring the issues. The *New York Times* and the *Washington Post* maintained a reasonably dispassionate editorial tone, and occasionally called both pros and cons to task. A good example of rabid opposition to Winkler's policy was the *Chicago Tribune.* A passionate supporter of the president's views was the *St. Louis Post Dis-*

patch. On the whole, Democratic papers supported the president, and Republican papers opposed his policy on the issue. Generally speaking, editorial opinion was more divided on the moral issues involved than on the strictly economic matters in question.

A peculiar difficulty confronting the student of this affair resulted from the burning of the U.S. Embassy in Graustark, a conflagration that consumed almost all the records of the affair kept there. According to a State Department spokesman, some of this data was reconstructed from memory by a three-man team of Embassy staff members. The reconstruction is classified and not available to scholars.

Many studies, scholarly and otherwise, have dealt with the question; a large proportion is spoiled by obvious prejudice. These prejudices are sometimes patriotic, sometimes related to political party affiliation, and sometimes related to the ancillary religious controversy between the United States and Graustark. The best analysis of the economic issues is Green, *Graustarkian Economic Aims,* although it is marred by his excessive dependence on the letter of statements in *Verity* and by his neglect of historical materials demonstrative of an undeviating Graustarkian policy in this field over many years. Best on the political-moral implications of the United States surrender to the Graustarkian Tri-State Formula is Smithers, *Appeasement Again,* which is admirably objective.

Example 3: From R. Shafer, Economic Societies in the Spanish World.

Society publications available for the period to 1821 totaled some 10,000 pages (more than 6,000 for Spanish Societies; more than 3,000 for American). Manuscript material in the Archivo General of Guatemala provided necessary additional evidence on the Society of that place. A considerable amount of evidence on the Societies was gleaned from non-Society publications of the late 18th and early 19th centuries. For Spain these were largely the writings of literary figures and government officials, as Jovellanos, Sempere y Guarinos, and Fernández de Navarrete. For America more information was derived from periodicals, as the *Gazeta de Guatemala,* the *Mercurio Peruano,* and the *Telégrafo Mercantil.*

Sources available for the Spanish Societies were a satisfactory sample for the present purpose; much more material is available in Spain. The materials for the American Societies were more nearly exhausted. The most important publications of the Havana and Guatemala Societies were exploited. It is doubtful that much can be added to the small printed product of the other American Societies. Manuscript sources in Spain and America certainly can provide further information on the American Societies, but it is doubtful that such information would seriously alter the picture of the American Societies presented here.

Previous studies of the Economic Societies are of restricted value. There has been no study of any magnitude of all the Societies—Spanish and American or of all the American Societies. Studies of individual Societies tend to be based on too little evidence, are usually badly organized, and spend much interest on origins, motives, and general attitudes, and relatively little on chronology, statistics, and physical accomplishments, to say nothing of a precise and orderly analysis of ideas and objectives.

G. Writing

Effective writing is a necessity for successful communication, as beginning researchers are told insistently by guides and instructors. The student must accept the seriousness of this injunction, and he must expect to be criticized (and downgraded) for defects of sentence and paragraph construction, grammar, spelling, punctuation, word selection, and allied matters.

A number of subjects treated earlier in this *Guide* relate to the final act of writing or communication: for example, the need for thorough digestion of evidence; the problem of organization, possibly aided by an outline; the form and types of footnotes. Here we add some injunctions that are valuable for their own sakes, and that will emphasize for the student the need for care in composition. As a practical matter, there is not time in the beginning course in historical method to devote much attention to problems of exposition. If the student's first research paper is returned with severe criticism of the writing, and he wishes to continue research, he must settle down to the study of usage he obviously neglected in earlier years. There are excellent guides devoted to the subject.[7]

The student must be clear that good writing is necessary to maximum performance of the historical task. As Pericles put it long ago, "A man who has the knowledge but lacks the power clearly to express it is no better off than if he never had any ideas." The student must be aware also that it is a common mistake of the beginning researcher to allow too little time for writing and re-writing. Many fine professional writers of historical prose have testified to the many times they have re-written passages of their works. Ask yourself: Have I said exactly what I intend? Is it possible that what I have set down might confuse or seem ambiguous to others? Remember that the first draft is a device for putting initial flesh on an outline or scheme of organization; subsequent re-writing may almost completely replace the initial wordage.

Of the many practices of good usage and style, the following may be stressed:

1. *Opening statement.* Historical papers and books usually open with a statement of intent; in addition, if it is properly constructed, it will set the tone of the work.

2. *General qualities.* Strive for accuracy, lucidity, thoroughness, and consistency in argument.

3. *Vocabulary.* Much of the success of exposition depends on the selection and use of words. (*a*) Emphasize nouns and verbs in writing. This means both selecting them with care, and making them bear the burden of the sentence. Adjectives and adverbs, thus, should be used sparingly. (*b*) A successful war on clichés and jargon will do as much as anything to give strength and grace to the paper, thus appealing to the interest of the reader and thereby probably improving clarity. A rapidly com-

---

[7] In the Preface we recommended Strunk and White. Also useful are H. W. Fowler, *A Dictionary of Modern English Usage* (2d ed., rev. by Sir Ernest Gowers; Oxford: Clarendon Press, 1965); Bergen and Cornelia Evans, *A Dictionary of Contemporary American Usage* (New York: Random House, 1957).

posed first draft inevitably will contain many clichés, commonplace expressions. It will also contain "tired" words, currently
so overworked, and in so many contexts, as to have lost much
of their force. Colloquialisms should be avoided. An important
task of re-writing is to reduce the number of all these types of
words and phrases, replacing them with words used in novel
ways. Jargon also must be fought. It was present in writing—
for example, theological tracts—before modern times, but it
is especially prevalent now. It has been said that "jargon is language which is more technical than the ideas it serves to express,"[8] as in much sociological literature. Such language from
specialized disciplines, and from bureaucracies that produce it
in confusion and profusion, often will convey insufficient or incorrect, meaning to the reader; even more often will it be irritating; and in any event nearly always it is unnecessary. There
is no need to "utilize" things, when "use" is available for use.
(*c*) Beware of "over-writing," that is, of becoming lush and
gooey. (*d*) Delete unnecessary words. Almost always it is possible to delete verbiage to advantage. Certain words are habitual
offenders: e.g., "very" creeps into expression much more often
than it is required. Also, it will be found that phrases used in
early drafts can be replaced with shorter phrases, or even with
single words by some reconstruction of sentences. (*e*) Take care
in using linkage words: e.g., but, because, since, however, although, also. Be sure you are using them in their precise
sense. (*f*) Abbreviations seldom are put into the text of a
paper; they are more acceptable in footnotes, appendixes, and
bibliographies.

4. *Spelling and punctuation.* Diligently look for mistakes
in spelling and punctuation. It is amazing how easily they can
be overlooked. When in doubt, consult a dictionary or manual
of usage. You cannot throw this burden onto the instructor, just
as the professional researcher cannot expect it all to be borne
by an editor. Great care and patience are nearly as important in

---

[8] Susanne Langer, *Mind: An Essay on Human Feeling* (Baltimore: Johns
Hopkins University Press, 1967), p. 36.

achieving proper spelling and punctuation as are knowledge and access to reference works. Sloppy practice in these realms not only may seriously alter meaning, but it tends to reduce general confidence in a writer's sense of responsibility and dedication to precision. "Pray" for "prey," or "council" for "counsel" are inexcusable. Reading a sentence aloud is a useful way of determining whether the punctuation contributes to the intended sense. Among the commoner rules to bear in mind are: (a) if you are not firm on the use of the semi-colon (and many people are not), you had better construct two declarative sentences separated by a period; (b) use a comma to separate the co-ordinate clauses of a compound sentence when a co-ordinating conjunction (e.g., but, for) is used, but if there is no conjunction, use a semicolon; (c) put a comma after a subordinate clause that precedes an independent clause in a sentence; (d) if you are not firm on the use of hyphens, see a usage manual.

5. *Construction.* (*a*) Be careful of verb tenses. This is a matter both of avoiding confusion and ambiguity, and of arriving at a pleasing style. Beware of mixing tenses in a paragraph; sometimes it is not proper. (*b*) Use the active (subject of the sentence performs the act) rather than the passive (subject is acted upon) voice. The active voice usually is shorter, clearer, and stylistically more pleasing. It is better to state: "The herald blew the trumpet at dawn, arousing the army for battle," than, "The trumpet was blown at dawn by the herald in order to arouse the army for battle." (*c*) Search for errors and ambiguities in the agreement of pronoun and antecedent and of subject and verb. This is a schoolday injunction, familiar to all beginning researchers at the college and university level. It will pay the researcher to review in his own mind what he has been taught about this and other aspects of usage. (*d*) Avoid misplaced modifiers; be certain that it is clear what word is being modified. (*e*) Write in the third person. If it is necessary to mention yourself, use such phrases as "the present writer," or "the investigator."

6. *The sentence.* Phrases masquerading as full sentences obviously must be altered. Aside from that rule, the most im-

portant requirement is that a sentence be clear beyond doubt. Be wary of mixing tenses and voices within a single sentence. It often will lend both force and grace to the composition to vary the length or the construction style of sentences. It usually helps to have close together nouns and the adjectives describing them, verbs and modifying adverbs, and qualifying phrases and the things they relate to.

7. *The paragraph.* The successful paragraph is a joy to writer and reader. It should begin with a topic sentence, clearly stating the matter to be discussed. It requires some ingenuity to provide variety in such opening sentences, to avoid a stiff and mechanical effect. It is helpful if the opening sentence also serves as a bridge from the preceding paragraph, but this sometimes is difficult to arrange satisfactorily. The argument or elaboration after the opening sentence should be relevant to the theme announced. Nothing is more common in student compositions than sentences in paragraphs that have little or no connection with matter immediately at issue. Delete such material. Also, the order of discussion in the paragraph is important: that is, the meaning of each sentence should flow from that of the preceding sentence. Abrupt changes of subject within paragraphs should be avoided. Possibly such a change suggests the need for a new paragraph. Remember, that there is no law on the length of paragraphs. Those of only two or three lines are much more common in journalism than in scholarly work, but some of that length are allowable in the latter. Finally, the paragraph should be concluded with a sentence summarizing or commenting on the subject-matter, and at the same time including an element which the next paragraph can echo. Thus, a large part of successful paragraph construction consists in *transitions*—between paragraphs, and between sentences within paragraphs.

8. *Quotations.* Be aware that the method and the style of quotations require care. First of all, keep quotations to a minimum, and especially do not throw the burden of interpretation on the reader. A good beginning will have been made if the research notes consist of summary and paraphrase rather than

long quotations, as we advised earlier in this guide. As for using quotations to give "flavor" to the paper, usually it does not pay unless very well done; and using quotations to make a point usually is inferior to your direct comment.

Do not appropriate anything without giving credit, by using quotation marks and indicating the source. There are three ways of putting quotations into the text. (*a*) As an integral part of the sentence: Moctezuma complained to Cortés, "You destroy our gods without explaining your own." (*b*) Following a colon at the end of the sentence: Moctezuma said to Cortés: "You destroy our gods without explaining your own." (*c*) When there are more than three lines of quotation, they are put as a separate paragraph, distinguished from the text proper by indentation, by smaller type, or by both:

You destroy our gods without explaining your own. And when we attempt to expostulate, you brand us on the face as slaves. How can we make a decision as men under these conditions?

Quotation marks are not required when this style is used.

Some other rules are important: (*a*) Put double quotation marks at each end of a quotation, and add single quotation marks for a quotation within a quotation. (*b*) Changes you make in quoted material (e.g., spelling, punctuation) must be indicated in brackets or in a footnote. When you supply words in a quotation, to improve the sense, they must be put in brackets: "When 'red beard' [Pedro de Alvarado] arrived at the place, he found 20,000 Indians drawn up for battle." (*c*) *Sic* (thus) is inserted in brackets in a quotation to indicate that something (e.g., bad sense or bad spelling) is thus in the original, when the reader might suppose the quotation to be inexact. (*d*) Omissions from quotations are shown by three dots; a fourth is added if at the end of a sentence; (*e*) Put the final quote marks outside of the punctuation mark. (*f*) Put the reference number outside the quote marks at the end.

9. *Errors of reasoning.* There are compositional faults that amount to errors or to the obscuring of fact. Many of these occur early in the data collection and analysis processes, and are

perpetuated in the exposition; some others are introduced during the process of final composition. Whatever the origin, they must be watched for during drafting. A few of the more common are: the non-sequitur; hidden or needless repetition or tautology; exaggeration; anachronism; inexact metaphor; ambiguity; sloppy definition; irrelevancy; argument by appeal to authority without regard for fact; triviality; shifting attention from the question to partisans of points of view so drastically as to obscure the central argument.

We end with the most difficult matter of all—style. The attainment of style, an individualistic mode of expression, must be the aim of every writer. It comes, if it comes at all, only with much labor. The beginning researcher, following the suggestions of this *Guide,* and of appropriate reference works, may certainly hope to attain clarity of expression; in addition, with much practice, and possibly the help of God, he may aspire to achieve some day that style which Edmund Wilson defined as a combination of "lucidity, force, and grace."

A

An assignment schedule

We do not use a common assignment schedule in all our classes in historical method. A schedule is set down here merely to indicate one way in which the elements emphasized in teaching historical method may be combined.[1] Of course, the arrangement and emphasis in this schedule reflect our judgment, based on experience, as to what is important. Above all, the schedule stresses: (*a*) the importance of the individual conference or tutorial session, and (*b*) attention to enumerated items of bibliographic and substantive research, analysis, and composition. We find that conferences organized around such specified expectations quickly diabuse the student of the notion that, after all, it is merely a question of a bit of reading, a few notes, and a weekend of cutting and pasting.

For a first conference, early in the term: (1) Do general reading on the subject selected for the research task. (2) Begin to make up bibliography cards from the card catalog and

---

[1] Some instructors prefer to emphasize the production of a rough draft as early as possible, so that it can be criticized and returned to the student for revision.

other bibliographic aids; take to the conference. (3) Have a few research notes.

For a second conference, near mid-term, bring: (1) An outline of the subject, no matter how modest. (2) All research notes, no matter how few—it is the method that will be checked with especial care. On at least a few of the research notes there should be the beginnings of analysis of the evidence, or, to put it differently, some consideration of the confidence that can be reposed in the material. (3) All 3 x 5 cards of the working bibliography, including cards on bibliographic aids. (4) Two or three examples of entries for a bibliography.

For a third conference, bring: (1) An outline of the subject (possibly cut down from the original topic). (2) All research notes, a fair number of which should include some analysis of the evidence. (3) All 3 x 5 working bibliography cards, some with annotations, and including cards for bibliographic aids. (4) Two or three samples of entries in a bibliography, with annotations.

Optional at the third conference or at special conferences, bring: (1) Sample bibliographic essay. (2) Sample portion of text with multiple citation footnote.

Students will turn in at the end of the semester: (1) Paper in proper form, with footnotes. (2) Bibliographic essay. (3) Annotated bibliography. (4) All research notes. (5) All working bibliography cards.

appendix

B

Bibliographic aids
for selected
countries

A large part of modern bibliography is organized by countries. There are, of course, many bibliographic aids dealing with large time or cultural periods such as the European Middle Ages, Ancient Mediterranean World, Pre-Columbian Amerinds, or with such topics of transnational interest as numismatics, chemistry, or the Negro, or with state or provincial political units, or with international organizations.[1] Here we offer highly selective lists of bibliographic aids for certain countries: A. United States; B. Great Britain; C. France; D. Germany; E. Mexico; and F. Kenya. The United States and Mexico lists are longer than the others to provide a wider coverage of examples, and not as an indication either of the relative importance of the countries or of the relative development of their bibliographic aids. It is naturally the case that aids are much better developed for some countries than for others.

---

[1] For example, the United Nations, Organization of American States, North Atlantic Treaty Organization. Cf. Brenda Brimmer, *et al., A Guide to the Use of United Nations Documents, Including Reference to the Specialized Agencies and Special UN Bodies* (Dobbs Ferry, N.Y., 1962).

The lists are intended to: (*a*) speed the early work of some students, since many will do research on the major countries treated here; (*b*) further emphasize for American students that the elements of bibliographic method apply to all countries; (*c*) show some examples of types of important bibliographic aids, in addition to those in Chapter IV (C); and (*d*) encourage research outside the "traditional" United States–Western Europe focus in this country.

The student also should look for bibliographic help in the American Historical Association's *Guide to Historical Literature*, which has excellent lists of bibliographic aids on many areas and specialized subjects. And Chapter IV (C) in this *Guide* contains bibliographic suggestions that should be pursued (for example, use should be made of guides to dissertations, periodical indexes, guides to reference books). These lists are intended more as a training device than as a reference to bibliography. They are especially helpful in demonstrating the categorization of bibliographic aids, the content of the categories, and the variation between countries.

1. The United States

Perhaps the single most important bibliographic aid for the student of United States history is Oscar Handlin *et al.* (eds.), *Harvard Guide to American History* (Cambridge, Mass., 1966), listing printed materials topically and chronologically. Excellent supplements to this, including more recent publications, are the bibliographies in the volumes of *The New American Nation Series* edited by Commager and Morris. The American Historical Association's Service Center for Teachers of History publishes useful bibliographic essays in pamphlet form. Two of these are *The American Revolution: A Review of Changing Interpretations,* and *The Progressive Movement, 1900–1920: Recent Ideas and New Literature.*

a. *General bibliographies.* Several older general bibliographies remain valuable. In J. N. Larned (ed.), *The Literature of American History. A Bibliographical Guide* (Boston, 1902), over 4,000 titles are analyzed. H. P. Beers (ed.), *Bibliographies in American History* (rev. ed., New York, 1942), gives bibliographies by chronological field (Colonial, Revolutionary, Confederation, National), as well as topical fields (economic, constitutional, diplomatic, social, cultural, history of science). A more recent and highly selective listing is the Library of Congress, *Guide to the Study of the United States of America. Representative Books Reflecting the Development of American Life and Thought* (Washington, 1960), which gives a short précis of each entry. Guides to special subjects include S. F. Bemis and G. G. Griffin (eds.), *Guide to the Diplomatic History of the United States, 1775–1921* (Washington, 1935); H. M. Larson (ed.), *Guide to Business History* (Cambridge, Mass., 1948); Robert E. Spiller *et al.* (eds.), *Literary History of the United States* (rev. ed., 3 vols., New York, 1953). *Writings on American History* has been for years an important annual compilation of books and articles, but it is not being kept current.[2] A useful guide to local history is Clarence S. Peterson, *Consolidated Bibliography of County Histories in Fifty States in 1961* (Baltimore, 1963).

   b. Manuscript and archival guides. Two major guides to manuscript collections in American history are Philip M. Hamer (ed.), *A Guide to Archives and Manuscripts in the United States* (New Haven, Conn., 1961), and the *National Union Catalog of Manuscript Collections* (1st vol. published 1962; several subsequent volumes). The most important depository of federal records is the National Archives in Washington, D.C., surveyed in its *Guide to the Records in the National Archives* (Washington, 1948). Many holdings in state libraries have been cataloged by the Historical Records Survey: e.g., *Guide to Depositories of Manuscript Collections in the United States: California* (Los Angeles, 1941).

   c. Guides and indexes or checklists to government publications. Working with government documents can be frustrating,

---

  [2] See Chapter IV (B) on this bibliographic annual and on many other bibliographic aids in the field of United States history.

and a friendly documents librarian can be helpful to the beginning student. Two useful guides on how to use federal documents are L. F. Schmeckebier (ed.), *Government Publications and Their Use* (rev. ed., Washington, 1961), and A. M. Boyd (ed.), *United States Government Publications: Sources of Information for Librarians* (3d ed., rev. by R. E. Rips, New York, 1949). There is no single good index or checklist for federal documents. The main indexes (Poore, Ames, and the *Monthly Catalog*) are listed above in Chapter IV (C). The states have their own guides or indexes to their documents. An index of special merit covering the period down to 1904 is A. R. Hasse (ed.), *Index of Economic Material in Documents of the States of the United States* (Washington, 1907–22), which surveys materials in California, Delaware, Illinois, Kentucky, Maine, Massachusetts, New Hampshire, New Jersey, New York, Ohio, Pennsylvania, Rhode Island, and Vermont.

d. Indexes of journals and newspapers. The best guide to scholarly articles concerning United States history appearing before 1958 is the *Writings on American History*. After that date, consult the indexes in *American Historical Review, Journal of American History* (formerly *Mississippi Valley Historical Review*), *Journal of Southern History,* and *William and Mary Quarterly.* For newspapers to 1820 see Clarence S. Brigham (ed.), *History and Bibliography of American Newspapers 1690–1820* (2 vols., Worcester, Mass., 1947). The later period is surveyed in Winifred Gregory, *American Newspapers 1821–1936, A Union List of Files Available in the United States and Canada* (New York, 1937). The Library of Congress has published its sixth edition of *Newspapers on Microfilm* (Washington, 1967), many of which can be borrowed or purchased.

2. Great Britain

Much the most complete and reliable biliography for British history can be drawn from the *British Museum General Catalogue of Printed Books* recently published (1965–66) in 263 volumes. They cover all of the Museum's acquisitions to 1955;

catalogs of each year's additions are being published beginning with 1963; but no volumes as yet cover 1956–62. Massive and unselective though this catalog is, it does not exhaust the printed sources for British history, especially those for the two centuries following the invention of printing. Early printed material should be checked for in A. W. Pollard and G. W. Redgrave's *Short-title Catalogue of Books Printed in England, Scotland, and Ireland . . . 1475–1640* (1926) and in D. G. Wing's sequel for 1641–1700 (1945–51).

Students of British history are well served by very extensive if not exhaustive bibliographies for each major period before 1789. Wilfrid Bonser has compiled *A Romano-British Bibliography, 55 B.C.–449 A.D.* (1964) and *An Anglo-Saxon and Celtic Bibliography, 450–1087* (1957). For medieval history the best general guide to articles, books and editions of texts published before 1915 is Chas. Gross's *Sources and Literature of English History from the Earliest Times to about 1485* (1915). Literary sources for the medieval period are listed in T. Duffus Hardy's *Descriptive Catalogue of Materials Relating to the History of Great Britain and Ireland* (1862–71) and in C. P. Farrar and A. P. Evans' *Bibliography of English Translations from Medieval Sources* (1946). The 16th, 17th, and 18th centuries are covered by three *Bibliographies of British History* produced under the joint auspices of the Royal Historical Association and the American Historical Association: Conyers Read on the Tudor period, 1485–1603 (1959), G. Davies on the Stuart period, 1603–1714 (1928), and Stanley Pargellis and D. J. Medley for 1714–1789 (1951).

The American Historical Association has also brought out in pamphlet form brief bibliographical essays on modern British history: Robert Walcott on *The Tudor-Stuart Period of English History* (1964), R. K. Webb on *English History, 1815–1914* (1967), and H. R. Winkler on *Great Britain in the 20th Century* (1960). A. F. Havighurst's discussion and list of "Paperbacks on British History" in the *Journal of British Studies* (VI, 2, May, 1967) is useful for teaching purposes. There are several means to keep up with current publication, among them the (English) Historical Association's *Annual Bulletin of Historical Literature*. The *English Historical Review* lists and briefly describes articles from a wide variety of journals annually in its July issue.

P. and G. Ford have performed a great service to modern British history by preparing a whole series of tools with which to approach the rich mine of information in the Parliamentary papers. Their *Guide to Parliamentary Papers* (1956); their reprint of Hansard's *Catalogue and Breviate of Parliamentary Papers, 1696–1899* (1953); a *Select List of British Parliamentary Papers, 1833–1899* (1953); and *Breviates of Parliamentary Papers* for 1900–16 (1957), 1917–39 (1951), and 1940–54 (1961). The British government issues an annual catalog of its publications entitled *Official Indexes, Lists, Guides, Catalogues,* for which Her Majesty's Stationery Office (H.M.S.O.) has produced two introductory guides: *Government Information and the Research Worker* (1952) and *Published by H.M.S.O.* (1960). Finally, there are many bibliographies—though never enough—devoted to specific aspects of British history, for example the Historical Association's *English Local History Handlist* (1952) and W. E. Houghton's *Wellesley Index to Victorian Periodicals* (1966) which unmasks their anonymous contributors.

3. France[3]

There are two great bibliographies that include nearly all books published in France from the 18th to the early 20th century: Joseph Quérard, *La France littéraire* . . . (18 vols., 1827–64, with title variation) covers to 1849; Otto Lorenz *et al.,* *Catalogue général de la librairie française, 1840–1925* (32 vols.). The following guides are devoted specifically to books and articles in history: P. Caron and H. Stein, *Répertoire bibliographique de l'histoire de la France* deals with works pub-

---

[3] Although these selections were made primarily with the history of modern France in mind, all the items also are useful for medieval French history, except the *Supplement F* to the *Bibliographie de la France*.

lished in 1920–1931 on the entire history of France (somewhat similar guides exist for publications back to 1866); the very important *Bibliographie annuelle de l'histoire de France du 5e siècle à 1939* began in 1955, appears currently with author and subject index, and extended its historical period forward to 1945 with the 1964 volume.

The student will sometimes find useful the bibliographies and the "present research problems" sections in the volumes in the series *Clio: Introduction aux études historiques* which has been published by the Presses Universitaires de France since 1937. This is particularly true for the more recent volumes on the 18th and 19th centuries, and for the newer series, *Nouvelle Clio: L'histoire et ses problèmes* issued by the same press.

To keep up with very recent scholarship the student can turn to *Biblio: Catalogue des ouvrages parus en langue française dans le monde entier* (October, 1933, to date) which appears both monthly and annually and has author, title, and subject entries. Unfortunately, there is no French periodical index. References to French articles may be found in the German publication, *Bibliographie der fremdsprachigen Zeitschriftenliteratur,* covering 1911 to 1964. In 1964, the title was changed to *Internationale Bibliographie der Zeitschriftenliteratur aus allen Gebieten des Wissens.* The *Bibliographie de la France* in its *Supplément F. publications officielles* (September, 1950, to date), covers publications of the national, local, and overseas governments. It appears irregularly in six or seven parts for a year and issues an annual index.

There are two guides to the *Bibliothèque nationale,* which is the repository for all books published in France. *The Catalogue général des livres imprimés* (195 volumes since 1900) has an author listing only, and had come down to the letter "U" in 1966; the *Catalogue de l'histoire de France* covers books and pamphlets published before 1875 on the history of France. The inventories of French archives are dealt with in H. Courteault, *Etat des inventaires des archives nationales, départementales, communales, et hospitalières au 1 Janvier 1937,* with *Supplément* covering 1937–55 by R. Boutier.

4. Germany

Bibliographic resources for German history are rich and varied, but as a result of the regime shifts of 1918 and 1945 also somewhat erratic in their publication record. The best general bibliographic aid is Friedrich Dahlmann and Georg Waitz, *Quellenkunde der deutschen Geschichte;* the editors are two major German historians of the 19th century. A new edition is being published, with the first two volumes appearing in 1967. Until all volumes have appeared, the best bibliographic source for more recent literature on the 19th and 20th centuries will remain Bruno Gebhardt, *Handbuch der Deutschen Geschichte,* two volumes, edited by Herbert Grundmann (Stuttgart, 1954–59). A more specialized but very useful compendium of current literature on post-1918 events is the *Bücherschau der Weltkriegbücherei* (which appeared under the title *Vierteljahresschrift der Weltkriegsbücherei* until 1942), and the bibliographies appended to each issue of the *Vierteljahrshefte für Zeitgeschichte.* The latter is also the best German periodical devoted to contemporary history. Two English-language journals are also of prime importance in the area of recent German history: the *Journal of Contemporary History* and *Central European History,* a new journal which appeared in the spring of 1968.

Researchers in German history will find a welcome index to the relevant periodical literature in the well-edited and complete *Halbjahresverzeichnis der deutschsprachigen Zeitschriftenliteratur* and *Halbjahresverzeichnis der fremdsprachigen Zeitschriftenliteratur.* Statistical data in German newspapers may be consulted in two annual compendia, *Der Leitfaden* for West German papers and *Handbuch der demokratischen Presse* for the East.

The major biographical compendia are the *Allgemeine Deutsche Biographie,* now seriously out of date, and the more recent, but also less inclusive five-volume set, *Die Grossen Deutschen.*

5. Mexico

Many important bibliographic aids for the study of Mexican history may be found in two items: the introduction to vol. I of *Fuentes de la historia contemporánea;* and Ramos, *Bibliografía de la historia.* Most important materials on Mexico of interest to the historian (except government publications) put out since 1935 are listed in the annual volumes of the *Handbook of Latin American Studies.*

a. Only a few of the many *library and manuscript catalogs and guides* are listed here: Biblioteca Nacional, *Catálogos* (11 vols., Mexico, 1889–1908); University of California, Berkeley, The Bancroft Library, *Catalog of Printed Books* (22 vols., Boston, 1964); New York Public Library, *Dictionary Catalog of the History of the Americas* (28 vols., Boston, 1961); Mexico, Departmento de Bibliotecas, *Directorio de bibliotecas de la República Mexicana* (Mexico, 1962).

b. Bibliographies. An excellent start on materials published in the colonial period may be had by consulting: Joaquín García Icazbalceta, *Bibliografía mexicana del siglo XVI* (Mexico, 1886); Vicente de P. Andrade, *Ensayo bibliográfico mexicano del siglo XVII* (Mexico, 1899); Nicolás León, *Bibliografía mexicana del siglo XVIII* (6 vols., Mexico, 1902–8); José Toribio Medina, *La imprenta en México, 1539–1821* (8 vols., Santiago, 1907–12). Useful bibliographies of bibliographies are Cecil K. Jones, *A Bibliography of Latin American Bibliographies* (2d ed., Washington, 1942); Nicolás León, *Bibliografía bibliográfica mexicana* (Mexico, 1923); Agustín Millares Carlo and José I. Mantecón, *Ensayo de una bibliografía de bibliografías mexicanas* (Mexico, 1943) and an *Adiciones* published 1944; new items after 1935 are in the *Handbook of Latin American Studies.* A fundamental guide is the aforementioned Roberto Ramos, *Bibliografía de la historia de México* (Mexico, 1956), with alphabetical listings of 4,776 items published to 1955, but not works on the Revolution. A splendid review of work since Independence is Robert A. Potash, "Historiography of Mexico Since 1821," in *Hispanic American Historical Re-*

view, August, 1960, pp. 383–424. Important on the Revolution is Roberto Ramos, *Bibliografía de la Revolución Mexicana* (3 vols., Mexico 1931–40; and reissued in 1959–60), mostly of publications to 1937. Much more thorough, better executed, and with good annotations, are the five big volumes (Mexico: El Colegio de México, 1961–1967) of *Fuentes de la historia contemporánea de México,* covering the years 1910–40, and listing books, pamphlets, and periodical articles. Very valuable is *Veinticinco años de investigación histórica en México,* published as special issues of *Historia Mexicana,* Nos. 58–59 (Oct., 1965–March, 1966) and 60 (June, 1966), pp. 1–782, done topically, covering the publications of the past quarter-century. The national bibliography (annual publication) of Mexico cannot be followed, even in recent years, in any one source. The *Boletín* of the Biblioteca Nacional does not cover all publication. Scattered years were fairly well covered by fugitive bibliographies. Some publishers' and booksellers' lists (especially Porrua, Robredo, and the Fondo de Cultura Económica) of recent decades are useful. The Banco de México, Nacional Financiera, and the Secretaría de Hacienda publish bulletins and other materials that help follow some classes (especially economic) of publication. There are many bibliographies of Mexican states: Genaro Estrada, *Bibliografía de Sinaloa, histórica y geográfica* (Mexico, 1926); Rafael Ayala Echávarri, *Bibliografía histórica y geográfica de Querétaro* (Mexico, 1949); Mario Colín, *Bibliografía general del estado de México* (Mexico, 1963). Three important specialized bibliographies among the many published in Mexico are: Ramón Beltrán and Luz García Núñez, *Bibliografía de la Secretaría de Hacienda y Crédito Público* (Mexico, 1943), covering the publications of the Treasury Department in 1821–1942, including some important studies; Juan B. Iguíniz, *Bibliografía de los escritores de la Provincia Mexicana de la Compañía de Jesús desde su restauración en 1816 hasta nuestros días* (Mexico, 1946), listing some 3,500 items; *El Instituto Nacional de Antropología e Historia; su contribución a la bibliografía nacional* (Mexico, 1962).

c. Guides to government publications are poor for Mexico.

There is no single government press, and no publication lists all government publications. The scholar must know the agencies and round up publications by using various lists and libraries. The holdings of the Library of Congress of the United States are the best in this country, but far from complete. Research in depth in Mexican government documents must be done in Mexico. Helpful for older materials is Annita Ker, *Mexican Government Publications: A Guide to the More Important Publications of the National Government of Mexico, 1821–1936* (Washington, 1940). The law and legal literature of some years ago is covered in John Vance and Helen Clagett, *A Guide to the Law and Legal Literature of Mexico* (Washington, 1945); and Clagett on the *Mexican States* (Washington, 1947). A good (but by no means complete) record of government statistical publications may be had from materials put out by the Dirección General de Estadística: e.g., *Bibliografía mexicana de estadística* (2 vols., Mexico, 1941–42); *Catálogo de estadística* (1937), and its continuations titled *Catálogo de las estadísticas nacionales,* still being published. Also useful on statistics is Rubén Gleason Galicia, "Instituciones que recolectan y proporcionan información estadística en México," *Ciencias Políticas y Sociales* (Mexico, July–Sept., 1963), pp. 277 ff.

d. There are no indexes of Mexican newspapers or popular magazines. Articles in the more serious and scholarly journals can be followed fairly well in the annual volumes of the *Handbook of Latin American Studies;* and in the issues of *Revista de Historia de América* of the Pan American Institute of Geography and History, *American Historical Review,* and *Historia Mexicana.* Many articles on economics and allied subjects are listed in the issues of *Mercado de Valores,* published by Nacional Financiera. The *Fuentes de historia contemporánea,* discussed above, covers periodical literature in 1910–40. Good coverage is found in two publications of the Columbus Memorial Library of the Pan American Union: *Index to Latin American Periodical Literature, 1929–1960* (8 vols., Boston, 1962); *Index to Latin American Periodicals* (Boston, 1961–). Information on Mexican periodicals may be found in: *Catalog of Mexican Periodicals* (Mexico: Departamento de Liberería,

Centro Mexicano de Escritores, 1959), with 1,450 entries, and
a Spanish edition the same year; Irene Zimmerman, *A Guide
to Current Latin American Periodicals. Humanities and Social
Sciences* (Gainesville, Fla., 1961), with pp. 132–163 on
Mexico.

   e. Guides to archives and archival materials that touch Mexico are quite numerous. Much of the rich documentation on the
colonial period is in Spain, and the guides to that material are
not listed here. Important is Agustín Millares Carlo and José I.
Mantecón, *Repertorio bibliográfico de los archivos mexicanos
y de las colecciones diplomáticas fundamentales para la historia
de México* (Mexico, 1948), listing guides, calendars, and indexes, plus documentary publications. On archives see Lino
Gómez Canedo, *Los archivos de la historia de América. Período
colonial español* (2 vols., Mexico, 1961), including Spanish
archives, and vol. I, 271–352, on archives and libraries of Mexico; Roscoe Hill, *The National Archives of Latin America*
(Cambridge, Mass., 1945); Ronald Hilton, ed., *Handbook of
Hispanic Source Materials and Research Organizations in the
United States* (2nd ed., Stanford, 1956). On materials abroad,
Agustín Millares Carlo, *Repertorio bibliográfico de los archivos
mexicanos y de los europeos y norteamericanos de interés para
la historia de México* (Mexico, 1959). The bibliography of the
United States must be examined for the many guides to United
States manuscripts that touch the history of Mexico. A number
of United States libraries have extensive collections of Mexican
manuscripts: e.g., see *Guide to the Latin American Manuscripts
in the University of Texas Library* (Cambridge, Mass., 1939).
A valuable new addition is Richard E. Greenleaf and Michael C.
Meyer (eds.), *Research in Mexican History. Topics, Methodology, Sources, and a Practical Guide to Field Research* (University of Nebraska Press, 1973).

6. Kenya

   So little has been done in the collection of the important oral
tradition of the peoples of Kenya that no bibliographic com-

pilation of the material would be justified. The principal documentary sources for Kenya's history are found in Portugal, Britain, and India, as well as East Africa, and they are written in Arabic, Swahili, Gujarati, and Hindi as well as English. The most complete guide is John B. Webster's *A Bibliography on Kenya* (Syracuse University Program of Eastern African Studies, 1967), which lists 7,210 books and articles.

Webster compiled his information from the following sources, which now need not be consulted for their records on Kenya history published prior to 1967: published catalogs of university libraries with unique Africana collections, such as Boston, Northwestern, and Howard Universities, U.C.L.A., and the School of Oriental and African Studies at the University of London; the published catalogs of the Library of Congress, British Museum, New York Public Library, and the Royal Empire Society; indexes to periodical literature, such as *Readers' Guide, Poole's Index,* and the *Annual Cumulated Bulletin* of the Public Information Service; bibliographies regularly included in periodicals such as *Africa,* the *Journal of Negro Education, Zaire,* and *African Affairs;* special collections such as L. J. P. Gaskin's *A Bibliography of African Art* (London: International African Institute, 1965); and lists of unpublished manuscripts, including the *Theses on Africa Accepted by Universities in the United Kingdom and Ireland* (Cambridge: W. Heffer, 1964) issued by the Standing Conference on Library Materials on Africa and the *List of American Doctoral Dissertations on Africa* (Washington, 1962) compiled by the Library of Congress.

Webster's compilation, however, was not exhaustive. It represents an intensive survey of the pertinent literature published in England, France, and the United States, and of the English-language publications in Kenya, but it is deficient in Portuguese sources, and it does not include any publications in non-European languages. Its listing of government documents is inadequate, and it does not mention any of the many important articles in the English-language periodicals of India, South Africa, and Rhodesia.

Because of these omissions, the historian must still consult
many other bibliographical aids relative to Kenya history. The
published records of legislative debates in Kenya, Britain, and
India have indexes at the back of each volume. The *British Ses-
sional Papers* contain annual indexes, and separate indexes have
been compiled for multiyear periods. Documents published by
the Kenya government are cited in the Library of Congress'
Official Publications of British East Africa: Part I; *The East
Africa High Commission and Other Documents;* and Part III,
Kenya and Zanzibar. Unpublished British documents can be
found in three Public Record Office catalogs: *List of Cabinet
Papers, 1880–1914* (London: H.M.S.O., 1964); *The Records
of the Colonial and Dominions Offices* (London: H.M.S.O.,
1964); and *List of Colonial Office Confidential Print to 1916*
(London: H.M.S.O., 1965). A "List of Manuscripts in the East
African Swahili Committee Collections, March 1964" has been
published in the *University College Library Bulletin* (Dar es
Salaam), vol. 24, 1964. Rhodes House, Oxford University,
issues annual lists of the private papers of British colonial admin-
istrators which it has collected since 1963 under the Colonial
Records Project. The East African pamphlet collection in the
former British Colonial Office Library has been microfilmed in
14 reels, and there is a two-volume printed index. Carbon 14
dates and sites, which are vital data on Kenya's iron age, are
published periodically in the *Journal of African History.* The
best atlas is the Kenya government publication, *Atlas of Kenya*
(Nairobi: Survey of Kenya, 1959). Two useful newspapers, the
London *Times* and the *New York Times,* have indexes. In
India one must still visit the National Archives to consult lists
of government files for material relating to Kenya. Syracuse University, which is in the process of obtaining a microfilm repro-
duction of the Kenya National Archives, in 1969 will publish an
annotated guide to the Archives material at Syracuse.

Additional reading on historical method

The following items, all in English, give additional information on the subjects covered in this *Guide,* and provide further bibliographic leads into the literature. See Chapter IV (B) and Appendix B for references on bibliographic aids. See the American Historical Association, *Guide to Historical Literature,* and Winchell, *Guide to Reference Books,* for further guidance. Four lists are offered here: A. Meaning and Scope of Human History; B. History of Historical Writing; C. The Older Auxiliary Disciplines; and D. Social and Behavioral Sciences and History. Items frequently contain material relating to more than one of these categories; but we list an item only once.

1. Meaning and scope of human history

The literature on these subjects is large, and increases rapidly. The following are only a few of the interesting treatises produced in recent years. The Cohen item, by a philosopher, is more carefully constructed and reasoned than most. Raymond Aron, *Introduction to the Philosophy of History: An Essay on the Limits of Historical Objectivity* (trans. from the French; Boston, 1961). Isaiah Berlin, *Historical Inevitability* (New York, 1955). Grace Cairns, *Philosophies of History. Meeting of East and West in Cycle—Pattern Theories of History* (New York, 1962). Edward H. Carr, *What Is History?* (New York, 1962). Ernst Cassirer, *The Logic of the Humanities* (trans, from the German; New Haven and London, 1960). Morris R. Cohen, *The Meaning of Human History* (La Salle, Ill., 1947). R. G. Collingwood, *The Idea of History* (Oxford, 1946). William H. Dray, *Philosophy of History* (Englewood Cliffs, N.J., 1964). David Hackett Fischer, *Historians' Fallacies: Toward a Logic of Historical Thought* (New York, 1970). Patrick Gardiner (ed.), *Theories of History* (Glencoe, Ill., 1959). Pieter Geyl, *Debates with Historians* (The Hague, 1954), and *Use and Abuse of History* (New Haven, 1955). J. H. Hexter, *The History Primer* (New York, 1971). Sidney Hook, *The Hero in History* (2d ed., New York, 1955), and Hook (ed.), *Philosophy and History* (New York, 1963). H. Stuart Hughes, *History as Art and as Science* (New York, 1964). Georg G. Iggers, "The Idea of Progress: A Critical Assessment," *American Historical Review,* Oct. 1965, pp. 1–17. Erich Kahler, *The Meaning of History* (New York, 1964). Karl Löwith, *Meaning in History* (Chicago, 1949). Gerhard Masur, "Distinctive Traits of Western Civilization: Through the Eyes of Western Historians," *American Historical Review,* April, 1962, pp. 591 ff. Bruce Mazlish, *The Riddle of History. The Great Speculators from Vico to Freud* (New York, 1966). Hans Meyerhoff (ed.), *The Philosophy of History in Our Time* (Garden City, N.Y., 1959). Murray G. Murphey, *Our Knowledge of the Historical Past* (Indianapolis and New York, 1973). Emery Neff, *The Poetry of History* (New York, 1947). Bernard Norling, *Timeless Problems in History* (Boston, 1969). Don Karl Rowney and James Q. Graham, Jr., eds., *Quantitative History. Selected Readings in the Quantitative Analysis of Historical Data* (Homewood, Ill., 1969). A. L. Rowse, *The Use of History* (New York, rev. ed., 1963). Social Science Research Council, *Generalization in the Writing of History: A Report of the Com-*

mittee on Historical Analysis of the SSRC (Chicago, 1963), and Theory and Practice in Historical Study. A Report of the Committee on Historiography (New York, 1946). Caroline Ware (ed.), The Cultural Approach to History (New York, 1940). Morton White, The Foundations of Historical Knowledge (New York, 1965). C. Vann Woodward, "The Age of Reinterpretation," American Historical Review, Oct. 1960, pp. 1 ff.

2. History of historical writing

Matthew A. Fitzsimons et al., The Development of Historiography (Harrisburg, 1954), covers nearly all human groups that have had a written history, and is an excellent starting point for references. Coverage is largely Occidental in Harry E. Barnes, A History of Historical Writing (2d rev. ed., New York, 1963); and James W. Thompson, with B. Holm, A History of Historical Writing (2 vols., New York, 1942). Noah E. Fehl et al., History and Society (Hong Kong, 1964), deals with Chinese, Israelite, ancient Greek, and modern Western historiography.

3. The older auxiliary disciplines

Two general treatments are Tom B. Jones, Paths to the Ancient Past (New York, 1967), and John M. Vincent, Historical Research (New York, 1911; reprinted 1929). For archeology see V. Gordon Childe, Piecing Together the Past: Methods and Theories of Archeology (New York, 1956); Glyn E. Daniel, A Hundred Years of Archeology (London, 1950). On chronology see J. C. McDonald, Chronologies and Calendars (London, 1927); Willis I. Milham, Time and Time-Keepers (New York, 1947); Stephen Toulmin and June Goodfield, The Discovery of Time (New York, 1965). Gilbert Doan, Searching for Your Ancestors. The How and Why of Genealogy (rev. ed., Minneapolis, 1948). On numismatics see Elvira Eliza Clain-Stefanelli, Numismatics—An Ancient Science. A Survey of Its History (Washington: The Museum of History and Technology, 1965);

Stanley E. Lane-Poole, ed., *Coins and Medals: Their Place in History and Art* (3d ed., London, 1894). For diplomatics and paleography see André Blum, *On the Origin of Paper* (tr. Lydenberg, New York, 1934); Sven Dahl, *History of the Book* (tr. from Danish, New York, 1958); Hubert Hall (ed.), *A Formula Book of English Official Historical Documents* (2 vols., Cambridge, 1908–9); William Mason, *A History of the Art of Writing* (New York, 1920); E. M. Thompson, *Handbook of Greek and Latin Paleography* (New York, 1893); B. L. Ullman, *Ancient Writing* (New York, 1932). On modern linguistics see John B. Carroll, *The Study of Language* (Harvard University, 1953); Otto Jespersen, *Language, Its Nature, Origin, and Development* (New York, 1922); Joseph Vendryes, *Language: A Linguistic Introduction to History* (London, 1925; tr. from French of 1921).

4. Social and behavioral sciences and history

Lee Benson, *Toward the Scientific Study of History* (Philadelphia, 1972). Bernard Berelson and Gary A. Steiner, *Human Behavior: An Inventory of Scientific Findings* (New York, 1964). Robert Berkhofer, Jr., *A Behavioral Approach to Historical Analysis* (New York: Free Press, 1969). Werner J. Cahnman and Alvin Boskoff, *Sociology and History: Theory and Research* (Glencoe, Ill., 1964). Thomas C. Cochran, *The Inner Revolution: Essays on the Social Sciences in History* (Toronto, 1962). Folke Dovring, *History as a Social Science: An Essay on the Nature and Purpose of Historical Studies* (The Hague, 1960). Maurice Duverger, *An Introduction to the Social Sciences* (New York, 1964), including a section on the methods and problems of sampling opinion by interviews and questionnaires. Wilson Gee, *Social Science Research Methods* (New York, 1950). Bert F. Hoselitz, *A Reader's Guide to the Social Sciences* (Glencoe, Ill., 1959). H. Stuart Hughes, "The Historian and the Social Scientist," *American Historical Review*, Oct., 1960, pp. 20 ff. Robert Hyman et al., *Interviewing in Social Research* (Chicago, 1954). *International Encyclopedia of the Social Sciences* (17 vols.; New York, 1968). Carl Jung, *Collected Works* (ed. by H. Read *et al.,* New York, 1953–64), especially Vols. V and IX, on oral tradition and the "collective folk soul." Mirra Komarovsky (ed.), *Common Frontiers of the Social Sciences* (Glencoe, Ill., 1957). Susanne K. Langer, *Mind: An Essay on Human Feeling* (Baltimore, 1967). Eugene Meehan, *Explanation in the Social Sciences: A System Paradigm* (Homewood, Ill.; Dorsey Press, 1968). Richard S. Rudner, *Philosophy of Social Science* (Englewood Cliffs, N.J., 1966). Edward Saveth (ed.), *American History and the Social Sciences* (Glencoe, Ill., 1964). Social Science Research Council, *The Use of Personal Documents in History, Anthropology, and Sociology* (New York, 1945); and *The Social Sciences in Historical Study* (New York, 1954). Pauline Young, *Scientific Social Surveys and Research* (3d ed., New York, 1956).

Index

243

This book has been set in 11 and 10 point Times Roman, leaded 2 points. Chapter numbers are in 24 point Craw Modern, and chapter titles are in 18 point Craw Modern. The size of the type page is 24 by 42 picas.